Daughters of Courage

Stephanie

DONNA FLETCHER CROW

MOODY PRESS
CHICAGO

© 1993 by
DONNA FLETCHER CROW

ISBN: 0-8024-4529-2

1 3 5 7 9 10 8 6 4 2

Printed in the United States of America

To the Peters
in the joy of friendship—
Mike and Lynette,
Misty, Becca, Abby, and Ben

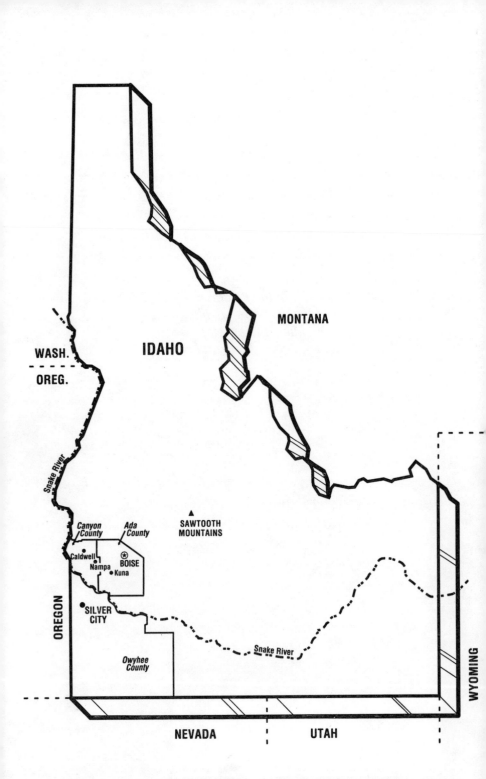

1

"Vote for Hamilton. Eliot Hamilton for state representative. Would you like a balloon?"

Stephanie handed a string to a three-foot tall, cap-pistol-packing cowboy, then smiled as the child strode across the park beside his mother. A red "Hamilton for the House" balloon now bounced above his head.

Stephanie smoothed her bouffant blonde hair and tugged at her Western-fringed, green miniskirt. Then she brightened her smile and approached the next set of strollers in Lakeview Park. Over in the rodeo grounds, the crowds were gathering for the third night of the Snake River Stampede, "The Wildest, Fastest Show on Earth," one of the five largest rodeos in the world, right here in Nampa, Idaho.

"Vote for Hamilton. Would you like a—" She stopped short and laughed. "Oh, hi, Grace. I didn't recognize you. Are these your grandchildren?"

Grace Sperlin Paterson was her mother's oldest and dearest friend. "Yes, Todd and Tessa. They've come down from McCall just to go to the Stampede with Grandma."

The children, whom Stephanie guessed to be about six and seven, murmured shy acknowledgments and held out their wrists for Stephanie to tie on balloon strings while Grace continued.

7

"Of course we'll be voting for your father. Seems he's been interested in politics ever since I knew him, and he's done so much for Canyon County—supporting education and fighting liquor by the drink."

"Thank you, Grace. Would you like a button?"

Grace took the red plastic button with "Hamilton" written across it in white letters. Although in her mid-fifties, she had kept the attractive figure Stephanie had seen in her mother's yearbook from Kuna High School. And, although now more gray than blonde, Grace still wore her hair in a swirl of waves in defiance of the sleek, back-combed styles everyone else wore. "Is your mother around?"

"Yes, she's somewhere with Daddy, shaking hands with the constituents."

"How's she holding up?"

"Loves it. I think Mother's more a natural politician than Daddy." She could have added, *Mother is perfect in this role as she is in everything else. What did you expect?* But it wouldn't do to let it be known that the Hamilton family had a case of the much talked-about generation gap. "Oh, here Mother comes now with Jennifer—Alex's daughter."

The years of peace and growing prosperity of the fifties, after Eliot returned from the war and earned his law degree, had given Elizabeth Hamilton the opportunity to develop into the elegant woman her tall, broad-shouldered form and thick black hair had always promised. Although her hair was gray at the temples, its sleek, Jackie Kennedy style emphasized her large, dark eyes. In her simple yellow linen shift she looked exceedingly young.

The old friends exchanged greetings, and Elizabeth introduced her seven-year-old niece to Grace's grandchildren. "Since I don't have any grandchildren, it's nice that my sister had her daughter so late in life."

Before Stephanie could take offense at the remark she felt was directed at her, the children ran toward the street

8

shouting. "Oh, goody, here it comes!" "The parade! Hooray, hooray!"

The adults rushed after them to keep them on the sidewalk, and the parade—billed as the longest rodeo parade in the world—passed before them on some of the world's finest horseflesh.

Todd and Tessa bounced up and down, waving their balloons at the flag-bearers and the queen and her court that headed the parade.

But Jennifer stood in open-mouthed awe. She didn't even blink until the raven-haired girl in a bright blue suit with red roses embroidered on it turned her prancing chestnut horse into the stadium.

"Oh." Jennifer sighed. "Someday I'm going to be Queen of the Snake River Stampede."

The saddle clubs were passing now, units of fifty to a hundred riders with perfectly matched, perfectly polished equipment, riding in precise formation.

Grace turned to the child who was still gazing after the departing princesses. "I was almost queen once." Grace's startling news brought Jennifer's head around with a snap. "Of course, it wasn't the Snake River Stampede then. It was the Nampa Harvest Festival—but this is what it's grown into. I was the princess from Kuna."

"Did you ride a horse?"

"No, I rode in a 1930 black roadster and sang and danced at the Pix Theater." Grace laughed. "Can you imagine?"

Elizabeth nodded. "Oh, yes. I remember it well. That was the day I realized I loved Eliot. And I was terrified he'd fall for you, you were so beautiful."

The women reminisced while the children exclaimed over the parade, and the riders smiled and returned their waves. The parade had progressed to its individual contestant section where riders competed for ornate blue rosettes proclaiming them "Best girl under ten," "Best boy under ten," "Best pair women," "Best pair men," and on to

"Best family group" and "Best comedy group," before Elizabeth got around to asking after Grace's brothers and their families.

"Is Fred showing any interest in that widow that's been chasing him?"

Grace sighed with exasperation. "Dear Freddie, he's so much like Daddy was—just wants to help everybody and be kind to everybody and take good care of his farm. But he's never found a wife to help him like Mother did Daddy."

"And Albert?"

"Patricia's father retired last year, so the whole ranch is theirs. They love it. I just wish we could see them more often—Ketchum's not that far away, but you know how it is."

Elizabeth agreed. It seemed she seldom saw her own family.

"Oh, did I tell you Albert's boy is in Saigon?"

Stephanie turned away. Oh, no. Here it came. Grace was a very nice lady, but nothing could be more irritating than hearing her go on about her clever, dedicated nephew.

"Carlton? The one who did so brilliantly in law school? I didn't know he was in the army."

"He enlisted this spring. Of course it broke Patricia's heart to have her only son go off to Vietnam, but he's very idealistic about doing his duty."

Saint Carlton the dutiful, Stephanie thought. Just turning her back wasn't enough to shut out the panegyric.

"I suppose he'll be reasonably safe in JAG. That's what Eliot did in World War II, wasn't it?"

Elizabeth started to answer, but the parade ended just then, and the children were tugging impatiently to get to their seats in the stadium.

Stephanie stood shaking her head as they disappeared into the crowd funneling toward the giant green stadium. Of course, Jennifer was only seven, and terribly

10

spoiled, having been born to Alex after her second marriage—when everyone thought she was too old to have children. Stephanie could understand her daydreaming about being a rodeo queen.

But what of those eighteen-to-twenty-two-year-olds who were actually doing it? Thirty-six of them this year from all over Idaho and western Oregon with nothing better to spend their time on than horses, queen contests, and cowboys. Didn't they realize this was 1968? Didn't they know that if the world was going to be made a better place their generation had to do it?

Did these young women have nothing better to do than pet their horses and wear fancy clothes? Hadn't they read *The Feminine Mystique?* Didn't they know Betty Friedan had shown women a way to greater fulfillment? What about the ideals Robert Kennedy and Martin Luther King had given their lives for?

That was why Stephanie had majored in political science at Boise State. That was why she firmly refused to get serious about any of the men she knew. But first she had to get a less stifling job. Could there be anything more out of character for a member of the Now Generation than working in a bank? The trouble was, what did political science majors who didn't want to be teachers do?

Well, they could work in political campaigns. She could start by getting her father elected to the state legislature. Even if he didn't understand the hippie's love movement and thought antiwar demonstrations were harmful for the country, she knew he was that great exception to the rule—someone over thirty who could be trusted. And for all her sympathies with those of her generation who marched in protest, she wasn't sure that was the best way. Protests seemed far too often to lead to violence. Just look at the terrible riots in Detroit and Watts last summer.

She could never become a hippie or a protester. Many of her friends had in the past two or three years. But she didn't believe in dropping out or in violent protesting. She was going to work inside the system. Politics was the answer. She didn't know how or when, but she was determined to become an office-holder. And then they'd see something—all those complacent middle-class Americans who just went along with the program—she'd show them what a dedicated woman could do to make people better. She would build new houses, playgrounds, schools . . .

Yes, the world needed changing—and she was going to do her share of the changing. And she was going to do it long before she was anything like her father's fifty-eight years old. But she would start with getting him elected to the state legislature.

"Would you like a balloon?" She turned to a little boy walking a very big dog, then gave his father a leaflet explaining Eliot Hamilton's campaign issues.

2

July melted into August. The long hot summer baked the Idaho desert, making Stephanie thankful that at least her bank job offered air conditioning. The political race heated up across the country. Every evening Stephanie returned to the apartment she shared with her friend Diane, who looked and sang like Joan Baez, to watch scenes of violence on the evening news.

"Come quick! They're interviewing McCarthy," Dede called as Stephanie opened the door.

Stephanie sank onto the sofa next to her friend.

Dede's bare feet, extending from bell bottom jeans, were propped on the coffee table. On the black and white screen the Minnesota senator, who was hoping to be nominated as the Democratic presidential candidate, was being interviewed in front of the Chicago hotel where he was staying during the convention.

Dede applauded his statements of strong opposition to the Vietnam war. But Stephanie sat with her mouth drawn in a tight, thin line as the camera shifted to scenes of violence on the streets of Chicago outside the convention. Just when she thought she couldn't take any more, the stock market report came on.

Dede switched off the TV and picked up her guitar. She began singing a song she had recently composed in honor of her boyfriend, Barry, who had gone to Canada to avoid the draft, and another friend who had been jailed when a protest turned into a riot.

Stephanie waited until Dede was about to start the second verse before she interrupted. "Dede, I know you're doing what you think is right, but there has to be a better way. All those people being violent in the streets of America isn't going to make people less violent in Southeast Asia—or anywhere else. There *has* to be a better solution."

Dede slashed a harsh chord across her strings. "Oh, I know, I know. Work within the system to make better people. Look, I tried sitting in the park handing flowers to people. That whole summer after I dropped out of UCLA I spent loving people. I could see the Movement wasn't getting anywhere, so I thought maybe if I came back to Small Town USA I could get people to listen—"

"Well, you don't seem to have any trouble getting audiences to listen to The Gathering."

"Oh, sure, they like our music, but nobody hears the words. Everybody is as complacent and apathetic here as anywhere else—more so."

Stephanie nodded. "I know, we're sheltered here—so far off the beaten track. But that gives us more chance to make a difference, Dede. Things are smaller, haven't gotten so far out of hand. That's why if we work right here for slum prevention instead of waiting until it has to be slum clearance—"

"What is this? Your Vote for Hamilton speech for the Kiwanis picnic?"

"*Oh!* Thanks for reminding me!" Stephanie darted into her room to change out of her prim navy blue dress with white collar and cuffs, almost a uniform for working in a bank. She put on a denim miniskirt and red and white gingham blouse.

Stepping carefully so as not to get grass stains on her white boots, Stephanie circulated among the fried chicken, corn-on-the-cob eating crowd. She smiled and handed out Hamilton materials like the seasoned campaigner she was quickly becoming. She loved it when people engaged her in conversation, asking about her father's views on issues of local interest. Although the Vietnam War was the central issue in the election—and most Idaho voters wanted to be assured that their candidates supported America's men in action—she was spared a continuation of her debate with Dede. A member of the state House of Representatives wouldn't be voting on national or international issues.

At last the lines of hungry picnickers were more or less settled at their butcher-paper-covered tables, and the piles of empty corncobs under the feet of all the little boys indicated they were reaching saturation point. The Western band that had been performing foot-tapping music all evening took a break, and the Kiwanis president introduced their speakers, Eliot Hamilton and his opponent, Benton Smith.

Smith at once launched into his favorite topic. The root cause of the social, economic, and civil unrest in the nation, he said, stemmed from inadequate educational opportunities for all.

"Well, if it isn't the lady herself—Stephanie Hamilton."

Stephanie turned. "Oh. Hi, Jim."

Jimmy Linzler had been the love of her life from the sixth grade until sometime in high school when she suddenly realized that there had to be more to fuel her one-sided passion than the fact that he had been the first boy to pull her braids in kindergarten. Or that when he had once kicked her chair in a program, she had turned around on the platform and slugged him.

Jimmy had managed to land a reporter's job with the *Idaho Free Press*. He played weekend soldier with the Idaho National Guard, a unit he had joined as soon as his graduation from the University had ended his student deferment from the draft.

15

Stephanie was now able to find even less about him to fuel a passion. But he was an old friend, besides the fact that he was reporting on her father's campaign speech. So she smiled.

"How about going to a movie when you're through here?"

She had to admit that his rich, Beatles-style hair and gleaming white teeth in a tanned face weren't unattractive. She did find the fact that she was an inch taller than he to be rather awkward.

"*The Graduate*'s playing at the Nampa-Caldwell Drive-in."

She started to make up an excuse about being too tired after an evening of campaigning, then changed her mind. "I'm not wild to see the movie, Jim. But if you're flexible, we could go hear Dede sing at the peace rally at City Hall."

"Hey, I'm not only flexible, I'm ecstatic. I just might get a story out of that, and the whole thing will be deductible."

"Does that mean you're offering to buy me a Coke? Jimmy, you really know how to talk to a girl." She looked at his notepad with its spare notes. "I'm surprised you'd choose to cover the Kiwanis picnic over a demonstration."

"Editor's choice, not mine." Jim shrugged. "If I had my druthers I'd be in Chicago. Now that's what I call action."

"I agree it's lively. But I don't agree that I'd want to be in on all the head-bashing I saw on TV tonight." She started to ask whether he thought McCarthy or Humphrey would be nominated, but Benton Smith was warming to his topic and Jim turned to his note-taking.

When the next speaker was introduced, Stephanie hoped it wasn't just wishful thinking that made the applause for Eliot Hamilton sound so much louder than that for his opponent.

"My fellow citizens, I invite you to join me in the challenge before us—to restore respect for the law and the rights of others by working to eliminate the causes of disorder while protecting lives and property through fair but firm law enforcement . . ."

When she was at last certain that nearly every adult at the picnic had been offered a brochure, Stephanie was surprised at how happy she was to escape with Jim. He parked in front of the square, red brick newspaper office. It was several blocks from the City Hall, but even so they could hear the music from the rally.

When they arrived, Dede—long black hair, beads, and fringed shirt all swaying in time to the music—was singing the protest song she had practiced earlier in the apartment. The audience was mostly high school students looking for something to do on a hot August evening. They clapped in rhythm and waved hastily made posters bearing round black peace symbols and declaring: Stop the Killing; An Immoral War; Make Love, Not War.

The speaker was a young man whose long hair was held out of his face with an Indian headband. He wore a beaded and fringed vest over dangerously low-slung jeans. He denounced the war, the American government, and people who thought differently than he did. Each denunciation brought a round of cheering and chanting from the crowd which, except for some scornful looks at the watching policemen, showed little sign of getting out of control.

Then Dede and her group began singing "Where Have All the Flowers Gone?" and the audience took up the refrain.

But Stephanie only mouthed the words. She looked at the sincerity on the faces around her. They wanted to build a better world. But what were they really accomplishing? Protest, even when it didn't break out in violence, didn't seem to be a convincing answer. The breeze blew a sticky, sweet odor to her. She turned in the direction of the scent. Mind expansion through marijuana and LSD were certainly not the answer, no matter what wonders Timothy O'Leary claimed for them. And working at a boring bank job wasn't the answer, either.

17

She expressed similar thoughts to Jim over their Cokes and onion rings at the Harmony House Cafe.

He looked at her through lowered eyelids and flashed his most wicked grin. "You could have my child."

"I guess that was supposed to be funny." She glared at him. "I'm not even outraged at the immorality of the suggestion—or the new morality—I suppose I should say. But I'm absolutely furious that you can't take my questions seriously." Suddenly he was the little boy who had jiggled her chair in the spring program. She almost hit him again. Instead she stood and marched out of the cafe.

Out of the cafe and straight into a street fight. The peaceful demonstration had suddenly turned ugly when some protesters, high on marijuana or beer, had taunted the policemen standing guard against just such an outbreak.

Stephanie screamed and ducked as a rock flew past her head. The rock missed, but she banged her head on a parking meter and staggered backward.

"Did one of those pigs hit you?" A protester helped her to her feet and thrust her forward into the melee. She screamed as someone aimed a beer bottle at a policeman. The officer retaliated with his nightstick.

Then a group of cowboys joined the fracas, swinging punches right and left at the antiwar demonstrators.

Stephanie looked around for a way out, but everywhere was chaos. Cries, angry shouts, and snarled threats accompanied the sounds of smashing, ripping, and breaking.

"Stephanie, Stephanie! Over here, Steph!"

Through a break in the brawl, she heard Dede shouting to her. She turned and darted forward. Just as she moved, a boy next to her lunged forward to strike at a policeman with a peace poster. Stephanie threw up her hands to avoid getting hit with the stake. A flashbulb exploded in her eyes.

3

Late the next morning Stephanie groaned when she tried to lift her head off the pillow.

"Best not to move yet." Dede, still in her gray flannel robe, hair tousled, stood by the bed.

Stephanie touched the bandage on her forehead. "Did you rescue me?"

"Mmm. With a little help from that snake, Jimmy."

"Snake?"

"Ssss." Dede hissed like a rattler. "He had to take a picture for his beloved establishment newspaper before he helped you."

Stephanie forced her eyes open. "The paper. Is it out yet?"

"Er—I'll get you some coffee if you can sit up."

Dede fled, and a few minutes later Stephanie, who had carefully pushed herself to a sitting position, smelled the reviving aroma.

"How come you aren't at work?"

Dede was a hostess for the noon shift at the Harmony House.

"Closed for repairs—just like you. Three windows smashed after you got it last night." She handed Stephanie the coffee.

"Nampa, Idaho—just like Chicago. And there I was last night thinking how safe we were." She tried to shake her head, but it hurt too much.

"I called you in sick too."

Stephanie took a long sip of coffee. "Thanks. For everything."

Dede shrugged. "Least I could do. It's too bad when innocent bystanders get hurt."

"Well, one line of thought is that there are no innocent bystanders—that we're all responsible for the mess the world's in. I don't know—I was just trying to discuss something like that with Jim last night when we had a fight, and I walked out on him. Talk about out of the frying pan and into the fire."

"Oh, so you and Jimmy were fighting. That explains it."

"Explains what?"

Dede held out the newspaper. "Are you ready for this?"

Stephanie's groan had nothing to do with the pain ricocheting in her head. The front page of the *Free Press* bore a glaring photo, unusually clear for a newspaper picture, of her hitting a policeman over the head with a peace poster. The cutline read: "Stephanie Hamilton, daughter of Eliot Hamilton, local candidate for the House of Representatives . . ."

"That rat! That—that—"

"Snake," Dede offered. "Except that one hates to insult the reptile world like that."

"But how could he? What is this? I never . . ." She crumpled the newspaper onto the bed as the realization of what this could mean to her father's election chances hit her. There would be little use trying to explain that it wasn't at all the way it looked. Who would believe her? And besides, she *was* there. Guilt by association would do it everytime.

20

It was no surprise that the story of the Kiwanis picnic gave a far more glowing account of Benton Smith's speech than of Eliot Hamilton's. It was no surprise, but it plunged Stephanie into deeper depression yet. Working for her father's election was her one solace, her one contribution to the better society she wanted to build. But she couldn't have sabotaged the campaign more effectively if she had been paid by the other side.

Laconically she turned the pages. There was little hope that even the comics would give her a lift, although she had been a "Maggie and Jiggs" fan since childhood and now never let a day go by without reading "Pogo." But she never got as far as the comics.

"Dede, come see this!" Why did the photo of that handsome, vaguely remembered face smiling at her from page three of the *Free Press* make her forget her headache? "It's Carlton Sperlin. He's the nephew of my mother's best friend. I think his grandfather tried to marry my grandmother about a hundred years ago."

Dede sat on the edge of the bed to read. The bumping reminded Stephanie of her headache.

"Distinguished Service Medal for rescuing three servicemen and a civilian from a flaming building in Saigon." She shrugged. "Well, at least I'm glad about the civilian. Pity that someone that handsome has to be in the army— what a waste."

Stephanie bit back a retort. Barry's going to Canada hardly seemed less wasteful. Instead she said, "He's in JAG—the legal department—it's his job to see that the war is fought with justice."

Dede snorted. "That poster must have whacked you harder than I thought! Justice? How can you have justice in an unjust war?"

Stephanie groaned and slithered down in her bed. "I don't know. I can't talk about it now. Maybe later." She closed her eyes.

Dede left, but the sleep Stephanie feigned eluded her. It seemed all she heard was that America was fighting an unjust war. What was an unjust war? Was there such a thing as a just war? Surely World War II had been just— Hitler had to be stopped. What about the stories in the Old Testament of God commanding the army of Israel?

Yet she hated war—all war. She had even argued once in a history class that the Revolutionary War should never have been fought. America would have gained her independence peacefully later. She was never sure she fully believed that, but it had certainly made an interesting class discussion.

But what did all that have to do with now?

War tore up everything the world should be: peaceful, loving, beautiful, happy. Yet those qualities couldn't exist without freedom and justice. And as long as there were would-be tyrants, it seemed that man would have to fight for freedom and justice. If there were just some other way to prevent tyrants. Some better way to make better people. Some way to prevent violence. Someday she would have a chance. Someday she would do something to build a better world.

She was just drifting back to sleep when she heard a knock at the door.

Dede answered it, and a moment later Elizabeth Hamilton walked into her room. Stephanie could see how perfect her mother looked, her silver-streaked, dark hair smooth around her head, her dark blue suit ribbed in white and adorned only with a silver circle pin. Stephanie groaned. This was not a good moment for her to be hit over the head with perfection.

"My dear, we're so concerned for you. Dede just called an hour ago, or I'd have been here sooner." She kissed Stephanie on the cheek. Her lips were cool and soft.

"I'm OK. Mother, it wasn't what it looked like. I wasn't really protesting. I just happened to be there."

Elizabeth pulled off her short white gloves and sat on a small wooden chair. "I know your father will be relieved to hear that. But he'll be more concerned to hear how you are."

"I'm OK. Like I said. Really I am. I didn't hit anyone, Mother. I was trying to keep from getting hit, but he got me. I'll probably be able to go back to work tomorrow. Just a headache. The cut's not very big." She realized she was saying that for her mother's benefit. She really had no idea how big the cut was. Had she had stitches, or had Dede bandaged her herself? She'd ask later.

Elizabeth was rummaging in her purse. "Here. I always carry aspirin. Believe me, one needs them constantly on the campaign trail. Getting beat over the head verbally can be almost as bad as being hit physically." She walked out in search of a glass of water.

Stephanie was amazed. Her mother always stood so straight and never flinched, no matter what was flung her way. She had no idea her mother felt battered by the opposition. When Elizabeth returned with the water, Stephanie obediently swallowed the round, white pills.

"Do you have a vitamin B complex? It would be good for your nerves. You've been looking peaked lately. And some calcium. Women should always take calcium. I'll get you some."

Stephanie smiled. "Yes, Mother." Then she felt she should make more of an attempt to reach out. "How's Boyd?"

"He seems fine. I got a letter last week." Elizabeth proceeded to tell Stephanie the latest about her brother, who was working on a Nevada cattle ranch. "I just wish he'd open up more. I always have the feeling he's holding back—keeping something from me."

The report was followed by a brief silence. Stephanie broke it. "Good picture of Grace's nephew in the paper. Nice that he won that medal." She didn't add that it would give Grace something more to brag about.

23

Elizabeth smiled. "It's wonderful. And wonderful about the people he saved. He's sure to have a hero's welcome when he comes home."

"Oh, is he coming soon?"

Elizabeth sighed. "I suppose it could be years yet if all of this keeps dragging on. Maybe this election will make a difference. If we can get a leader with vision."

Elizabeth's visit left Stephanie feeling more confused than before—and over issues far closer to home than the rightness or wrongness of war. Why had she felt so suddenly depressed over her mother's estimation that it could be years before Carlton returned? Of course, it was depressing to think of the war dragging on, in spite of the fact that both Nixon and Humphrey declared that they had solutions for the situation. Her first thought, however, had not been for the hostilities overseas. It had been for the face in the newspaper that seemed to show such compassion in his eyes.

And then she thought of her mother—the glimpse she had had of vulnerability in a woman she always thought invulnerable.

Mother was always so strong, the one they all leaned on, the one who kept everything going when Father was involved weeks on end in a big case or campaigning for some issue to improve the community. Mother always took everything in her stride, it seemed. Nothing ever ruffled her well-coiffed hair. But Mother needed aspirin too. And she really had come up just to see how Stephanie was, not to reprimand her for unseemly behavior.

4

The bad publicity had its effect. The next poll showed Hamilton falling behind his opponent.

With the coming of autumn, cooler temperatures helped reduce the violence the long hot summer had spawned in the cities. The nation focused more sharply on the coming election. Most polls showed the Humphrey/Muskie ticket running about even with Nixon/Agnew, and no one felt quite certain what effect George Wallace's third party movement would have on the outcome.

As important as the national election was, however, the Hamilton family centered all their efforts on Eliot's election.

"Oh, I don't believe this! Have you seen Benton's latest statement on the water project development fund?" In her agitation Stephanie almost shouted, although her father was sitting in the chair next to hers in the family room of the Hamilton home.

"Yes, that's the first item I want to discuss at our strategy meeting tonight. Of course our water board must aggressively support projects to protect Idaho's water, but if we create a development fund the expenditures must be on actual projects only."

"Of course!" Stephanie bounced forward in her chair, and her hair swung farther over her cheeks. "Benton's plan for an unlimited fund would be crushing for the taxpayers. Can't people *see* that?"

Eliot ran a hand across his own sleek hair, now more gray than the shining blond it had been in his youth. "That's exactly the message we've got to get out. I'm so glad to have you on the team, Steph."

"Even after what happened last month?"

Stephanie had spoken to every group in the district who would listen to her, trying to explain that the whole incident was a mistake. Unfortunately, her own ambivalence over the war showed through when she was questioned by hawkish constituents. And it seemed that in this case one picture was worth many thousands of words. Eliot's ratings had never fully recovered.

"Dinner, you two." Elizabeth entered, wearing a ruffled apron over her blue and white striped dress. She looked flawless as always in spite of having spoken to two women's clubs that day before grocery shopping and then preparing dinner.

And as always, Stephanie bristled at the Donna Reed image. She would never make pie crusts in a ruffled apron. No one told her she had to, but the fact that her mother did such things with one hand metaphorically tied behind her back never failed to grate on Stephanie. She tossed her head and marched to the table in her short, hot-pink shift with lime green trim.

"Are you going to the meeting, Mother?" Stephanie asked after her third bite of pot roast. No matter how much she might reject her mother's lifestyle as outmoded, she couldn't help enjoying her delicious cooking.

"I don't think so. Political strategy isn't really my department. I think I can accomplish more by staying right here and praying for you."

Eliot reached across the table and took Elizabeth's hand. "That's my girl. I can always rely on your prayers." He looked up at Stephanie. "Your mother always knows what's most important."

Stephanie slowly lowered her forkful of mashed potatoes and gravy as conflicting emotions surged through her. Well, yes, God was important. She'd been taught that from infancy, and she believed it. But she couldn't believe that running to God and whining that the world was in a mess and He should fix it was enough. Surely we were supposed to get out there and do our part to make it all better. How could her mother be so smug and self-righteous in her yellow and white kitchen and carpeted living room when people were starving to death?

"But you take it easy tonight for a change, my dear. You've always done the work of three women, but I don't think any of us realized how much work this campaign would be."

Eliot's words made Stephanie look at her mother. Really look.

Where had all those wrinkles come from? Her mother's rich brown eyes were bright with intelligence and caring, but the circles under them spoke of fatigue.

Stephanie felt a stab of guilt. Who was she, with her easy—if boring—bank job and no one to care for but herself, to criticize her mother? She thought of the stories she had heard from both parents of their struggles during the Depression. Would she have had the strength to hold up through the hardships her mother had known?

She jumped to her feet. "Sit still, Mother. I'll make the coffee to go with the cake."

Later that evening Stephanie sat on a straight chair in the living room of Eliot's campaign manager, wishing the short skirt on her A-line dress wouldn't keep crawling upward. She felt even more guilty about her mental criticism of her mother.

"Elizabeth's speeches to the PTA groups seem to be one of our most successful forums." Gene Cunningham, manager of the Hamilton for the House campaign, straightened his yellow and orange psychedelic-print tie. "People generally seem to support the idea of Boise State College

27

becoming a university, but they are very worried that it will take funds away from our local schools. Elizabeth has done a great job of explaining your formula for apportionment, Eliot."

And no one said that it was almost, but not quite, enough to make up for his daughter's stupid blunder.

The meeting was interrupted by the doorbell. Stephanie was amazed when Grace Paterson walked in, her silver hair waved softly around her face and her lavender floral dress unfashionable, yet graceful, below her knees.

"Hello, Grace. What a surprise." Stephanie's greeting joined that of the others.

Grace took the chair next to Stephanie's, and Stephanie suddenly realized how her entrance had electrified the room. All these seasoned politicians seemed to be holding their breath, waiting for what this gentle lady had to say. Why *was* Grace here?

"Well, gentlemen, I won't keep you in suspense. It wasn't easy, but I got it!" She held out an envelope. "I don't know whether to blame the United States Postal Service or the US Army, but between the two of them I had three letters returned from Manila, marked addressee unknown, before they finally located Carlton. You'd think if they could find him to give him a Distinguished Service Medal they could find him to deliver a letter.

"But anyway—" she pulled a letter from the envelope and handed it to Eliot "—once my letter caught up with him, he didn't waste any time before answering in glowing terms."

"'It gives me great pleasure to endorse Eliot Hamilton for a seat in the Idaho State House of Representatives,'" Eliot read aloud, then scanned the letter silently before handing it to Gene. "A fine letter."

Gene Cunningham gave his boyish grin and ran a hand over the flattop he clung to. "Well, this ought to set things straight in the minds of any voters who think you've strayed from the fold, Eliot. Listen to this" —he read to the room— "'At a time when the Great Society has broken down, when lawlessness runs rampant in our cities, our foreign policy has failed, and we find ourselves bogged down in a war without positive direction, Idaho needs the vision of a man like Eliot Hamilton. The lives of the nearly 30,000 Americans lost in Vietnam demand that we elect people of the highest caliber to public office. I have known Eliot Hamilton all my life. He is such a man. Please join me in voting for him.'"

The room was silent.

"Well, now! That from our local war hero ought to just put us over the top." The campaign treasurer grinned over his horn-rimmed glasses.

The room buzzed with ideas of how to make maximum use of this endorsement. They finally decided to buy a half-page ad in the *Free Press*. They would print the full text of the letter along with a photo of Carlton and his honor citation, as well as run TV ads of Grace reading her nephew's letter.

"How much should we make of the fact that he wrote this from a military hospital where he's recovering from serious wounds?" Gene asked. Even his flattop and psychedelic tie managed to look sincere when he wrinkled his forehead.

"Isn't that a little crass? Capitalizing on his pain?" Stephanie spoke more sharply than she meant to.

The political pros and cons were tossed around the room until Grace brought the debate to a close. "It's something he made no reference to in his letter to me that came with this. I don't think he'd want it mentioned. Also—" she bit her lip, as though uncertain what to say "—I don't know . . . there seems to be some sort of mystery about it all. It's probably just military red tape, but not even my sister-in-law, Carlton's mother, has been able to learn much from his CO. I think we should let the letter and its writer speak for themselves."

On the first Tuesday after the first Monday in November they could only hope that it was enough.

Stephanie, in a new black-and-white striped, A-line, knit dress that made her blonde hair seem brighter than ever, helped her mother set bowls of popcorn and chips around the living room and family room.

Her parents had built this home fifteen years earlier on a hill south of Nampa, when Eliot decided to subdivide the farm he had bought as an investment after the war. The view of the wide green Boise Valley stretching to the Sawtooth Mountains to the northeast was one Stephanie had never tired of in all her growing-up years. A half-acre alfalfa field stretched down to the road. Now, in November, this was short brown stubble, but it would be sweet and green again in the spring, beckoning to Stephanie to go lie flat on her back in the middle of it as she so often had when a child.

She paused before the picture window, holding a bowl of potato chips. It was dark out now, and lights winked at her from across the valley. But in Stephanie's mind she saw the piercingly blue sky with just one fluffy white cloud ringed with a frame of alfalfa—her favorite childhood day-dreaming vista.

"Riots and crime tear our lives apart." From the television in the family room the words of James McClure, candidate for the US Congress, jarred against her idyllic childhood memories. "The hour is growing late for America. The wounds are deep, and their effective healing can only be accomplished by the wisdom, patience, and personal commitment of each American."

The weight in Stephanie's chest was so heavy she couldn't catch her breath. She had felt it often, this wave of longing, like a kind of homesickness, to be *doing something,* to work for making the world a better place. If only she knew *what* to do, *how* to go about helping people.

"Government must prudently weigh needs against resources and understand the difference between words and deeds. The future will be built by those who work for it—not by those who only promise it." McClure finished his speech. The drone of reporter interviews began, interspersed with election results from the East Coast, where the polls had already been closed for almost two hours.

So far the presidential race looked close, but Stephanie's mind was on her new determination to find a way to get more involved. Especially now that the campaign was over and she wouldn't even have this small outlet.

The lights of a car turned into the lane. In a few minutes Gene Cunningham and several other loyal workers were at the door. The next hour or so was a blur of cheers and groans. The returns began to pile up, and more friends dropped by to cheer for Eliot Hamilton, who seemed to be pulling ahead in a tight race.

Stephanie whirled between helping her mother hostess, trying to watch the analysts on TV, and visiting with their guests. She was closest to the door the next time the bell rang.

"Grace. Come in. Looks like your letter did the trick. We're better than a hundred votes ahead—oh!" Stephanie squealed with delight and held out her arms. "Grammie! What a wonderful surprise!" She darted down the steps to clasp the arm of the frail figure that Harold Paterson, Grace's husband, was assisting up the walk.

At eighty-four, Kathryn Jayne Allen was the beloved center of every family occasion. Throughout the Hamilton children's childhood, Stephanie and Boyd had spent countless happy summer days on Grammie's farm in Kuna, run by their uncle Clarey. They rode Jughead, his patient, dappled gray horse, with their older cousins Tommy and Susie. They ate Grammie's homemade bread and listened endlessly to her stories of times past. The fact that she had left her home tonight indicated the importance of the occasion.

Stephanie bent to kiss the soft, wrinkled cheek. "I'm so glad you came!"

A neighbor sprang to his feet to give his seat in front of the TV to Kathryn.

31

"My, my, isn't this something?" She smoothed the skirt of her navy blue dress printed with red and yellow flowers. "First time I voted was for Calvin Coolidge. I could have sooner, but there was always so much else to worry about closer to home. But that Coolidge was a fine fellow. I always thought Grace Coolidge was one of the prettiest First Ladies we ever had. It was such a shame about their son that died in the White House. Just seemed to take the spirit out of the president. The young people were doing the Charleston, and he got a blister on his foot—we didn't have antibiotics in those days—the simplest infection could be tragic."

Stephanie bent over the chair to get every word but was suddenly distracted when a cheer went up. The latest Canyon County results were posted: Hamilton had widened his lead.

"About time to get down to headquarters, I should think." Gene Cunningham looked at his watch. "They'll be wanting interviews from the winner."

Eliot shook hands with his friends around the room, then paused when he came to Grace. "Thank you. It was your letter that put us over the top. Polls showed it three days after we started running the ads."

Gene was right behind him, shaking hands in his bumptious, boyish way. "That's right. How *is* that heroic nephew of yours?"

Grace shook her head. "Haven't heard anything. His mother is practically distraught, knowing her son is wounded but not being able to learn anything about it."

"Well, I wouldn't worry unduly." Gene pumped her hand again. "We know he was well enough to write a prize letter, and soon as we have a new man in the White House we'll get things straightened out over there." He led the way to the door.

Stephanie slipped on a short red jacket, kissed her grandmother good-bye, and hurried out after her father.

Elizabeth waved them off. "Run along, you three. We'll stay here and watch you on television."

Campaign headquarters was a rented store on Main Street.

"Pity they tore down the Dewey Palace to make room for a modern motel," Stephanie said. She thought of the stories her mother and grandmother had told her of attending parties at the grand old hotel on similar occasions. "I guess that's what they call progress." At least Elizabeth had purchased a scrolled pediment from one of the Ionic columns surrounding the porch. It now stood in Grammie's living room, supporting a glass coffee-table top.

Gene opened the car door for Stephanie, she came back to the present, and they walked toward the building. People milling about on the sidewalk recognized Eliot and stepped forward to shake his hand and congratulate him. He greeted everybody and thanked them for all their help —a speech he repeated countless times throughout the evening.

Inside, red, white, and blue bedecked party-ers cheered and blew whistles with each victorious posting. Television sets blared the coverage of each of the three networks over a background roar of loyal party workers and hangers-on competing to express their views and celebrate the fruits of months of hard work. Both Boise television studios were represented by reporters with bulky portable cameras, while radio and newspaper reporters walked around with tape recorders and notebooks. Someone stuck a Coke in Stephanie's right hand as she waved to a friend across the room with her left.

"How about an exclusive?" a familiar voice said close to her ear.

She turned with such a start she almost sloshed the speaker with her Coke. When she saw who it was, she wished she had. She even considered tossing it at him. "And why should I ever speak to you again, James Linzler?

That was the dirtiest piece of yellow journalism I've ever seen."

He ducked his head and a curl fell across his forehead. "I guess I owe you an apology. Dede told me what happened—after it was too late. The truth is, Steph, I honestly didn't know. I walked out of the restaurant, snapped a picture of the fracas—basic reporter's instincts—then Dede screamed, and I saw you lying in the street with your head bleeding. When I developed the picture I wrote a cutline for what I thought happened. After all, you're Dede's roommate—why shouldn't you be influenced by her views?"

Stephanie stared at him. Was it possible? He looked so sincere. "Doesn't sound like you need an interview. Just make up your story on the basis of what it looks like is going on here."

"Not forgiven, huh?" He toyed with his wide necktie of swirling geometric shapes. "All right. To show you I wish you nothing but the best, I'll give you a hot tip—absolutely free. Then you can give me that interview or not—it's up to you."

She didn't agree, but she didn't turn her back either.

"Are you ready for this, baby?" He squared his shoulders and all but puffed out his chest. "I've been offered a real plum. First of the year I move to Boise and go to work for United Press International. How's that for local boy making good?"

"Congratulations, Jimmy."

"Yeah, thanks. You remember my sister Penny—graduated the year before we started Nampa High? Don't know if you heard she went off to UCLA and married a lawyer."

Feeling lost in his story, Stephanie shook her head. She really wanted to be greeting friends and watching campaign returns, not hearing Jimmy's family history.

He took her motion as an invitation to continue, however, "Name's Arnold Bartmess. He joined a big law firm in Pocatello—making a mint, I can tell you. Anyway, the point is, he has big connections—and I'm talking *big*. All it took was a word in the right place, and the job was mine."

"Er—yeah, well, congratulations." She took a step backwards.

"No, wait. You don't get my point at all. How many times have I heard you say you hate your job, that you want something more involved, more *now?* Well, listen, baby, the media is where the action is. Nothing and nobody influences the way people think more than we do. Talk about involvement, talk about now, talk about power. So— I'm offering you a chance to get in on the ground floor."

She still just stared.

"Don't get it yet, huh? You're the first person I've told, see? No one knows my job's up for grabs. And if you come in with a knockout application—and when were you ever anything less than a knockout?—right after I hand in my resignation, and I give you a really good recommendation . . . baby, you're a shoe-in."

As offensive as she found Jim's boasting and his terminology, Stephanie was intrigued by the idea. At last, an escape from her humdrum job! Newspaper reporter! Why hadn't she thought of that? She had loved working on *The Growl* for the Nampa High Bulldogs. She had even taken an intro to journalism class her sophomore year in college. Suddenly it seemed incredible to her that she had never considered a career in journalism. She looked at the journalists in the room. They certainly were where the action was. And what a great way to use her political science major.

Slowly she nodded, but before she could speak a trumpet fanfare called everyone's attention to the podium where Eliot Hamilton and the other successful local candidates were being introduced to give short victory statements.

Eliot took his turn, handsome in his dark blue suit and red tie spangled with blue and white stars. "And I pledge to continue working for the safeguarding of our water, the preservation of our scenic splendors, and the welfare of all our people."

Stephanie felt her own heart swell with pride and thought how proud her mother must feel watching all this on television. The thought crossed her mind that perhaps they weren't as dissimilar as she had believed.

Then her attention went back to cheering for her favorite politician. Out of the corner of her eye she saw Jim scribbling in his notebook and thought that in a few months she could be doing that. She cheered even louder, for she suddenly realized that the night had brought two Hamilton victories—an office for her father and a new job for herself.

Eliot came down from the platform, and she ran to hug him. Behind them on the broadscreen television Richard Nixon and Spiro Agnew stood with arms extended, fingers spread in the victory sign.

5

"And so, although I pledge to our friends here and abroad that the United States will remain a presence in the Far East"—President Nixon gave his characteristic jowly nod to emphasize the importance of his announcement—"it will forthwith be our policy to reduce the number of US military forces abroad. We will assist smaller nations to defend themselves through military and economic aid, but the Asian nations will have to carry the main burden of their own defense."

Stephanie and Dede sat with their TV dinners cooling on their laps, glued to every word.

Dede tossed her long black hair out of her eyes. "OK, Tricky Dicky—we're gonna hold you to it. We want out of there." Discarding her dinner, she picked up her guitar and strummed a few experimental notes. "Maybe I can write a song around that. 'Get us out, get us out, we want out now.'"

"I don't think it'd make it at Woodstock."

The president's speech over, NBC news had turned to an account of Jackie Onassis cruising the Mediterranean with her new husband, and Stephanie crossed the room to turn the TV off.

"Oh, Woodstock." Dede began strumming "Lucy in the Sky with Diamonds." "If they have another happening like that, I have to be there—even if it means hitchhiking across the whole United States. Though there is talk of trying to get something together out this way."

Stephanie adjusted the white headband keeping her hair in place and put a coat of white gloss over her tangerine lipstick. "Well, I'm off to make my last round of the hospital reports." She picked up her notebook. "See you later."

"I thought a reporter's life was supposed to be all glamour and excitement—major fires, dinners with the governor—not who had an emergency appendectomy and who got run in for having a dog without a license."

Stephanie sighed. "Yeah, I know. And then there was the story I filed from the police register about somebody losing a black and gold Afghan. How was I supposed to know it was a dog?"

"Can't you get your editor to send you to Cape Kennedy for the moon landing?"

"I'll be lucky to get time off to watch it on TV, let alone cover it." She slung a leather bag over her shoulder and went out the door. It was true her reporter's job held neither the glamour nor the scope she had envisioned, and she had taken a cut in pay with the change. But she found the work easy, and even routine court reports were more interesting than her old job. The part she liked best was the opportunity to exert her creativity in feature writing—like the piece she was working on for next week about pioneering in Idaho's desert. She had interviewed two old-timers who had come to the desert just after the turn of the century and endured life in the dirt and the sagebrush for years before the coming of irrigation water.

She thought about her project as she drove her little green Mustang on her rounds. This weekend it would all come together for her when her family gathered to celebrate the anniversary of their favorite pioneer's coming to Idaho. Now eighty-five, Kathryn Jayne Allen was one of the oldest living Idaho pioneers, and Stephanie planned to use her grandmother's celebration as the centerpiece for her article.

She looked forward to the event with mixed emotions. Working together as a family last summer and fall for Eliot's election had seemed a good experience for them all. It had been an opportunity to close some of the generation gap that appeared to be inevitable in even the closest of families today. Since then, however, they had seen each other only at Christmas, the opening of the new session of the legislature in January, and at Easter. Her brother, Boyd, hadn't even come for Christmas.

Thoughts of Boyd followed her up the broad sidewalk to the hospital, where she would check the emergency room reports as she did twice each day. She hoped Boyd would come for Grammie's party as he had promised. She didn't understand his estrangement from the family. They had been so close as children.

As far as she knew he had not fought with either of their parents, although she knew they were disappointed that their only son had chosen to drop out after only two years of college. She supposed that Boyd must have feelings similar to some of her own, although probably directed toward their father rather than their mother. Eliot was just so successful, so great at everything he did, that Boyd must feel it was an impossible act to follow—one he didn't even want to follow. Yet at the same time he was probably feeling guilty that he wasn't trying.

Stephanie knew that feeling. By the time her mother was Stephanie's age, she had achieved her career goal of becoming a teacher and was married. Not that Stephanie had any desire to be either a teacher or a wife, but she felt that by the age of twenty-eight she should have achieved *some* goal.

Two days later she was still feeling uneasy as she drove to Kuna for the celebration. At least she felt good about the way she looked. Her new soft gold miniskirt and vest, her long-sleeved ivory blouse, made her feel feminine

39

and classy at the same time. She also knew that the wide gold bar sweeping her hair behind her right ear was the perfect accent for her blondness.

She pulled into the parking lot of the newly remodeled church on Kuna's Main Street—the church where both her mother and grandmother had been married. She walked into the fellowship hall that still smelled of fresh paint.

The first thing to catch her eye when she entered the busy hall was the center of calm at the front of the room. Sitting in her favorite overstuffed chair, which her son had brought from home, was Kathryn Esther Allen, Queen for the Day.

"Grammie!" Stephanie bent to kiss her. Being with Grammie was always being at home. "Your new dress is beautiful!"

Kathryn smiled as she smoothed the wide lace collar of her blue and lavender flowered dress. "Thank you, my dear. Your mother and Alex and Mavis bought it for me, but I expect your mother was the guiding hand."

Stephanie smiled. "Yes. She usually is." She held out a blue and yellow gift-wrapped package of bath oil and powder. "Hope you like these—they're my favorite."

Before Kathryn could reply, Elizabeth and her sister, Alexandra, wheeled a three-tiered birthday cake across the room, and everyone started singing, "Happy birthday to you . . ."

"My, oh, my." Kathryn's voice quavered when she attempted to speak loudly enough to be heard throughout the room. "It's not really my birthday yet, you know. It's really the anniversary of Papa's and my arrival in Kuna." She paused. "I've never forgotten how awful *that* was. It was 106 degrees, and I'd never been in sagebrush before, and Papa's brother wasn't there to meet us because his wife had just died . . ."

She paused again to shake her head. "Oh, my, those were some days, and here I am rattling on while all those candles are melting my cake." She looked at her two great-grandchildren. "Rachel, Esther, can you two blow these out for me before someone brings in a fire extinguisher?"

Fourteen-year-old Rachel, who bore the name of their Scottish ancestress and her father Tommy's red hair, led her dark-haired, ten-year-old sister to the center of the room. At another signal from Kathryn, Jenny Fulmont—Alexandra's daughter—her brown braids tied in blue ribbons—joined them as did Grace's grandchildren. They began huffing and puffing at the eighty-five candles.

Elizabeth was crisp and cool in a white sheath dress, navy piping bordering its square collar and brass buttons lining the front. She stepped forward to cut the cake and handed the first piece to Kathryn. "Now, don't you wait to start eating this, Mama. We know how fond you've always been of sweets."

Kathryn set down the glass of pink punch Alex had given her and took the cake. "That's what I attribute my long life to." Her laugh was shaky, but it still held the joyous ring it had when she was a girl.

Stephanie, who was taking careful mental notes for the feature story she would file later, prodded, "Tell us your real secret, Grammie."

Kathryn's eyes sparkled as she shook her head. "There's no secret." She patted the large black book resting on the low table beside her chair. "It's all right there in the Bible. Only thing that makes it a secret is the fact that folks don't read it anymore. But I'll tell you what I've learned. You have to be strong. Strong inside. You have to be a survivor. I never quit. I just did what I had to do and kept on—with my head up when I could. But if I couldn't hold my head up, I kept on anyway. And I kept praying."

Kathryn paused for so long that Stephanie thought she was finished and started to say something. But Kathryn held up her hand. "And I'll tell you another thing. I never told anyone before, but now that you're all here, it seems like a good time. Something it seems like we don't hear

41

much about anymore is praying through. But it used to be that when something was really important—important in terms of eternity—we didn't just pray about it, we prayed *through.*

"We prayed and prayed and kept on praying until we had an assurance from God that He hadn't just heard us but that He would grant what we asked. You have to be mighty careful with that kind of praying—I've heard stories of people who made terrible mistakes by praying for the wrong thing—but one thing we can always be sure is the will of God is the salvation of our children."

Kathryn's voice took on the strength of a much younger woman. "So I prayed through for every one of my children and my grandchildren." She looked around the room. "I prayed through that I'd see every one of you in heaven."

Most of those she spoke of were standing before her: Big, kind, Clarey with his little, dark Mavis and their grown, married children, Tommy and Susie. Susie, with the soft brown hair and round eyes that always made her look like a surprised, trusting child, stood beside her precisely tailored husband, Bob Newman, in his narrow-waisted, bell-bottom suit, his dark brown hair trimmed well above his collar. No antiestablishment long hair was going to keep him from climbing the corporate ladder.

Kathryn's second daughter, Alexandra, her hair still as blonde and bouncy as in her childhood but with her blue eyes covered by horn-rimmed spectacles, stood by Leonard Fulmont, her tweedy, college professor husband. Nine-year-old Jennifer shifted from one foot to another and twirled her pigtails. Her mother kept telling her to be still.

Then Elizabeth and Eliot . . .

With her grandmother's words gripping her mind, Stephanie looked at each one. Yes, it was really amazing in these days when all values were being overthrown that every one of these people professed a vital personal faith. What a testimony to Kathryn's life. And the many, many friends that had come today too: Grace and Harold Paterson; Albert and Patricia Sperlin, the war hero's parents, down from their ranch in Ketchum—and on around the room—all these lives had been touched and influenced for good by one little woman who had simply tried to live her life by the Bible.

Then Stephanie's throat tightened. What about the ones not here? What about her Uncle Boyd? Was he in heaven with the infant Eldon her mother had so often told her of? At least it was a comfort to Kathryn to think so. But what about the other Boyd, Stephanie's brother? No one spoke of their disappointment at not seeing him today, but she knew it weighed especially heavy on her mother.

And finally the question she couldn't escape. What about herself? Where did she place the faith of her fathers in her own life? But that was the trouble, wasn't it? It was just the faith of her fathers. She knew that although she hadn't openly rejected the traditional Christianity she had been reared with, it would have to become truly her own if it were to sustain her through eighty-five years as Kathryn's had her.

She jerked as her grandmother's voice echoed her thoughts. "You know, the Bible talks about the faith of our fathers—or is that just a song? Anyway, I know the Bible says that the sins of the fathers are visited on the children unto the third and fourth generation. But I've always believed that the righteousness of the mothers could go just as far." She nodded, looking at each one around her. "And I don't think I was very far wrong." She passed a thin, blue-veined hand over her forehead. "That's enough speech-making for now. But I do have such wonderful memories."

Elizabeth stepped up to serve the cake, and Alex began ladling punch.

As the crowd shifted, Stephanie found herself standing next to the Sperlins. She asked them first about their daughter Julia. Stephanie had vague memories of having met her just once when they were in grade school. But

43

Elizabeth mentioned her occasionally, so Stephanie felt she knew her.

"She's managing a shop in Spokane," Albert said. As with all the Sperlins, Stephanie had to look way up when he spoke. "Women's dresses," he added.

"Not a shop. A boutique." His wife, Patricia, tossed her sun-streaked hair. "I think that means everything in it is very high-fashioned, and she can charge about double for it all." Her smile was brilliant in her tanned face. It was easy to see that life on the cattle ranch agreed with her perfectly.

"We all appreciated Carlton's letter so much last fall." Stephanie wanted to ask about the enigmatic hero but wasn't sure a direct question would be tactful. She didn't know how his recovery was progressing.

"So glad we could have a part in helping," Albert answered. "Your father's doing a fine job in the legislature. We need more men like him."

Stephanie agreed, but that wasn't the direction she had hoped the conversation would go.

Then Patricia spoke. "He'll be home in a month or two. I can't believe it. I've missed him so much."

"How is he?"

"Oh, he's fine!"

"Fine. Just fine." The Sperlins spoke in tandem, very quickly, then turned to greet other guests.

Stephanie stood blinking. What was going on? If he was so fine why did they run from the topic?

"Steph, it's so nice to see you!" Susie, in a white-collared blue dress, batted her blue saucer eyes at Stephanie.

"Oh, hi, Sue. What are you doing these days?"

"We're moving. What an awful job. We found a darling little house in the Highlands, overlooking the golf course, but it needed so much work—paint, wallpaper, everything. With Bob gone so much it's been a full-time job for me. We're just about organized now, though. I'd love to have you come see me the next time you're in Boise.

We even have a spare room. You could stay over if you had meetings to go to or something."

Stephanie thanked her and answered her questions about life as a reporter. Then Susie answered Steph's question's about Bob's job as an engineer for Morrison-Knudsen—the world's largest construction firm, based right there in Boise. That seemed to cover it. Neither cousin seemed able to think of much more to say.

Stephanie couldn't help liking her cousin. Nobody could possibly dislike Susie. But Stephanie also couldn't help finding her irritating. She was so old-fashioned. It was like she was frozen in the fifties. Susie could have been the daughter on the "Donna Reed Show." And Stephanie could never get away from the uncomfortable feeling that that was the way *she* was supposed to have turned out.

Stephanie turned to the punch bowl. "Would you like me to serve for a while, Aunt Alex?"

Almost as a reflex, Alex handed her a cup of fruit punch. "Sure, I wouldn't mind a chance to sit down, although it's not a very arduous job. We really could let people help themselves to refills. I don't know why they're so slow. I'm afraid people will want to leave before the big surprise."

"Surprise?"

"Oh, I assumed Elizabeth would have told you."

She rushed on before Stephanie was forced to explain that communication between her mother and herself wasn't all that it might be. "We have a special guest coming. All the way from Scotland. Let's see, I think she'd be your second or third cousin or something—I haven't really worked it out."

"Good grief! That *is* a surprise. I didn't know I had a Scottish cousin."

"Fred Sperlin's delegated to bring her from the airport. But she's not the surprise. We're trying to hold the surprise until they're here too."

Stephanie started to ask more, but a jaunty horn-tooting outside told them they had new arrivals. A minute later

45

the doorway of the fellowship hall was filled with six-foot-three Fred Sperlin ushering in a five-foot-two lass in an emerald green dress.

"Howdy, folks. This here's Miss Fiona Buchanan come all the way from Scotland to celebrate with us."

Fiona was immediately the center of attention—for everyone in the room except Stephanie. She was looking the other direction. Still standing in the foyer, framed by the doorway, the sun making an aureole of his golden hair, was a man who must have stepped straight from the legends of Greek gods. What could Apollo possibly be doing in Kuna, Idaho?

Then on second look, Stephanie revised her appellation. Not Apollo, but a young King David. And not too young —about thirty-five, she judged, as he stepped through the doorway. But where had he come from? This was a gathering of family and close friends. She was sure she had never seen him before.

Meanwhile, everyone else moved to make the Scottish cousin welcome. Fiona was smiling at the chorused greetings. Stephanie, wrenching her attention from King David to Fiona, now thought of Snow White with her raven black hair and eyes, snow-white skin, and red lips. Stephanie tried to sort out in her mind just where this beautiful girl fit in the family tree.

She knew that Kathryn's husband, Merrick Allen, had come from Scotland. She had heard Grammie tell about her honeymoon to meet his family in Selkirk. It seemed that Merrick had a sister. She searched her mind for a name—Rowena, maybe. A sister who had a son that inherited the estate.

It must have been that son's son that Uncle Boyd had gone off with to join the RAF in the '30s. *Ian.* She suddenly recalled his name. So Fiona must be Ian's daughter—or possibly niece or cousin? It was so complicated. She longed for a piece of paper to work it all out on.

46

So had the golden mystery man come with Fiona? Her boyfriend? Husband? Brother? Why did Stephanie shrink so from any designation that would make him unavailable? What did she care about this or any man? She had her career. She had her goals. None of them required a man to bring fulfillment. And yet . . .

At the front of the room Elizabeth was presenting Fiona to Kathryn, and Stephanie moved closer to hear.

In a charming gesture Fiona had dropped to her knees beside Kathryn's chair, and Kathryn held a slim white hand in both of her wrinkled ones.

"So you're little Robbie Bruce's granddaughter. He was just a lad when I met him—making his first riding . . ." Her voice trailed off as her memory followed it. "Do they still do that?"

"Oh, yes. It's grand!"

"I'll never forget it—the horses took off like thunder with the skirl of the bagpipes and everyone singing and cheering. I was just a girl then, and I'd never seen anything like it. And the flag. Do they still cast the flag?"

"Aye. Every year."

"My Merrick cast the flag that year. It meant so much, because it was a signal he'd been forgiven by his family. Oh, but that was such a long time ago." Her voice wavered, and Stephanie thought she saw a tear shimmer in the pale eyes. "Such wonderful memories. Oh, how I wish I could share them with all of you—especially you little ones." Kathryn smiled at the children gathered around. "The world was such a different place then."

"I'm so glad you said that, Mama." In her most efficient chairwoman manner Elizabeth stepped forward. "I think that's a perfect opening for me to give you all the great surprise I've prepared for this day."

She stood beside Kathryn and placed a hand on her shoulder. "Mama, you've always been such an inspiration and source of wisdom to us. And as much as we love hearing your stories, we know you won't always be with us to tell them."

"Well, now, I just might hold on longer than you think." Kathryn's blue eyes had faded to a pale gray, but they hadn't lost their mischievous twinkle. Then she looked serious. "Sometimes, though, I think I'd like to see Papa and my Merrick and our little Eldon—sometimes I wonder if he'll still be just six weeks old in heaven."

"Well, Mama, we know even you can't tell us about the future, but you sure have a lot to tell us about the past. So that's why I had copies of this printed up." She stepped to the side of the room and lifted the long white cloth that Stephanie had supposed covered a pile of gifts—to reveal a stack of red-bound books. "Now whenever one of us wants to visit with you when you're not available, Mama, we can just sit down and read your book." She placed a thick, paperback volume in Kathryn's hands.

"Land sakes a' mercy, what's this? Don't tell me you had those old notebooks I scribble in *printed up?*" Kathryn turned the heavy book over and over in her hands. Then she let it come to rest in her lap and laced her thin fingers on top of it.

The book was as thick as an epic novel, for she had kept her journal for almost seventy years. The first entries in her girlish scrawl told of the trip she and her papa made by train from Nebraska to Idaho in the summer heat of 1902. She had spared nothing in recording her horror at arriving at their new home. They had found a dilapidated wooden sign that said KUNA. It had marked a handful of scattered homestead shacks, a graveyard containing some twenty graves where the first settlers had all died of diphtheria, and, as far as she could see in every direction, miles and miles of brown, dusty sagebrush. That had been the only time on the whole journey when the seventeen-year-old girl had wanted to turn around and run.

She hadn't written every day, of course. Sometimes there were gaps of weeks, months, even years. Many days she had written only a line or two—especially when the children were small or Merrick was sick or during the Depression when she was too exhausted to write more. And yet, maybe some of those two-line entries told the most. She shook her head. "Mercy me. I just can't believe I wrote a book."

"That's exactly what you did, Mama. And I can tell you all" —Elizabeth looked at their family and close friends gathered there— "I never had more fun in my life than I've had these past months reading Mama's diaries and putting them all together for you. But I do think you should all go together to buy me a new pair of glasses." She turned to Kathryn as everyone laughed. "Your writing wasn't always very clear, Mama." And to prove it she had included some facsimile pages from Kathryn's own hand.

"Well, I just don't believe this." Kathryn shook her head. "I wondered what you were doing when you asked for those old things from the attic. When you asked if I minded the whole family reading them, I sure didn't think you had anything like this in mind. I don't know—I think you could spend the time a whole lot better reading the Bible."

Nine-year-old Jennifer, Kathryn's youngest grandchild hugged her grandmother. "Never mind, Grams. I think I might like some of your stories better."

Fiona took advantage of the little break in the proceedings the child's remark offered to turn to Kathryn. "I hope you don't mind, but I brought another friend with me."

Kathryn looked around with interest, and Fiona waved to the man at the back of the room. As he came forward Stephanie admired the classic cut of his tweed suit and the way the rust fleck in the fabric and the matching tie brought out the copper lights in his hair.

"This is David Fraser." Fiona presented him to Kathryn. "He's the closest thing I've ever had to a big brother, and he's going to be working right near here in Boise."

The conversation went on—something about his working for the Ministry of Agriculture in Edinburgh and doing some kind of job exchange with the Idaho Woolgrowers Commission. But Stephanie was still focusing on his name. How extraordinary that she had dubbed him David and that was his name. At the same time she was trying not to focus on the strange way her heart was thumping.

Elizabeth took charge again. "Now, I know you're all anxious to get your own copies of Mother's book—especially to see what pictures I chose for the middle. If some of you wondered why Alex and I were asking about old photos a few months back, now you know."

Stephanie wrenched her attention back to Elizabeth. As usual, her mother really was absolutely amazing: the efficiency, the organization, the perfection with which she did everything. What a wonderful thing this book would be for their family and close friends, and how superbly Elizabeth had managed everything, with apparently only the slightest help from Alex. And as always, her mother's excellence made Stephanie want to crawl in a dark corner. It was certainly no wonder that her mother had never fully approved of her—that she had never quite come up to the mark—how could anybody come up to *that* mark?

As she watched everyone congratulate Elizabeth on another wonderful accomplishment, Stephanie thought back, trying to pick out the milestones in their generation gap. Her freshman year at Northwest Christian College. It wasn't the fact, as everyone had assumed, that both her parents had left brilliant records there, nor the fact that both her Aunt Alex and Uncle Leonard Fulmont were on the faculty, that caused her to transfer to the state college. It was when she had called home to tell her mother she had made straight A's and Elizabeth had asked, "Why aren't they A pluses?" She had said it as a joke, but Stephanie knew she meant it.

Elizabeth hadn't said anything when Stephanie declared her political science major instead of becoming a teacher like her mother. But Stephanie hadn't forgotten the innumerable times she had heard her mother say, "I always think teaching is the nicest profession there is for a woman."

That hadn't caused a major break, but when Stephanie turned down Davey's proposal after graduation—Davey Brewington, son of one of the leading pioneer families in Kuna, nephew of a close friend of her mother's, and Elizabeth's hand-picked candidate for son-in-law—the rift had widened with a grating creak.

The final thing, of course, had been Boyd's going away. Stephanie and her brother had fought remarkably little growing up. Why had they had to have a row the night before he left? Stephanie couldn't even remember what it was about now. Had his leaving really been her fault? She knew her mother thought so, and no matter what she did, she couldn't make it up to her. She wasn't a particularly great daughter. She certainly couldn't be both daughter and son.

She moved forward to receive her book. "What are you thinking so hard about, my dear? Your forehead's all wrinkley."

Stephanie smiled at her grandmother and reached out to take her hand. It was as frail as a toothpick sculpture. "Oh, Grammie, I was thinking about Boyd. I wish he were here."

Kathryn nodded. "Yes. They told me he was working on a ranch. But I don't think that's right. He never came back from the war."

"Oh, Grams . . ." Stephanie hugged her, aware of the thinness of her shoulders. Kathryn's mind was usually as clear as a bell. She almost never forgot anything or got confused. But the loss of the son who flew raids over France for the RAF in 1940 had left a gap in her life that her mind now sometimes filled with the grandson who was also missing.

And then, right in the midst of their reminiscing and exclaiming over Kathryn's memoirs, they were not just

51

jerked back to the present but were thrust ahead into the coming decades. Clarey, along with several of the other guests, had been keeping an eye on the small black and white television set in a side room. Now he burst into the hall. "They did it! They just walked on the moon!"

Everyone's attention shifted again—Stephanie's back to David Fraser as he followed Fiona around the room.

6

The next day Stephanie postponed the writing of her pioneer feature article to get to know their Scottish visitors better. After all, this was news, so over a cup of tea—brewed strong and served with milk and sugar the way they liked it—she took notes as she visited with Fiona and David at Elizabeth and Eliot's home.

"And so how did you come to suddenly show up on our doorstep, so to speak?" she asked Fiona.

"Ooh, it was a thing I'd always wanted to do. I've dreamed of it ever since I can remember." The charm of Fiona's broad vowels made Stephanie smile at the simplest statements. "It was my faether, you see. He talked so much about your Boyd when I was growing up. I always wanted to meet my American cousins. I knew you'd all be as nice as this man my faether thought so much of. So when my grandmother died last spring and left me some money, I knew what I wanted to do. I'll be marrying soon—" she paused and bit her lip, while Stephanie's heart did a flip "—at least I hope it'll be soon. We canna' wed until Callum takes his degree at University and has a position."

Stephanie let herself breathe again. Callum. That was fine. "How long will that be?"

Fiona shook her head, and her close-cropped, dark curls bounced. "It may be a wee while yet. But my Callum's worth waiting for. And I have my work." She held her breath for a moment. "Oh, but wouldn't it be wonderful if you could come to Scotland for our wedding!"

Stephanie agreed, thinking how much such a trip would mean to Grammie. Then she encouraged Fiona to tell more about Callum and her job as a music teacher before they got back to talking about their families.

"And did you know your uncle was in love with my mother too?" Fiona asked.

"No. I had no idea. I really don't know much about Uncle Boyd at all. But I'd be surprised if even Grammie knew that. I don't think he was very good about writing after he went to Scotland."

"Well, you wouldn't be surprised if you saw my mother. She's still beautiful. But I've seen pictures of her when she was a girl—red hair hanging below her waist, and laughing all the time. Apparently both my faether and your uncle were in love with her. She must have led them a merry chase. Barbara, her name is—a very 'Bonnie Barbara Allen' she'd have been if she'd married your Boyd."

Then Stephanie turned to David, her pencil poised. "And just what will you be doing in Idaho, Mr. Fraser?" She hoped she sounded professional.

He leaned back, and the ivory cushions of Elizabeth's sofa made a perfect background for his red-gold coloring. He smiled the slow smile that gave an upward curve to all of his long face. "Call me David. After all, I've always stood as a big brother to Fiona, so that must make us the next best thing to cousins."

Stephanie smiled back. She could think of something better than cousins.

"I'm very pleased"—he gave the slightest roll to his r's —"about being here. I'll be working with your wool growers, teaching them some of our Scottish methods and learning some of your techniques to take home."

"And you'll be in Boise?"

"Oh, aye. That'll be my headquarters, so to speak, but I think most of my time will be spent on sheep ranches—working right with the beasties and their owners."

For all his friendliness and relaxed manner, David was not an expansive talker. Stephanie had to coax every bit of his story out of him. But finally she got a fairly complete picture of how working with the sheep on his family's estate of Heatherleigh, which marched with the Buchanan's Woodburn, had led to his taking a degree in veterinary science at Edinburgh University. His specialty was in woolgrowing in temperate climates—which made him a perfect candidate to do the exchange sponsored by their Min of Ag and the Idaho commission.

"How long will you be here?" Stephanie held her breath. An exchange program could be anything from two weeks to two years.

"I've committed to stay a year. Since our work is climate-sensitive, I'll need to be here for all the seasons. Then we can extend if all the parties want to."

"And your family?" Stephanie prompted, then reminded herself she must keep taking notes in order to give the conversation an official air.

David answered readily, telling about his older, married sister, Eliza, her children, and his two younger brothers still working with their father at Heatherleigh.

Stephanie would have liked to probe deeper, but that seemed to be as much of his personal life as their guest wished to divulge.

Two weeks later Fiona went back to Scotland, taking with her many copies of Stephanie's story. It had run in the *Free Press* with a picture of Fiona and David wearing tams in their clan's tartans. Fiona vowed to read every word in Kathryn's book and write to them all often.

"Oh, my dear, how I wish I could be going back with you—just one more time." Stephanie was amazed at the depth of longing in her grandmother's voice as she hugged

Fiona good-bye. It seemed that Fiona's visit had brightened all of Kathryn's girlhood memories of her honeymoon and the early days of her long and happy marriage to Merrick. How wonderful it would be if Grammie could go back.

But Stephanie was very glad that one person did not go back. Bob and Susie helped David find a small, inexpensive apartment in Boise, and several family occasions throughout that fall brought Stephanie and David together. He was always so friendly, always seemed to single Stephanie out for special attention, but he never asked her for a date.

Her heart jumped every time he winked at her, as he often did. It even affected her after she saw him do it to others, so that she knew it was little more than a habit. And no matter how sternly she reminded herself that a man in her life was a complication she didn't need—nothing more than a hindrance to progress toward all her goals —she still found herself at every family dinner making an extra effort to say witty things to their Scottish guest so that he would wink at her.

It was amazing that the simple presence of one charming man could make such a difference in Stephanie's life. Suddenly the sum total of her days was made up of more than newspaper reporting and worry about the turmoil the world was in.

David was from another world—a world of green hillsides dotted with sheep, of whitewashed, thatched-roofed crofters' huts set beside rushing streams, of ancient ballads and poetry. A world he never seemed to tire of sharing with them, especially when Kathryn encouraged him to "speak a bit of Bobby Burns like my Merrick used to do."

Thanksgiving dinner was the best Stephanie could remember in years. For once she had come not just out of duty or a sense of family loyalty. There was nowhere else she wanted to be more than right there in the old family house in Kuna—listening to the poetry of Robert Burns from the lips of the visitor to whom the whole family was showing a real, American Thanksgiving:

> "Ye banks and braes o' bonnie Doon
>   How can ye bloom sae fresh and fair?
> How can ye chant, ye little birds,
>   And I saw weary fu' o' care?
> Thou'lt break my heart, thou warbling bird,
>   That wantons through the flowering thorn'
> Thou minds me o' departed joys,
>   Departed never to return."

Stephanie saw Kathryn brush a tear away with her thin, blue-veined hand. "Stephanie, why don't you take David for a walk? I know that's what they'd do in Scotland after a meal like this."

As much as she wanted to do just that, Stephanie felt she must protest. "Oh, but there's all these dishes—"

The remains of pumpkin, mince, and apple pies sat on the table in front of them. On the sideboard to the right, the carcass of a twenty-some-pound turkey still lay surrounded by bowls of potatoes, dressing, gravy, cranberry sauce.

"Nonsense, dear, out you go." There was no arguing with Elizabeth's chairwoman manner. "There isn't room for us all to work in the kitchen at once anyway. There will be plenty to do when you get back."

"It's a nice walk to the pond at the bottom of the south forty," Kathryn suggested, then smiled. "When I was a girl, folks used to walk along the railroad tracks just for something to do on Sunday afternoons."

In a few minutes, bundled into warm woolen jackets, scarves, and gloves, Stephanie and David crunched across the frosty ground. The alfalfa fields ran rows of brown stubble between the irrigation furrows. To their left, last summer's onion field lay a mass of small, brown mounds that could have been dug by a corps of hyperactive gophers.

57

At first she encouraged David to talk about his work.

"Oh, aye, I'm enjoying it fine. Your farmers' ideas are much more modern than ours. I'll have ideas and aplenty to take back with me—but getting our farmers to adopt them will be something else."

"So you like it here?"

"Oh, I like it fine. It's a grand opportunity. But—"

"But naturally you miss home." At last she had an opening to turn the conversation to something more personal.

For a while he talked about his sister and brothers, drawing for her a charming picture of their rural life in the Scottish Borders.

"In some ways not so different from here—cattle and land are pretty much the same wherever you farm—but here there's so much more frenzy to be new, to be doing, to be going. At home it's more peaceful inside."

"Inside?"

"Inside people. Less striving for hurry inside them."

Stephanie's foot slipped on a frosty patch of stubble.

He took her arm to support her over the rough ground. When the path smoothed out a bit he still held her. "And it's greener. Green even where it isn't irrigated."

But she didn't want to talk about the landscape. She wanted to talk about the people. Especially about one certain person. Only she couldn't imagine how to broach the subject. "Your brothers—will they be marrying soon, do you think?" That seemed the best she could do.

It was enough. Suddenly it was as if that she had turned the key. David wanted to talk. "Aye. Gordie is probably married by now. They only waited until I was gone, I'm sure."

"You mean your brother got married, and no one even told you?"

"They meant it as a kindness. It's a long, old story, but I'll tell it if ye wish. The pond's still a long way ahead." He pointed to the circle of bare trees they were heading towards.

"Perhaps the telling will keep us warm." White steam puffed from his mouth as he spoke.

"Yes, please." Stephanie gave him her most encouraging smile.

But in the end, it was a short tale indeed. He and Mary had been sweethearts since early days in Selkirk grammar school. Gordon, two years younger, had always teased them mercilessly but had made himself available to help Mary with anything she might need when David wasn't around. Especially when David went off to university.

It was years until he earned his doctor's degree, but Mary waited. She was patient, happy to go to parties with Gordon when David was away. At last David returned with his degree and a good job. So they set the wedding date. He was so happy to have his long-held dreams coming true that he didn't notice the least reticence in Mary.

The night before the wedding she confessed. It was Gordie she loved. David gave her a parting kiss, took back his ring, and applied to work in America.

"And 'there I took the last fareweel o' my sweet Highland Mary.'" Never had Burns been quoted so coldly.

He told it all in short sentences with no show of emotion. His fierce control told Stephanie how raw the pain still was. She pulled off her red wool mitten and slipped her hand in his inside his pocket. Although already side-by-side, it seemed that every step brought them closer to each other. Stephanie rested her head against his arm. She wanted him to know how much she cared.

He seemed to discern her message, for when they came to the ice-covered pond he took his hands out of his pockets and put his arms around her. His kiss was like nothing she had ever experienced before. The two of them were a blaze of ecstasy in a world of icy frost—a glowing ruby set in a ring of cold diamonds.

7

The following weeks and months Stephanie felt like a schizophrenia victim. Her days were filled with reports of police emergencies and student demonstrations. These were on a far smaller scale than those that filled her television screen in the evening, as the fighting in Southeast Asia spread to Cambodia, but they were disturbance enough for their small community. At the same time, her mind held images of green, rolling hillsides where baby lambs tottered behind their mothers and daffodils changed to daisies as spring turned into summer.

While Stephanie longed to be rambling on those misty hillsides with one very special Scotsman quoting Robert Burns to her, Dede continued composing protest songs and singing them almost nightly with her group, The Gathering.

In spite of the spread of the war, however, President Nixon continued his program of Vietnamization. He brought thousands of troops home, many of them to Idaho. Stephanie, with the energy and determination that had always won her success, threw herself more fiercely than ever into her reporter's job and began an in-depth series on how the changes in the war were changing lives in Idaho.

Never mind that David had been gone since early spring, working on a sheep ranch in the eastern part of the state. His letters were infrequent but well worth waiting for. They were filled with the same Celtic touch of poetry as his speech when he described the sheep and people he worked with. He shared a little of his homesickness for his own moist, green hills. And some homesickness for her?

Stephanie hoped so. She read his closing line for the twentieth time. "I miss ye lass."

Then another side of her personality took over and argued. What did she think she was doing, mooning about like this over a man she barely knew? Hadn't she always said she didn't need a man? Not even one whose wistful blue eyes bore the stamp of so much pain that she longed to wipe away?

Thursday was an exceptionally hot day in late August, especially for Stephanie, whose little green Mustang didn't have air conditioning. She had driven to Boise early to interview a war returnee in the Veteran's Hospital. Then she had an extended interview with several officials in the Veterans' Administration, so she wound up driving home to her likewise un–air-conditioned apartment in the hottest part of the day. The backs of her legs, where her short blue and white checked skirt had slid up, stuck to the vinyl car seat. Sweat ran down the back of her neck onto her white cotton blouse that had once been crisp.

Dede, in tank top and cut-off jeans, was sitting under an elm tree in the front yard of their apartment house, working on the chords for her newest song, when Stephanie pulled up in front. "You're late. Your editor called three times. He has an interview for you. He said to tell you four o'clock." She glanced at her watch. "That gives you about nine minutes."

"What?" Stephanie slammed the car door behind her. "I've been doing interviews all day. I'm exhausted. Why can't Mark do it?"

"He said it's an old friend of yours. Besides this Vietnamization in Idaho thing is your baby."

61

Stephanie sighed and started toward the stairs. She'd call Mark Brown and tell him just how she felt. If it was her baby, she could set up her own interviews. There was absolutely no way she was going to do another session today.

Fifteen minutes later she was in Mark Brown's office, her pencil poised over her stenographer's pad, struggling to look as fresh and think as clearly as if it were ten o'clock in the morning. At least the editor's office was air-conditioned, and he had provided iced Cokes for her and her subject before leaving them alone.

Them. As soon as Mark had told her who the subject of this article was, she knew she was licked. After all, Carlton Sperlin was the area's most decorated hero, and his letter of endorsement had won the election for her father. But she just couldn't believe Mark would thrust her into a situation like this unprepared. She was meticulous about studying her subjects ahead, never going to an interview without prepared questions. Except this time.

"Er—how long have you been back now, Mr. Sperlin?"

"Almost a year." He answered her questions politely but without the expansiveness that could have saved her fumbling.

She uncrossed her legs when she saw him glance at her knees. He looked so maddeningly cool. His black hair was gleamingly in place, his white shirt unwrinkled. He hadn't even removed his pale blue sport jacket that matched his blue and silver tie. "And you've taken a job with a large law firm in Boise?"

He nodded and named the firm. Then, with a spark of the twinkle that never seemed to be very far from his dark eyes, he took pity on her. He began to talk openly about how glad he was to be home, how much the support of his family and friends had meant to him in the dark days of the war, in contrast to how disspiriting the news of the antiwar demonstrations had been.

His words were succinct and highly quotable, but Stephanie chewed the end of her pencil a moment. She

62

didn't want to take a political stance in these articles. And if she did, she wasn't at all sure that was the stance she would take. Then she shrugged. After all, she was a reporter. It was her job to report. She wrote down his statements verbatim.

Then she remembered the questions that had surrounded the injuries that had led to his discharge. "We so appreciated the letter you wrote for my father two years ago. If I remember correctly, you wrote that from a hospital. Can you tell us more about your wounds and recovery?"

The eyes went from sparkly to serious. The little smile that played around the corners of his mouth most of the time faded to hard lines. He thought for so long she decided he wasn't going to answer her question. Then he leaned forward and spoke with a sincerity she hadn't heard in his voice before. "The grace of God was all that pulled me through. Without His strength and the prayers of my family and friends there's no way I'd be here today."

She scribbled a note. "Yes, I'm sure faith is very important at a time like that, but I'm sure our readers would like to know—"

The door behind her opened, and Mark Brown walked in. "Got enough have you, Steph? Thanks so much for stopping by, Carlton." He shook hands with the man, who had risen to his feet. "I know how busy you are. We were lucky to catch you in town today."

Carlton turned to thank Stephanie for the interview, although she thought she was supposed to be thanking him. Then the two men left the office, and she saw Carlton's limp. Ah, the war wound he didn't want to talk about. It probably bothered him that such a thing would spoil his perfection.

She was tired and hungry, but at least it was cool here. She might as well write her stories while her notes were fresh. She turned to the electric typewriter on her desk. Her stories normally came easily. Once she had her research done and the slant picked for a piece, Stephanie almost always found that the words fell into place. It wasn't so much a matter of finding the words as of looking at the pictures in her head and describing them, interspersed with quotations from her interviews.

But tonight she was having a problem. The jungle battlefields of Vietnam and Cambodia kept appearing in her mind as heather-covered sheep pastures in Scotland that would then slide into sagebrush rangeland where bands of sheep grazed on tender green foliage under pale bushes. Then when she was transcribing her notes of the interview in the VA hospital, the wan face of the young man with long brown hair, whose leg had been amputated at the knee, kept taking on the features of Carlton Sperlin.

Stephanie switched off the typewriter and slammed her notes in a desk drawer. It was the last straw when Carlton's black hair turned to red-tinted blond in her mind and she typed the name *David* in her story.

She and David had been together only once all summer—at a family Fourth of July picnic overrun with young cousins setting off firecrackers and dancing with sparklers that spit black ash into the potato salad. He had entered thoroughly into the American spirit and waved a small flag while they watched the parade of riding clubs and floats.

He had seemed far more patriotic than she felt. And even though she was delighted with his news that his visa had been extended for another year, she had felt none of the closeness she would have liked to resume with him. Even when they had found a brief moment of privacy and he gave her the kiss she had been longing for.

She told herself skyrockets had gone off, but it was mostly wishful thinking. And now he was doing some sort of ewe fertility experiment on a ranch in Montana that would keep him there through lambing season next spring or longer.

That was just as well, she insisted sturdily, because they were now facing the off-year elections of 1970. She would have her hands more than full with reporting on the local situation and campaigning for her father's reelection. The seesaw challenge was constantly there. She struggled to keep the pulse of a nation beset by riots—protestors raged against unemployment and inflation as well as the war—at the same time reflecting that the local situation was considerably calmer than it had been two years before.

Eliot Hamilton was easily reelected to a second term in the Idaho state legislature. Carlton Sperlin continued building his career as a successful Boise lawyer. David Fraser sent occasional postcards from his adopted sheep ranch. And Stephanie Hamilton found that even the life of a journalist could be dull, dull, dull.

8

It wasn't until the next summer, however, that Stephanie got the big break every reporter dreams of. A group calling themselves the Universal Life Church announced that they would hold their first annual church picnic at Farragut State Park in northern Idaho. The published prospective program for the Fourth of July weekend began each day with morning prayer, followed by such events as music from the church choir and a string quartet, then speeches by various bishops and ministers. Nevertheless it was rumored that this was going to be the biggest and best rock festival since Woodstock. And Stephanie was assigned to cover it.

Dede was beside herself with excitement. "What a beautiful happening. If only Barry could be there. It's just a few miles below the border. Do you suppose he could sneak down from Canada?"

"I think it would be insane. If he does, don't tell me. I don't want to be responsible." Then Stephanie burst out laughing. "Dede, have you *read* this program? Can you believe, a Universal Life Church barber shop quartet and progressive jazz band?"

Dede read over her shoulder. "Universal Life Church bake-off! What a send-up!"

"ULC old-time fiddler brigade," Stephanie read. "And ULC skittles band! These people have a sense of humor." Dede laughed. "Yeah, and smart, too."

"What do you mean?"

"Well, when the little old ladies in pink tennis shoes get bent out of shape about all these long-haired, dope-smoking hippies coming into their nice clean state, the organizers can show them this program. Who can object to a church picnic complete with pageant, choir, and orchestra?"

Stephanie frowned. "Dede. Do you know something I should know? What about the letters people have been writing to the paper that this is really going to be a drugfest?"

Dede scoffed. "Come on! You know how reactionary the establishment is. Sure, there'll probably be some marijuana smuggled into the park—why not? It's everywhere else. But come on, it's a church picnic. Just because it isn't Presbyterian or Methodist or something stuffy like that, who's to say what makes a church? These people call themselves ministers—so they're ministers." She picked up her guitar and began singing Carole King's latest hit, "You've Got a Friend." She paused between verses. "Want to ride up in Flower Power with the group?"

"Sure. Thanks." Stephanie wondered why she felt so uneasy. It sounded so simple when Dede explained it. She looked in the mirror. She would be thirty next December. Was she already over the hill? Was it true you couldn't trust anyone over thirty? Or even almost thirty?

She turned to the mail on her desk. The stamp with Queen Elizabeth on it made her catch her breath. How could she have failed to notice a letter from Scotland? Then a cold tightness seized her. David. He couldn't have gone back without telling her? *Without asking her to go with him,* she almost let herself think.

Then she smiled as she looked more closely at the handwriting. From Fiona, of course. Steph ripped the thin, blue aerogram open. David never talked about Mary and Gordie, so Stephanie has asked Fiona about them in her last letter.

Fiona's letter bubbled just as she did in person. Callum had finished his university degree and found a fine job in Glasgow. At least it would be fine—he loved the work for a large export firm—but it would be some time yet before they could afford to marry. Salaries there were terribly low and inflation high.

As happy as Stephanie was to hear about her cousin, she scanned ahead. Fiona's wedding plans were not the ones uppermost in her mind. She found it in the last paragraph. "I saw Mary yesterday. No, she and Gordie aren't married yet. She said she's off to London to look for a secretarial job."

Stephanie wondered. Did that mean Mary had decided not to marry Gordie? Or just that she was saving money to get married on? Did David know? Was he delaying his return to Scotland until after the wedding? Did that mean he was still in love with his Highland Mary? Could Stephanie be competition to a girl likened to one immortalized as a national heroine?

As the Fourth of July weekend approached, however, she had little time for introspection. The controversy the approaching event generated was more than enough to keep an enterprising reporter busy. The conflicting viewpoints fascinated Stephanie, who had always seen it as part of her job to get at the truth of whatever was causing a dispute.

And there was no lack of opposing views here: Farmers and people who lived in the small towns around the park worried about litter and property damage. PTAs and mothers' groups expressed concern over the nudity and free love that such gatherings were noted for, and their effect on the morals of minors. Law enforcement officers issued press statements regarding their limited ability to deal with a large influx of drug pushers. The planners reiterated that it was a church picnic. What could be more harmless, more all-American on the Fourth of July?

The plans went forward. Weather forecasters promised blue skies and sunshine for the weekend.

Stephanie was tossing jeans and a hairbrush into her duffle bag when the phone rang. "Hullo, Stephanie, it's David. Remember me?"

The soft Scots voice that she hadn't heard for months made her ears smile, not to mention what it did to her metabolism. But his next words brought a frown to her forehead. "We've finished all the work on the fertility tests. I'll be in Boise this weekend. Can we go to a picnic together or something?"

It was a testimony to Elizabeth's early training of her daughter that Stephanie did not swear at this dirty trick of fate. At least not out loud. She had been dreaming of this man for months, and the one weekend he would be in town she had the most important assignment of her career.

"David, I'm so sorry." She thought fleetingly of inviting David to go with her—he had said "picnic"—but she was pretty sure it wouldn't be an event he would enjoy. And she did have to work. "Can we possibly arrange to get together when I get back?" Then she caught her breath at a terrible thought."You aren't on your way back to Scotland, are you?"

"Not immediately. But soon, I expect. Don't worry. I won't go without saying good-bye."

And she had to leave it at that.

9

"Oh, what a fabulous place!"

Stephanie viewed the stately Ponderosa pines ringing the entrance to the four-thousand-acre state park. To their right, the bright blue waters of Lake Pend Oreille glistened through the pines. It was almost—but not quite—enough to make her forget her disappointment over not getting to see David this weekend.

She looked ahead to the park as the van inched forward. Stephanie had done her homework, so she knew that Farragut had originally been built during World War II as a naval base. Inductees got their boot training here in the sixty-five-mile-long lake, well-protected from enemy attack. More recently the park had achieved fame as the site of the 1967 Boy Scout World Jamboree. But the thousands of young people from all over the United States and foreign countries who were now converging on the park knew this place hadn't seen anything yet. This was going to be a whole new kind of happening.

"Yeah, it'll be great if we ever get in." Kelly, drummer for The Gathering, was driving the yellow, flower-splotched van. He swore as the motor, tired of idling in the long waiting line, gave a cough and died. "You'd think this park would have more than one entrance." All around them, on the dusty road and the grass beyond, people on foot and in vehicles of every description funneled toward the gate.

All six people in the van breathed a sigh of relief once they were in the vast park. Its wide-open green vistas, although covered with groups picnicking and listening to music, still left room for comfortable moving about, unlike the thirty-five acres of solid humanity photographers had filmed at Woodstock two years earlier.

Kelly drove further in and finally found a camping spot protected by a thicket of pines. Stephanie piled out of the van behind Dede, then waited while the four fellows, all long-haired, shirtless, and wearing bell-bottom jeans, got out.

Dede dived back in for her guitar and a bottle of wine. "Come on, let's mellow out and make some music." She shook her head to get her long, straight hair out of her face.

Kelly and the bearded Bo each held old blankets, while Aaron and Eric pulled a box of food from the back of the van.

"Great," Stephanie said. "You guys do your thing. I'm a working girl." She patted her voluminous denim shoulder bag containing all her necessities for the weekend, first and foremost of which were notebook and pencils. She had also put in rain gear in case it should decide to pour here as it had at Woodstock. She noted the au naturel looks all around her. The fact that her bag also contained make-up made her feel uneasily like an uptight member of the establishment. She was glad that she had let her hair grow and quit back combing it since being captivated by Ali McGraw's free-swinging style in *Love Story* last year.

"Let's put this stuff back and just walk around together for a while," Dede suggested. "If you go off news-hounding now you'll never find us again."

It was a sensible suggestion. People were still pouring into the park. Aaron pushed his glasses back up on his nose and took out the ULC brochure with a map on the back. "Let's go over this way to the amphitheater."

The crowds became thicker as they left the parking and camping areas. Janis Joplin's posthumous hit, "Me and Bobby McGee," issued from the loudspeakers around the amphitheater. Behind that was the Hog Farm, the picnic headquarters.

When a long-haired man dressed like a Viking stepped out of the Hog Farm, Stephanie knew it was time to go to work. "Listen—" she turned to Dede "—when you guys settle on a spot, somebody go back and leave me a note on the van."

The others were already drifting toward a booth marked Drug Info, so Dede waved and hurried off.

Stephanie turned to her subject. "Hi. Can we talk?"

"Hey, baby. I'm easy. Mungo the witch doctor, they call me."

Stephanie noted the yellow arm band, which marked volunteers. "You're working here?"

"Sure. Want to help. Do all I can to help my brothers and sisters. That's what it's all about, isn't it? Love and freedom. That's the whole thing."

"What do you do—specifically, that is?"

"Good trips. That's my bag. I want everyone to have a good trip. I'm an organic doctor. I feed the work crews. Keep the workers on their feet. These are beautiful, loving people—they need help to keep going."

Stephanie nodded. Already she'd sensed the relaxation and freedom Mungo talked about. It was warm. Everyone moved slowly, eating, drinking, singing. This was the hassle-free environment the organizers of the picnic had promised.

"What do you do if someone's having a bad trip?"

"I talk to them, soothe them, calm their aura. People whose psyches are in harmony with nature aren't likely to have bad trips. Sometimes I administer a mushroom tonic if they need something extra."

Stephanie longed to be writing all this down but was afraid the appearance of her notepad would cut off the interview. "What about the locals who were concerned about litter and drugs—things like that?"

"Listen. People are basically good. These are beautiful people—inside the park and out. Inside themselves and out. As soon as we met with the establishment bigwigs and assured them we meant no harm, they were great."

"No hassles from authorities?"

Mungo reached up to grasp a curving horn and pulled his helmet off, then shook out his full, blond hair. "Would you believe even pigs can be beautiful when they aren't hassled? We promised to provide our own security inside the park, and we've done it. We'll leave it better than the Boy Scouts."

A blonde girl in a white T-shirt, wearing her yellow volunteer band Indian style around her head, called from the Hog Farm. "Mungo, we need help." The concern in her voice was the only uptight note Stephanie had heard since entering the park.

Stephanie walked on, realizing her own pace had slowed to the directionless amble of those around her. She noted the first-aid stations, water supply stations, drug information centers. Behind her in the amphitheater someone was singing a James Taylor–style song.

The first report she would file was taking form in her mind: People need to get together and have a good time. There is nothing to be afraid of. That was the assurance she wanted to give the writers of those uptight letters to the *Free Press*. If they could just see these people enjoying each other—she observed couples everywhere with their arms around each other—if they could sense the freedom. As far as she could see, people sat and lay in groups, feeding each other, sharing their drinks, singing to each other. "A Beautiful Picnic," she would head her report and hope the headline writer would follow her cue.

She sat under a tree for a few minutes to organize her notes, then, dusting off her jeans and pulling down her yellow jersey, she strolled off. An interview with a picnicker and maybe a musician should round off her story for tonight. She could probably find a phone in the park headquarters or walk into the little town of Bayview to file her story—then just relax with everyone else for the rest of the evening.

She found her last interviewee near one of the information booths. A girl in her late teens who had come to Farragut from New Mexico with a carload of friends. Annie peeked at her from under shaggy bangs, her blue eyes dreamy as she puffed on a long white joint.

"What can I say? It's beautiful. The area is beautiful. The weather is beautiful. The people are beautiful. What did we come for?" She swept the park with her arm. "What did they all come for? To enjoy each other. What more could you ask?"

"Perfect! Thank you. Have a great picnic, Annie." Stephanie had her story. Tomorrow she would have to run down some hard facts, such as how many people were there. Ten thousand, thirty thousand, or more? But for tonight she could just experience being. Dede and The Gathering were on the list of those who would provide free entertainment at the amphitheater, and she would enjoy it.

In spite of the noise and hard ground, Stephanie slept well that night and awoke, cozy in her sleeping bag, to the fresh mountain air and the sound of birds chirping in the pines above her.

As soon as she sat up, Eric thrust a cup of coffee into her hands. She grinned her thanks, then, hugging her knees inside her sleeping bag with one arm, sipped slowly.

If only life could always be so hassle free. Maybe this was the answer she'd been looking for. Maybe she should really drop out, make a complete break with the uptight world she'd grown up in. That must be what her brother had done. Maybe this was why he hadn't been home for so long. He was too busy being.

This was a whole different way of thinking. An entirely do-your-own-thing style of living and system of values. Was this what David had talked about as the difference in attitudes in his own country? In groping for the new, had these people found an older way? She could picture herself relaxed like this on one of the heather-covered hills David had described.

She slithered from her bag and stretched. "Ooh, think I'll go down to Buttonhook Bay for a wash-up." She picked up her towel and soap and set out for the designated swimming area on the tip of Lake Pend Oreille.

Refreshed and invigorated from the icy water, with tendrils of damp hair clinging around her tingling cheeks, she strode back up the path. The morning sun shone warm on her head.

Stephanie slowed as she heard a soft cry. At first she thought the sound was a dog's whimpering, since many picnickers had brought their pets with them. Then she realized the sound of distress was coming from a young woman. Stephanie turned off the path to where a group was gathered around a girl lying curled in the fetal position, crying out and clawing at her own back and head.

"What is it?"

"Bad trip," a young man with matted black hair answered. "There're some dishonest merchandisers around here—lace their stuff with strychnine."

"*Strychnine?* Why would they do that?"

"It's a white, odorless powder. Cocaine should be mixed with lactose, but sometimes strychnine's cheaper and easier to get. They don't usually use enough to do much harm, but sometimes they miscalculate."

"So you're saying she's been poisoned? Somebody get help!" Stephanie looked around for someone in charge. Two people were bending over the girl, whose cries had now become shrieks, but she beat off any attempt to help her. "Where are the medics?" Stephanie's voice rose. "Has anyone gone to a first-aid station?"

"Yes, they're coming." An authoritative male voice made Stephanie jerk around. "Now everyone get back and give her some air. Don't fight. You're only distressing her."

The medics were just behind him. Two fellows in jeans, T-shirts, and yellow arm bands hoisted the girl, whose shrieks had now turned to sobs, onto a litter. Her hair fell away from her face, and Stephanie gasped. "Oh, no!"

The man who had brought the medics turned to her. "Do you know her?"

"It's Annie. No. I don't know her—not really. I only interviewed her yesterday. But she was so sweet. She was having such a beautiful time. She was so sincere and so innocent. And now—" Stephanie stifled a sob with a hand over her mouth.

"Sweet, sincere, innocent." The man's voice sounded tired with just an edge of bitterness. "Yes. Aren't they all? Sweet, beautiful, and deluded. Except for the ones who are dishonest."

She opened her mouth to argue that most people were good, when something sparked her memory—something about the way she had to crane her neck to look up at him, or maybe it was the way one eyebrow arched cynically over the dark eyes. His crisp blue-and-white striped sports shirt alone was enough to set him apart from the sea of grubby T-shirts.

"Carlton Sperlin." She blinked in amazement. The last person she would ever think of seeing here.

He clasped the hand she held out as a reflex. "Sure, I remember you. Stephanie Hamilton. You did the *Free Press* interview last summer. It was a good series."

They were alone now that the medics had departed with the freaked-out Annie and her friends.

"What are nice people like us doing in a place like this?" He grinned again. She thought she'd never seen such white teeth. It was evident he hadn't made do with a wash-up in the lake this morning. "Had breakfast yet?"

She shook her head.

"Good. There's a very cozy little cafe in Bayview."

Without waiting for an answer he led her to a sleek white Charger in the parking lot.

"But what about Annie? Will she be all right?" Stephanie had to step double-time in order to keep up with his long stride, in spite of the limp that caused him to drag dust over the polish of his left loafer.

He opened the door for her, then went around and slid behind the wheel. "We can hope so. There are volunteer nurses and at least one doctor, so hopefully she'll get something better than Mungo's mushroom tonic. I just wish the scoundrels who allowed this thing could see what they've done." He put the car in gear and headed for the gate.

"What do you mean? I thought the organizers were all here."

"I mean the real powers. The political bigwigs who made a deal with the organizers. 'You keep your drugs in the park, and we won't hassle you' is what it amounted to. A law enforcement nightmare."

"You've got to be exaggerating. What happened to Annie was terrible, but I'm covering this for the *Free Press*. I've observed, done interviews. It's a very mellow thing. Pretty well organized. People pick up their own trash. I mean, the locals were so paranoid about this attracting motorcycle gangs and there being a lot of violence. I haven't seen a single fistfight."

"And you'll probably tell me you haven't seen a single drug deal as well."

"That's right. I haven't."

"Right. We'll have breakfast, then I'll show you the facts of life." He parked at a little white building with ruffled curtains at the window and led her inside.

"You haven't explained what you're doing here," Stephanie said after ordering a scrambled egg and English muffin.

"George—that's George Barton, senior partner of the firm—is a real crusader. He's very concerned about Idaho being left with permanent drug problems as an aftermath of all this. Since the official position seems to be 'if you don't see it, it didn't happen,' he asked me to come up and find out what's really going on."

"And you're convinced it's all really sinister?"

"All? No. Most of these kids are exactly what you said—mellow and innocent. Trouble is, there's no one here to keep the other ones from doing their thing as well."

Suddenly Stephanie didn't want to talk about it. She turned her attention to spreading strawberry jam on the English muffin the waitress set in front of her.

Once they were back in the park, however, their difference of opinion loomed between them. He led her to a booth marked Drug Information. Beneath it was a smaller sign, "Tell Us About Your Trip."

Carlton Sperlin stood well back and observed silently for some time as people came and went from the booth.

Stephanie, who was accustomed to drug information meaning informing people as to facts about the harmful effects of drugs, began to realize that something quite different was going on here. "What is this?" she asked.

"That's what I'd like to know. One of the organizers said the purpose of the booth is to analyze drugs and be a place where users can report on the quality and description of the drugs they've taken. An undercover agent told me yesterday, though, that its real function is to tell people where to get particular kinds of drugs."

"Maybe they're just being realistic," Stephanie argued. "I mean, in a crowd this size you *are* going to have people using drugs and people selling drugs. It's inevitable. And since there are unscrupulous people selling bad stuff like Annie got hold of, people should be warned."

Carlton shook his head. "You sound just like the organizer I talked to. 'A lot of people feel that the right thing to do is to take drugs, so they take them. None of us want to enforce our standards of morality on others.'

"When I asked him if all this didn't really amount to an endorsement of drug use and had he ever considered trying prevention instead of mop-up, he went back to his song and dance about imposing morality on others. I shudder to think what our world would be like without any imposed morality—theft, murder, rape." He did shudder, then turned with a swift, bright smile. "Sorry. I know I come on too heavy. Blame it on my war experience."

He took her arm. "Come on, let's go see what kind of music they're playing. One group last night was really pretty good—not too original, but at least they sang on key."

She was surprised he would know what was original, but she didn't say so. Instead she turned her attention to the throng of celebrants jiving with the music on the stage. When the Jimi Hendrix number came to an end, thousands of voices screamed and continued dancing.

A young man wearing only jeans and a feathered headband jumped onto the stage and grabbed the mike. "This is unbelievable! I feel like I've been peaking for hours! This is a whole new thing for the world!"

Dino, seemingly one of the organizers, blond hair long and wearing a blue shirt, leaned across the speaker's shoulder to yell into the microphone. "He's not high on drugs, boys and girls—he's stoned on the tremendous atmosphere of love prevalent in this gathering. He's tripped out on freedom. He's stoned out on his brothers and sisters. This is the revolution!"

The first fellow took the mike back. "It's time more people were turned on. The establishment knows its days are numbered. We're knockin' on their door!"

Suddenly remembering she was there to work, Stephanie pulled her notebook out of her bag and began scribbling as fast as her fingers would move.

Dino spoke again. "That's right, boys and girls." He held up a hand for attention. "Next time—and there are going to be lots and lots of next times—we're just getting started." Prolonged cheers greeted his announcement. "Next time, we feel we should eliminate any selling or merchandising of anything. We don't want to bust the people who are selling bad dope—we want to make them unnecessary by having everything free. Everything should be free at the next picnic. Everything! Free dope, free food, free wine, free beer, free music. Complete freedom!"

Stephanie was too busy writing to cheer if she had chosen to, but one part of her mind was questioning. It sounded so good, so logical. But was it realistic? Could life be that way? Didn't someone have to pay ultimately? Who was supporting these kids? Where would they be if their parents weren't paying?

But the next announcement left her with no time for analysis. A girl with a yellow arm band ran on stage and spoke to Dino. He turned back to the mike. "OK, boys and girls, here's our chance to demonstrate that we believe in the caring and freedom we're celebrating. We've got a request here for some marijuana for the medics. They've been working hard all day taking care of you—let's take care of them."

People cheered and surged forward to deposit little packets on the stage. The girl scooped up a handful and ran back toward the Hog Farm.

Carlton shook his head. "And to think that our public officials sanctioned this. This is going to open up drug problems that our state will have to live with for years."

Stephanie shrugged. "It's just marijuana. I mean, I certainly wouldn't use it, but it hasn't really been proven any more harmful than cigarettes or alcohol."

"'No more harmful than cigarettes or alcohol.' Is that supposed to mean it's all right? That *they* aren't harmful?"

She was amazed at the vehemence in his voice. She thought she had been making a casual observation, one you could read in the paper almost any day, but he spoke with the fervor of an evangelist.

She tried a different tack. "I don't see how the officials could have said no. I mean, who could refuse a church picnic on the Fourth of July?"

His response was no less definite, but there was less agitation in his voice. "Church. What a put-on. This do-your-own-thing-religion where everyone is his own minister is the farthest thing possible from everything Christ lived and died for."

"What are you talking about? All I've heard this weekend is the importance of love. What could be more Christian than that?"

"Personal commitment to God. The willingness to sacrifice to do His will. When Christ said the truth shall make you free, He was talking about freedom from sin, not the right to sit in a park and smoke pot."

Stephanie started to interrupt, but he went on. "And what about the self-denial, sacrifice, and servant-heartedness that're at the center of the Christian life? All you see here is rampant self-indulgence and me-ism."

Stephanie struggled not to show her discomfort at the direction the conversation was going. "So if you were in charge here, what would you do? Arrest all thirty thousand of them?"

"If I'd been in charge it would have been clear from the first that the drug laws would be enforced. I would have given every support to our law enforcement officers, not tied their hands. We've never had cocaine in Idaho before, but you can count on it—we will now. Drug-dealing channels are being opened up all over this park."

Stephanie was horrified. Horrified at the picture he was painting of lives being ruined before her eyes. Multiple Annies filled her imagination. And she was horrified at her own confusion. Carlton spoke for everything she had been raised to believe, all the traditional values her family stood for. And yet she was attracted by the freedom and peace these people espoused—even if it was a different sort of freedom.

Her confusion expressed itself as anger. "So who elected you the law and order candidate, Mr. High and Mighty?" And she stalked off, missing David and his relaxed, understated ways more than ever.

For some time she wandered aimlessly, trying to sort out her feelings as she jotted down details of the scene around her for the story she would file tonight.

"Well, if it isn't Brenda Starr, girl reporter, scribbling away like a good little news hound. Want to interview someone really in the know?" She almost walked into a man in a purple tie-dyed shirt.

"Jimmy! What are you doing here—working or picnicking?" She wondered if he ground out his cigarette so quickly to keep her from smelling something besides tobacco.

"Listen, baby, a real reporter is never off duty. But that doesn't mean we can't have a little fun on the side. How about a stroll down to the bay? It's getting hot. A quick dip would sure feel good."

"I didn't bring my suit."

"Who said anything about swimming suits? No one down there lets such old-fashioned conventions hamper them. Or up here, either, for that matter."

A large group walked in front of them, all topless. Many wearing very little on the bottom. Stephanie felt like a prude turning her head away, but she couldn't help it. She had an idea that Jim was enjoying the view. She was glad she wasn't with Carlton. Somehow it would have been so much more embarrassing with him. Or maybe not. He would have turned away with her—and provided a distracting lecture on enforcing the state's obscenity laws.

"I'm getting hungry. Let's go find Dede and the gang." She started walking swiftly, hoping to outrun the agitation she felt.

"Whoa! Mellow out. What's the matter with you?"

"I don't know. I just don't think I'm the right type for a rock festival."

"Rock festival!" Jimmy threw up his hands. "This isn't a rock festival, lady. You need to read the story I filed this morning. 'The Universal Life Church picnic is much more than a rock festival,' I said. 'This is a celebration of life, not a plastic outdoor opera. This isn't Woodstock revisited, it's on a different level of consciousness.' Pretty good, huh?"

"Sounds good." But she spoke without enthusiasm. Her attention had been caught by the American flag she saw being flown upside down. She had seen others similarly displayed, but this was the first to be accompanied by a Vietcong flag.

Rock music blared from the amplifiers, people yelled around her, a sticky, sweet-smelling cloud hung over everything. It was too much. "I'll see you later, Jim. I'm going to sit in the van and write my story." She headed for the parking lot almost blindly.

But once in the van, in spite of the relative quiet she still couldn't think. Who was right? What was right? She wanted to work for a better world, but what kind of world? Suddenly there were no rules, no generally agreed standards. The picnickers said to do your own thing, find what was right for you. But what was her thing? What was right for her? She thought how vastly different all this was from their family gathering almost a year ago. How the people in the park would laugh at the old-fashionedness of all that.

Well, not all the people in the park. Carlton wouldn't laugh. Instinctively she was certain that he would say that the love and freedom at Kathryn's party were more valid because they built up, they didn't tear down. But was he right?

Or David with his Old World attitudes—was he right that things might be better if they were less new?

Having thought of Kathryn made her long to be able to talk to her grandmother. What would she say about all

83

this? Of course, Grammie wouldn't understand. Her world was a different place. But Grammie had lived through many changes in her world.

Then Stephanie recalled an entry she had read in Kathryn's journal just a few days ago. It hadn't made much of an impression at the time—at least she didn't think it had—but now she remembered a few lines written at a dark time during World War I: "The world seems such an unfriendly place. So very different from the one I grew up in. Why does everything have to change? Perhaps so we can learn to rely on the God who never changes, and listen to His unchanging promises."

It worked for Kathryn. Stephanie wasn't sure it would work for her, but she felt calm enough now to write her story.

10

Stephanie arrived home hoping David would still be there. She wanted to forget long-haired druggies and their philosophies of freedom almost as much as she wanted to forget Carlton Sperlin and his law and order ideas. She wanted to escape.

And that's exactly what she did—right into the arms of David Fraser. After his first kiss, he held her at arms' length and looked her up and down. She wore a little red sun suit that showed off her long, tanned legs and almost shoulder-length, streaky blonde hair.

"'O my Luve's like a red, red rose
That's newly sprung in June; O my Luve's like the melodie
That's sweetly played in tune!'"

Her heart leaped. Was it just his love of quoting Burns? Or did he truly feel love for her?

"I've good news for ye—at least, I hope it's good." He held her hand, and they strolled through the rose garden in Lakeview Park where she had suggested they go.

At his announcement she looked up at him. The sun struck lights of fire in his hair, renewing her first thoughts of him as Apollo or King David.

"Yes?" She was breathless.

"I've been invited to teach as a visiting professor at the University of Wyoming—good veterinary department there—so I'll be staying on in the States for another year."

"Oh, that *is* good news." She tried to sound enthusiastic, but she wondered. Had he sought the delay because he wanted to stay closer to her? Or because he, too, had heard that Mary was still unwed, and he didn't want to face that painful situation?

Now Stephanie's letters came to her from Wyoming. Long letters about his work—but nothing about his feelings. Never once since Thanksgiving Day by the pond had he talked about his feelings. But he had shown her, hadn't he? Each time they had been together, his kisses had meant more to her. And she could hope hers did to him as well, judging from how fiercely he held her. But she could only surmise.

She tried discussing it all with Dede.

"What?" Dede's fingers struck a clanging chord as she set her guitar aside. "What can you be thinking of? Are you just going to give up like that and become a middle-class housewife like your mother? What about your goals? Your ideals? What about the cause?" Dede paused for breath.

Stephanie was silent.

"Are you seriously thinking of moving to *Scotland,* for goodness' sake?"

"I haven't been asked," was all Stephanie would say. But she knew what her answer would be if David ever did ask.

And if he didn't? He'd been away three weeks already, and she hadn't heard from him. Just how much could she chalk up to Scottish reserve?

Dede returned to her music, and Stephanie walked from the room. She picked up Kathryn's book and turned to the pages telling of Kathryn's honeymoon to Scotland. Merrick didn't sound so very reserved.

Stephanie closed her eyes and daydreamed of fleeing from all of her problems to that green, misty land. She reread Kathryn's decision that they should return to their home in Kuna. Stephanie shook her head. She doubted that she could have made that decision. It was interesting to wonder where they'd all be now if Grammie had decided differently.

In the coming days and weeks, questions about David Fraser, his feelings for her and hers for him, took precedence over the list of questions about the governing of Idaho and the direction of America that she dealt with every day. It seemed, however, that the harder Stephanie struggled for answers, the more the questions piled up.

By September 1972, questions seemed to be all anyone had. Or was it, rather, that so many people were yelling answers at her that she couldn't hear them? That seemed the more likely scenario, she thought, as she surveyed the stack of newspapers around her. Each headline screamed another black-letter assertion. The country was again in the thick of a presidential election, which meant that the Hamilton family was in the midst of a legislative race. Stephanie found that her newspaper job, which required her to be in the thick of the political action, made working for her father easier. And yet harder. She had to avoid any conflict of interest as she worked to keep her reporting objective.

Today, though, she was free from worrying about local tax, education, and land-use issues. She wrestled with the challenging assignment her editor had handed her—to write a summary of the year's events. Mark Brown would then use her article as a springboard for his editorial supporting his favorite candidates.

"At least I got the easy part," she said to Dede, who had just turned off "All in the Family." "I'd hate to have to write an editorial that made sense out of the mess of this year's headlines."

Dede picked up a handful of newspapers. "Hmm. Instead of going at it chronologically, you might try grouping events by subject, like: Shirley Chisholm first black woman to run for president; first women run in Boston Marathon . . . Nixon goes to China to open relations; Nixon goes to Moscow to sign SALT . . . Heaviest bombing of the war launched against Hanoi and Haiphong; last US ground combat unit withdrawn from Vietnam . . ." She tossed the papers on the floor and leaned back on the sofa with her feet on the coffee table.

"Yeah, that's not a bad idea." Stephanie flipped back her hair, which had now grown to well below her shoulders. "McGovern backs Eagleton 1,000 per cent; McGovern announces Eagleton's withdrawal . . ."

"Hey, take it easy on my friends."

"This is a news report—purely unbiased. Mark Spitz wins seven gold medals in Munich; Palestinian terrorists kill Israeli athletes . . . Does 'Agents arrested breaking into Democratic headquarters at Watergate hotel' balance 'Jane Fonda returns from Hanoi'?" She grinned at Dede's frown. "Never mind. Bad joke."

Stephanie returned to her work.

Dede turned the TV back on but kept the last of the "Sonny and Cher Show" low so as not to bother her roommate. When the local news came on at ten o'clock, Dede broke her silence. "Can you believe the political hay this man is making out of that Farragut picnic?"

"Huh?" Stephanie turned to the television. "Oh, Carlton. Yeah, 'The Farragut Fiasco,' as he calls it, makes a good law and order issue for the attorney general race."

"I notice you're not campaigning for him, even though he's some sort of old family friend, huh?"

"Well, I'll probably vote for him. It's just that with working for Dad's re-election and my job and all—enough's enough."

"Do I detect a certain amount of ambivalence on the issue?"

Stephanie sighed. She got up from the floor and dusted off the seat of her navy blue pantsuit. "No, not in the least." She turned to listen to the last of his statement.

"Well, all right. I am a little ambivalent. I really respect the man. He's absolutely sincere in his beliefs—not one of those politicians out to grab power for himself. I'm just not sure I believe in the same things he does." She thought for a minute. "No, that's not right. I think we have the same goals. As members of the same party, I know Hamilton and Sperlin support the same issues. I'm just not sure we'd go about getting there the same way."

Dede clapped. "Well spoken. Was that the daughter of a seasoned politician or what? Now what does it mean? That Carlton Jules Sperlin's views are as outmoded as the horse and buggy, but that he's probably the most striking-looking man you've ever seen?"

Stephanie just looked at Dede with her mouth open. Then she turned back to consider the face on the television screen. Of course, she preferred David's golden Adonis looks, but it was undeniable: soon-to-be-elected Attorney General Sperlin had the chiseled features and the tall, raw-boned build she had often heard others recall about his grandfather Jules, whose name he bore—yet with a sleek sophistication of black hair and intelligent dark eyes.

His father, Albert, and his Uncle Fred Sperlin reflected similar family traits. But she had heard Kathryn say that being around Carlton was like having dear Jules back again. And Grammie would know. Stephanie had read in her journal how close she had come to marrying Jules. She shook her head firmly. This was nonsense. She didn't believe in voting on the basis of how good-looking a candidate was, nor even on the fact that his grandfather was almost your grandfather. And it certainly wasn't helping her get her article written.

She turned to her newspaper clippings as Dede began singing, "I Am Woman."

Election day, November 7, 1972, brought very few surprises. Richard M. Nixon and his running mate, Spiro T. Agnew, beat the McGovern/Shriver ticket in the biggest landslide in history, carrying forty-nine states. Hamilton was easily reelected, and Carlton Jules Sperlin was Idaho's new attorney general. A few days later Henry Kissinger announced that the Vietnam cease-fire was stalled, Apollo 17 set off for the moon, George Bush was named chairman of the Republican party, and the Hamiltons and Allens put politics aside to celebrate the holidays.

A skiff of snow two weeks before Christmas put Stephanie in such a holiday mood that she came in singing "Jingle Bells." She hung her short, fake-fur coat in the hall and tossed her hat on the shelf.

Dede was sitting at the kitchen table, wearing a black sweater pulled over her jeans.

"Dede, you've been crying!" Stephanie hurried to her friend, then saw that her eyes were shining, but not with tears. A letter bearing a Canadian stamp lay on the table. "Barry?"

Dede nodded. "I'd heard by the grapevine that he was going to become a Canadian citizen. I'd even heard that he still thought of me—but I didn't know. Everyone was so paranoid about getting arrested that he never wrote—if only I'd known how he felt, it would have made waiting so much easier." She held out the letter.

Stephanie read. "So you're going to him? Now?" She looked around, but there were no packed bags by the door.

"I'd go tonight if there were a bus north. Day after tomorrow at the latest. Oh, I'm so happy!"

Stephanie hugged her friend. She had never seen her so ebulient. She had the feeling one must need a visa or something, that you couldn't just move to a foreign country —no matter how often she herself daydreamed of moving to Scotland. But Dede was too excited to worry about such details. It would probably be all right if they married. She wondered whether that was what Barry had in mind. But she was glad Dede was happy.

90

It was some time later when she saw that Barry's letter wasn't all the mailman had brought. "I don't believe it! It's from Boyd!" She tore open the envelope and pulled out a card with a jolly red Santa on it.

"'Doing great, buy something for Mom and yourself with the enclosed. Your cowpoke brother,'" she read. "Well, he never was much of a correspondent. At least we know he's alive." She opened the folded check he had enclosed—$100. Her eyebrows shot up. He was doing well. How could he afford to be so generous on a ranch hand's salary?

Then she turned over the last letter and saw its foreign stamp. This was certainly the day for flourishing romances. Fiona had written two pages in her blocklike letters telling about her upcoming wedding to Callum and how they wished their American cousins could come visit them.

Well, why not? Stephanie thought. Kathryn had been longing to go for years, especially since Fiona's visit. This would be the perfect time. April, Fiona said. Immediately Stephanie's mind filled with the images of green hills and lambs that never seemed far from her thoughts. The more turbulent the conditions in America, the more hectic her own job, the more she longed to escape into that greenness. Taking her grandmother to a family wedding would be the perfect excuse.

The apartment seemed cold, dark, and empty when Dede was gone, so Stephanie was more than happy to accept her mother's invitation to move home a few days before Christmas and stay until the new year. Since the Hamilton home was only two miles south of town, it was just as easy for Stephanie to get to work from there. She even gave brief consideration to the idea of moving back permanently. It wouldn't take much remodeling to add a kitchen in the finished basement. It already contained a beautiful guest room with a sitting room and a bath.

She could pay her parents rent, and it would be a convenience for them to have a house-sitter when they both spent long hours in Boise during the legislative session. They often rented a motel room near the end of the session when the days ended late and started early and no one felt like making the hour-each-way commute. But then she considered the fact that she had just had her thirty-second birthday. She was too old to go home to Mama.

Except at Christmas. She unpacked quickly and ran upstairs. "Mmm, that smells great! I love gingerbread. Let's decorate cookies tomorrow. Remember the great cookies we made when I was little?"

Elizabeth gave her a forced, tight smile.

Thinking her mother found her an interruption, Stephanie started to leave.

"Don't go, Steph." Elizabeth pressed a hand to her temple. "I'm sorry, I just . . . "

When Elizabeth's voice caught in her throat, Stephanie realized how drawn her mother looked. "Mother! What is it?"

Elizabeth came around the counter and sat on a stool next to Stephanie. "I don't know—I hope I'm just being silly—but I'm so worried about your father. He's been having pains in his arm. It's that old injury."

Stephanie reached over and patted her mother's hand. She remembered the story about the plane crash her parents had been in at an air show years and years ago. She never thought about the scars on her father's face and was always surprised when someone asked her about them. "Has he seen Doctor Mangum yet?" The son of the man who had taken care of Eliot after the plane crash was now their family doctor.

"He promised he would after Christmas—he's been so busy getting ready for the session. I don't know—maybe you can talk to him. Urge him to get some rest."

Eliot came in late that night. "Sorry about making you wait dinner." He set his briefcase down and rubbed his arm. "Court ran late, then I had to confer with my clients, then return a list of calls . . ."

Stephanie took her cue. "Isn't there any place you can cut down, Dad? Get one of your associates to carry more of the caseload?"

"I'm trying, but I want to get this Jones case finished before the session. Then I can concentrate on all of this." He waved a hand toward his desk in the corner.

Stephanie had already noted the files there labeled "Dam Proposal," "Mining Laws," "Farm Policy"—issues she knew he would be voting on when the legislature convened next month. She supposed she should encourage him to get away from it all, but the subjects were so intriguing to her.

Eliot pulled his coat off, loosened his tie, and sank into his favorite lounge chair, pushing back to elevate his feet.

Stephanie sat in the rocker across from him. "What about this Mountain Home Project, Dad? Do you think they should build a dam on the South Fork of the Boise River?"

When Elizabeth entered the family room to call them to dinner twenty minutes later, she just stood in the doorway, hands on hips, shaking her head. "You two are the limit. Stephanie, I wanted you to get your father to relax, not hash out all the major issues of the coming session."

Stephanie looked up guiltily from the litter of files and clippings spread around her on the floor. She had pulled out items to ask her father about. "I'm sorry, Mother. But I'm sure he's right to oppose the building of a dam for purely power purposes. Irrigation needs are the key. And this plan would make any additional upstream use of water impossible—"

"Come on, you two," Elizabeth interrupted. "You can solve the problems of the world just as well on a full stomach. Then I want you both to get to bed early."

They followed her obediently and spent most of dinner reviewing the aftermath of the war on poverty and the

93

current welfare situation, an issue that Stephanie, with her burning desire to help people, felt strongly about.

In the coming days, however, political issues paled even in the Hamilton household as baking, package-wrapping, and tree-trimming filled every moment. The mantles in both living room and family room bore thick boughs of evergreen and clusters of red candles. Elizabeth's handmade crèche held center stage on the living room coffee table.

Stephanie took over adorning the floor-to-ceiling pine in the family room, while Kathryn, spending the day with them while Mavis went shopping, looked on.

"Oh, look at these!" Stephanie pulled a string of fluid-filled, glass candles from the tissue paper. "I love bubble lights. I used to watch them for hours when I was a child."

She was determined to do everything she could to make this a perfect Christmas. There would be no arguments with her mother—not even the unspoken sort she was most used to where she would simply walk out of the room in response to her mother's disapproval. This would be a perfect Christmas. One they would always remember.

"Yes, certainly I remember those." Kathryn smiled. "We all thought they were the most magic things we'd ever seen. It was impossible to get nonessentials like Christmas decorations during the war and even right after. When they started making things like that in the fifties it was such fun.

"Of course, when I first came here we didn't even have Christmas trees. My papa brought home a huge sagebrush bush." She stopped and a soft smile brightened her face. "And he brought home Merrick too. That all seems so long ago."

"Ready for a break?" Elizabeth bustled in wearing a white apron over her rose dress and carrying a tray of tea and cookies. She poured a cup for Kathryn, then noticed the fuzzy, red pipe-cleaner Santa Claus Stephanie had just hung on the tree. "Oh, remember that? Put him up higher, Steph. He's been on every tree you've ever had."

Stephanie moved the ornament as her mother continued.

"I got him tied to a package the year you were born. What a time that was—just three weeks after Pearl Harbor —right in the middle of Nampa's first blackout. We couldn't get to the hospital."

She broke off her reminiscence to survey the tree. "You need a few more ornaments on the lower left branches, dear."

Stephanie turned wordlessly to follow her mother's directions, then picked up a box of silver icicles. Another of her favorite memories was lights shimmering on the icicles whenever anyone walked by the tree.

"Oh, no, dear. Let's not have tinsel this year. It always gets so messy. Come sit down and have a cup of tea."

Stephanie bent forward to take a cup. Her hair fell over her shoulder and brushed the teapot.

"Stephanie, go brush your hair," Elizabeth said. "That new gold barrette of mine is on my dressing table. Why don't you put it in your hair?"

Stephanie jerked to her feet. So much for her vow not to leave the room in irritation.

She heard the doorbell ring while she was brushing her hair. A few moments later she walked back into the room, then stopped stock-still.

"David!" She flung herself into his outstretched arms. After all, he was standing under the mistletoe her mother always hung in the entryway.

His kiss was brief, but the warmth of it stayed on her lips as he murmured, "'So fair art thou, my bonnie lass,'" then crossed the room to greet Kathryn. How handsome he looked in tweed slacks and an ivory wool sweater pulled over a white shirt. Just the knot of his red and black Fraser tartan tie showed at his throat.

95

David accepted a cup of tea from Elizabeth and settled comfortably on the sofa.

"What do you think, David? This girl here has been trying to talk me into taking a trip to Scotland in the spring," Kathryn said.

"Wonderful!" He turned to Stephanie so sharply he almost sloshed tea into his saucer. "I can't think of a grander plan."

"You know about Fiona's wedding?" Stephanie asked.

"Indeed I do. And I know something else." He grinned, allowing their suspense to build.

"Yes?"

"I'll be there to meet your plane."

"You mean you're going home for Fiona's wedding too? Why don't we fly together?" Stephanie asked.

"Nay, I'll be there long before. I've found that teaching is what I truly love to do—far more than field research or being a vet—and I've been offered a post at the University of Edinburgh that starts spring term, so I'll be off in a few weeks."

Elizabeth refreshed their cups, and the conversation continued about David's plans until he turned to Stephanie. "That's a beautiful snow going to waste out there. Care for a wee stroll?"

If he had needed to repeat the invitation, there wouldn't have been time before Stephanie had slipped into her fuzzy white coat, pulled a red knit tam over her ears, and grabbed her long red scarf and mittens. "Be warned, I have a deadly aim with a snowball."

They went out laughing. But all thoughts of snowball fights left her mind when they were less than halfway down the lane and David drew her to him in the warmth of his arms. "Stephanie, my love, don't wait till spring to come to Scotland. Marry me and come now—right after Christmas. Think how wonderful it would be to be in Scotland on New Year's Eve with the haggis going in to the bagpipes and everyone singing 'Auld Lang Syne.'"

As soon as she could catch her breath she cried, "Wait! Are you proposing marriage or inviting me to a Hogmanay?"

"Oh, forgive me." His Scots accent got deeper in his confusion. "I canno do it in my own words. I must borrow Burns's:

"'So fair art thou, my bonnie lass,

So deep in luve am I; and I will luve thee still, my dear,

Till a' the seas gang dry—'"

They stood in the middle of the tree-lined lane. Snow-covered fields stretched smooth and white on either side of them. She snuggled against the roughness of his wool jacket. "No girl ever had a lovelier proposal."

"Does that mean yes?"

"Of course it does."

He gave a jubilant shout, lifted her off her feet, and swung her around. The world spun a crazy, sparkling white as she squealed in response.

He set her down, removed his glove, and pulled off her left one. The ring he slipped on her finger was a fiery red ruby circled with diamonds. "I hope you don't mind. This is a Scottish-style engagement ring. We don't go so much for the plain diamonds like you do here."

"It's wonderful." She held her finger out to catch the sparkle of the pale winter sun. "It's perfect. It's like the first time you kissed me. Do you remember—by the pond? I thought then we were like the warmth of a ruby surrounded by frostlike diamonds."

"I chose the ruby because my love's like a red, red rose."

"Let's go tell Grammie!" She grabbed his hand and headed toward the house.

"Shall we take her with us now? Or could your mother bring her over in the spring?"

Stephanie stopped. What was she thinking of? There was so much to decide. So much to arrange. She couldn't just pack up her whole life and move to Scotland in ten days. Then she looked at the man beside her. Yes, she could. She continued running toward the house.

Kathryn and Elizabeth were ecstatic at Stephanie and David's announcement. They all hugged and cried and exclaimed. Then Elizabeth slipped away to call Eliot to tell him their daughter's news.

"But don't tell anyone else," Stephanie warned. "It'll just be our secret until we announce it Christmas Eve."

"A very special secret, indeed." Kathryn clasped her hands together, her eyes shining.

That was one of the best parts. Kathryn adored David. Elizabeth adored him. For once Stephanie could please her mother—really come up to what was expected of her. And she was pleasing herself, she added quickly.

It was much later that night, when Stephanie found she couldn't sleep, that doubts set in. Was there the slightest chance David had asked her to marry him because he didn't want to go home and face Mary? Was the ring he had given her the ring Mary had once returned to him?

She easily dismissed such minor, unworthy speculations. The more serious questions wouldn't go away so quickly. Could she really give up everything—all her plans and goals, her home and country? Was her decision at least in part the running away Dede had accused her of? Fine thing for Dede to talk. Her fiancé had run. But she wasn't making decisions for Barry. She was making them for herself. She had spent all of her adult life believing she would someday make her world better. This world, the one she lived in right here in Nampa, Idaho. Could she abandon all that?

She closed her eyes, and her mind filled with a picture of David's classic hero features. Yes, she could go.

11

For Christmas Eve, two days later, Stephanie pulled a red sweater on with her floor-length black velvet skirt and carefully tied her hair back with a red ribbon at the nape of her neck. No arguments about hippie hairstyles were going to ruin her Christmas. Nothing was going to ruin her Christmas with David. She twisted the ring around her finger with her thumb. So far their engagement was still a delicious secret. The few people who had noticed her unusual ring had been put off with an "early Christmas present" explanation.

But tonight, when the flame burned low on the plum pudding, Eliot would make the announcement. She went out to arrange a stack of records on the record player while her mother put the finishing touches to a steaming pot of the clam chowder that had become a family Christmas Eve tradition. Stephanie sifted through the albums. Here they were: The Boston Pops, Johnny Mathis, the Ray Conniff Singers —her favorite Christmas albums from her college days.

Clarey and Mavis were the first to arrive, with Kathryn, looking festive in a red and gray dress.

"Merry Christmas, Grammie." Stephanie kissed her under the mistletoe, greeted her aunt and uncle, then waited expectantly. David was right behind them. Her Christmas was complete.

Susie and Bob burst in, laughing and shaking snow out of their hair.

"Whoa!" Bob grabbed Susie in the midst of unwinding a red and green knit scarf from around her neck and kissed her under the mistletoe. "Thanks for the help, Aunt Elizabeth." Bob turned to kiss his hostess on the cheek. "Susie might not have allowed that if you hadn't provided the trimming."

"Silly!" Susie cried, and to prove that she had no objections to kissing her husband she flung her arms around his neck and gave him a very thorough kiss.

Still laughing, they went on into the other room.

Stephanie smiled at David. She hoped their marriage could be as special as Bob and Susie's seemed to be. She slipped her hand inside his. How could she have ever thought she didn't want a man in her life?

Then Tommy arrived with his family, and the circle was complete. In keeping with their long-standing tradition, the family linked hands around the room, and, while "Silent Night" sang softly from the record player, Eliot led in prayer. When Stephanie opened her eyes she had the momentary impression of the room being filled with stars. Candles flickered on the mantle and tables and lights from the tree were reflected in the eyes of the younger family members.

"Oh, I'm so glad it's all so beautiful. I have to hold every minute in my heart." Susie turned to Stephanie.

"Yes, Christmas is always so special," Stephanie answered vaguely.

"That's true, but I mean especially this year because it'll be so long until Bob and I are together again." A tear shimmered in the corner of her round blue eyes, eyes that matched the sapphire dress she was wearing.

"What?" Stephanie felt at a loss.

"Haven't you heard? He's going to South America next week. It's this huge engineering project for M-K. He'll be gone for at least six months."

"Oh, Sue, can't you go with him?" Stephanie couldn't imagine having David go off to another country without her, and it must be even worse for Susie.

She shook her head. "No housing for dependents. It sounds dreadful. I think they'll be living on some rock pile in Argentina. It's supposed to be chock-full of minerals."

Stephanie squeezed her hand. "You'll make it." When Susie moved on to fill her plate, Stephanie thought how wrong appearances could be. Sue, who appeared to float through life in an old-fashioned housewifely haze, had fears and emptiness in her life too.

When she noticed that most people seemed to have finished with the main course, Stephanie slipped out to the kitchen to help her mother unmold the plum pudding. Elizabeth didn't like much help in the kitchen, but Stephanie could work around her without getting in the way. "Oh, it's beautiful, Mother. Just a little more sauce on this side—"

But Stephanie's words were drowned by a cry from the living room. She rushed in ahead of her mother. Her father lay on the floor, clutching his chest, his face an ashen gray.

"Daddy!" She fell to her knees beside him, then made room for her mother. "Somebody call an ambulance!" she cried to the faces that seemed frozen around her.

Stephanie had always thought herself cool and capable in emergencies, but now she could do nothing. She was aware that her mother was praying beside her and Clarey was loosening Eliot's shirt collar, but she could do nothing. She was vaguely aware of the doorbell ringing and more voices. Then the door banged again. There was more commotion as the medics came in and put her father on a stretcher. Someone pulled her to her feet, bundled her into her coat, and all but carried her to the car.

When she was tucked in beside her mother, a concerned face looked in at them. "We'll be praying for Eliot.

For you all." Then he shut the door, and Clarey drove off behind the ambulance.

Stephanie blinked. "Carlton? That was Carlton Sperlin, wasn't it? What was he doing here?"

"I invited Grace and her family over to sing carols with us after dinner." Elizabeth's voice was thin, and she was shaking.

Stephanie put an arm around her mother.

The harsh lights shone starkly on the white walls of the empty waiting room in the new Medical Center as Clarey guided Elizabeth and Stephanie to where they had been told to wait. Elizabeth took the chair her brother ushered her to and sat rigidly upright, gripping the brown, vinyl-covered chrome arms. Her face was as white as the wall behind her.

Stephanie crumpled onto a peach-colored, upholstered sofa. She wanted to yell at her mother to relax, unbend, cry. But Stephanie felt the walls would shatter if she lashed out. Certainly the walls she had built around herself would.

Then the elevator opened, and two familiar figures emerged. Grace went straight to Elizabeth and took her in her arms. When Stephanie saw her mother sink against her friend, she realized too late that she should have been the one to offer her mother that comfort.

She turned away—to face Carlton, who had folded himself quietly into the chair beside her. "Stephanie, I wish there were something I could do."

"You have. Thanks for getting me here."

He nodded.

She felt she should say something more. "Poor Mother . . ."

"I'll see what I can do." He looked around, then picked up a Gideon Bible, and moved closer to Elizabeth.

"The Lord is my shepherd . . ." The familiar words of the Twenty-third Psalm spread like a balm over the room. Stephanie felt her own tensions easing. "Yea, though I walk through the valley of the shadow of death, I will fear no evil; for thou art with me; thy rod and thy staff they comfort me."

The words also created in Stephanie's mind an echo of the passages she had read in her grandmother's journal. When Kathryn had suffered anxiety and hardship in the early days of her pioneering, those words had given her courage. For endless months Kathryn had seen no glimpse of green pastures or still waters, and yet the Shepherd had always been beside her.

Softly in the distance carolers began singing, "While shepherds watched their flocks by night, all seated on the ground, the angel of the Lord came down, and glory shone around . . ."

Stephanie winced. She wished she could be as certain of the glory as those around her were. Her take-it-for-granted faith seemed to be enough for everyday life, but in a crisis like this—

"Mrs. Hamilton?" A small, well-starched nurse came into the waiting room, and everyone froze. "Your husband's resting easy now. He's very weak, but he'd like to see you."

Stephanie couldn't believe her ears. He wasn't dead! He had looked so ghostly in his agony on the floor, fighting for his breath, pasty, blue-gray against the gold carpet. She shook her head to rid her mind of the vision. *Oh, thank You, God.* She breathed one of her infrequent prayers.

Elizabeth rose unaided before Carlton could spring to his feet to help her. She walked steadily down the corridor.

Grace filled the echoing silence in the waiting room with soothing, undemanding talk about what a fine man Eliot was, what a strong woman Elizabeth was, how much they had contributed to the church and community with their lives. Stephanie was grateful she had nothing more to do than nod occasionally.

When the nurse came back, Stephanie was on her feet before the white-clad figure could speak. But when she did, Stephanie was too shocked to move.

"Mr. Sperlin, he'd like to see you. Just a few minutes. We mustn't tire him."

Carlton? Her father was asking for *Carlton* with what might be his last breath? Not his daughter. Not a relative. Not even a close friend—a mere acquaintance, a political ally. Why Carlton? Why not her?

Eventually she sank back into her chair, but she refused to look at Grace, who had brought the interloper with her. Maybe five minutes passed in stony silence, maybe ten. That was part of the horror of it all—the timelessness—being suspended there in that stark, silent room, without any idea of how long it would all go on. Or what to expect next.

At last the prim little nurse reappeared on her silent shoes. "Miss Hamilton."

Inside the dimly lit room Stephanie saw her father, as white as the sheets that covered him, tubes running from his arm and nose. Elizabeth was sitting in a chair on the far side of the bed, her hand holding his. At first Stephanie thought Carlton had gone. She saw him, then, standing quietly in the far, dark corner.

"Daddy?" Stephanie tiptoed to the bed and touched his shoulder tentatively.

He turned and gave her a weak smile. "Stephanie . . ." His voice was raspy, barely above a whisper. "You tell her, Elizabeth."

"Your father has a job for you." Elizabeth's voice was steady. "He wants you to fill his seat in the House."

Stephanie was stunned. "Me?" She looked at the three faces watching her. "I—I—I don't understand."

Elizabeth looked to Carlton. "Your father hopes to get back to the House, but not this session. Under Idaho law, if a legislator is unable to serve, he can appoint his replacement."

Stephanie nodded as it began to make sense to her. "Yes, I've heard of wives filling in for their husbands . . ."

"We discussed that possibility, but your mother lobbied for you."

"Mother?" Stephanie looked at her mother wide-eyed. "Mother chose me?"

"Well, who better, dear?" Elizabeth gave her a gentle smile. "With your brilliant mind and your head for politics I know you'll do as superb a job of that as you do of everything else."

Outside the carolers had returned. "I heard the bells on Christmas Day their old, familiar carols play, and wild and sweet the words repeat, of peace on earth, good-will to men."

Her mother said that? Her mother thought she was brilliant and did a superb job of things? Her mother had faith that she could fill her father's seat in the legislature?

"And in despair I bowed my head," the carolers continued. "'There is no peace on earth,' I said, 'for hate is strong, and mocks the song of peace on earth, goodwill to men.'"

It was true. There was no peace. The world was filled with hate. But she believed in good-will to men. Here was her chance to work for it. For the goals she had so nearly abandoned.

With a shock Stephanie realized that this was the first time since her father's heart attack that she had given a single thought to David Fraser. Could she really dismiss him so completely from her life? Could she send him back to Scotland without her and stay here to fill her father's shoes as best she could?

"Then pealed the bells more loud and deep: 'God is not dead, nor doth He sleep; the wrong shall fail, the right prevail, with peace on earth, good will to men.'"

Stephanie leaned across the bed and kissed her father. "I'd be honored." And never once did her unannounced engagement cross her mind.

12

Two weeks later, however, Stephanie's ambivalence about her new office was shifting heavily from delight to frustration. She shut out the voice of the man speaking at the other end of the long table. She looked at the ring on her finger and heard again David's parting words at the airport:

"'And fare thee weel, my only Luve,

And fare thee weel a while! And I will come again, my Luve,

Thou it were ten thousand mile!'"

Yes, ten thousand miles was about the distance between them now, but he would not be coming to her. She would go to him when all this was over. But right now the mountain of legislative work to be climbed before she could go to her love looked far higher than Everest.

And Carlton Sperlin was the great white polar bear blocking the way to even her first step upward.

She clenched her fists and fought to hold onto her temper. Eliot Hamilton had been known as a legislator who approached even the hottest issues with cool reason, and Stephanie desperately wanted to be a capable successor to her father. But she also wanted this bill.

The deep red drapes and carpet, the rich dark mahogany paneling, the flames crackling in fireplaces at both ends of the majority caucus room all created a warmth and coziness that were at direct odds with the cold fury the speaker roused in her. The deep, resonant words of the attorney general's oration captivated everyone in the room—everyone except the newly appointed state representative from Canyon County. Nothing in their previous, sporadic acquaintance had prepared her to find Carlton Sperlin quite so impossible to work with.

"So we can see that the problems with this proposed bill are not only economic—we simply can't afford such a project. But they are also practical—the project would not produce the results claimed for it."

Stephanie jumped to her feet, although committee members usually spoke seated. "Mr. Sperlin, what about the social costs? The cost of crime? The cost of juvenile delinquency? The cost of child abuse? Are you considering those in your cold, calculating statement that 'we simply can't afford such a project'? I would submit that we can't afford not to have it!" She sat down, but her eyes were flashing and her cheeks were flushed with the heat of emotion, a heat that not even the January snowstorm swirling outside the windows could cool.

The chairman gaveled the state legislators gathered around the table back to order, and the discussion went on to other matters of upcoming legislation of special interest to the party.

Still seething, Stephanie eyed her opponent, sitting so coolly across the table from her. "To think that a man who looks like a cross between John Wayne and Prince Charles could be such a Grinch. Earlier that morning, driving to the capitol through the softly falling snowflakes that were refurbishing the grimy leftovers of December's white Christmas, Stephanie's spirits had soared. For the first time she could really believe she was a legislator, part of the action, not a mere observer and reporter as she had been in her role of newspaperwoman. She was on her way, her foot on the first rung of the ladder of success that it seemed she had dreamed of all her life.

She resisted the temptation to push harder on the gas pedal as she thought of attending her first official meeting—an organizational party caucus being held even before the official opening of the legislature to solidify party support for the most important bills to be presented from their side of the floor.

But now her high spirits foundered. The arrogant words of this man ripped apart the one piece of legislation she was determined to support heart and soul.

As the most junior of the junior legislators, Stephanie knew her role should be one of being seen and not heard until she learned her way around a little better. But this was her bill, and she wasn't going to sit there quietly and let some sanctimonious, high-and-mighty official tear it to shreds before it had even been assigned a number. Of course, it wasn't officially her bill—she certainly hadn't drafted it—but it so perfectly filled many of the ideals she believed in that, as soon as she read it, she had adopted its passage as her personal crusade. She felt that, if she could aid the passage of this bill, her entire term would be a success—a mark to leave behind her before she turned her back on this life and took up a whole new one.

And here was this man, Idaho's attorney general—their party's highest elected official since the governor was from the other party—personally attacking her bill. Attacking *her.*

From across the table she leveled her most searing look at him. She was fully aware of the power of her emerald green eyes to cut an opponent. She'd been doing it with great effect since high school debating days, but this time the effect was diminished by her opponent's quirking one eyebrow at her and then having the audacity to wink. Did he think she was a child to be pacified with a funny face? She almost expected him to produce a lollipop next. Well, he'd soon see that Eliot Hamilton knew what he was doing when he sent his daughter to the capitol to fill his seat. She was no pushover. She would go to the wall fighting for what she believed in.

"Mr. Chairman, I move we adjourn for lunch," a rotund, bald legislator sitting down the table from Stephanie said. His motion was met with murmurs of approval and several calls of "Second." Hearing no one opposed, the caucus chairman adjourned the meeting until two o'clock.

Stephanie went into the cloakroom and slipped into her black wool maxicoat. It had a double row of bright brass buttons that matched the highlights in her hair. She pulled a warm, creamy knit cap down over her neatly trimmed pageboy—more fitting to her new station than her old, almost-hippie look. She flipped one end of a long, fringed scarf over her shoulder, then turned quickly as the motion produced a startled cry.

"Oh, Fran, I'm so sorry! I didn't hear you come up behind me. Did I get you in the eye?" She reached out in concern to a small, dark-haired, older woman she had met frequently during the fall campaign.

Fran laughed. "No, no. You just surprised me. I wanted to ask you to join us for lunch." Fran indicated a group of fellow legislators that Steph knew only by reputation and was looking forward to getting to know well.

"I'd love to. It must be great to be starting your second term—to know the ropes and really be able to function."

"It is a good feeling," Fran agreed, "but you'll be amazed how quickly you'll get up to speed. And you showed this morning that you aren't the least bit shy about jumping right in."

"Oh dear, you mean my maiden speech? I know I should have kept my mouth shut, but he made me so mad with all his cold, calculating dogmatism. Doesn't the attorney general realize those are *people* in those slums? I had no idea he was so arrogant. I hope he won't prove as impossible to work with as he looks, or we could have a very stormy session even without the opposition party."

Stephanie finished pulling on her gloves, expecting Fran to reply. But at the startled look on Fran's face she swung around to find herself face to face with the subject of her tirade.

"Let's see what we can do about those storm warnings over lunch," he said, holding out his hand. "With the weatherman doing his worst outside, we don't need a chill in the chambers."

There was nothing for Stephanie to do but shake the extended hand, but she needn't accept his invitation. "Thank you, but I'm lunching with Fran Lawson and several others—"

Before she could finish, Fran interrupted. "Oh, that's all right. We'll catch it later." With a wave of her hand, Fran was halfway across the cloakroom.

Stephanie watched her retreat with a look that said, "Just wait until you need my support on something!" But she turned back to Carlton with her brightest political smile. "How's that for party loyalty?"

He gave her the little half smile that must have been worth several thousand votes last November. "I'd say the representative from Payette was very quick on the uptake."

"And the representative from Nampa?" Stephanie couldn't resist probing just a bit to see what he had thought of her speech this morning—if one could dignify her outburst with such a title.

"The newest member of the House isn't afraid to speak her mind. I'm afraid that's an all-too-rare quality in politicians these days." He took her elbow gently to lead her to the door. Short of digging her heels in (and digging into a marble floor would be quite a trick), Stephanie had no option but to accompany him gracefully.

At the top of the capitol steps he paused and unfurled a black umbrella to protect them from the swirling white flakes that filled the air, then took her arm to help her down the slippery steps.

110

She stole a sideways glance at his charcoal gray over-coat with its black velvet collar. Again she was reminded of her John Wayne/Prince Charles characterization. How did a man raised on an Idaho cattle ranch manage to look as if he bought his clothes on Saville Row?

"How's your father?" he asked as they paused at the street light.

"Doing very well, really. He and Mother have rented an apartment in Palm Desert until Easter. Doctor Mangum's very hopeful that with complete rest he'll be OK."

"And your mother?"

"Mother's ecstatic to have Daddy all to herself. I've never seen her so relaxed." And Elizabeth's relaxing had eased tensions between her and her daughter, but Stephanie didn't add that.

By now they were across the street and entering the gleaming brass and glass doors of Hotel Boise. The elevator took them to the top floor and delivered them to a quietly sophisticated restaurant.

The waiter led them to a table by a window that looked out catercorner across the block to the eagle atop the capitol dome and then beyond to the snow-covered mountains projecting up into the pale gray sky. He placed a leatherbound menu in Steph's hands, and she surveyed her surroundings.

"Oh, what a view!" she said. "And I love the art deco touches—and this dusty rose and dark blue color scheme. Oh, and look at the tinned ceiling."

The room managed to keep its quiet atmosphere even though it rapidly filled with patrons, all of whom, it seemed, recognized and greeted the attorney general.

"I'm glad you like it. Maybe you'll find it easier to forgive me for interrupting your luncheon plans."

"Oh, well, anything for party unity." There was nothing to be gained now by telling him what she really thought of him and his tactics—she'd just go along and see what came of the situation.

"I'm glad to hear you say that. I wouldn't have bet on it this morning."

"I hope you don't have some idea you can change my mind just by having lunch with me." The words came out as more of a taunt than she intended.

He looked at her levelly with his dark, intense eyes. "If I thought that little of your mind or your ideals I wouldn't bother having lunch with you, not for the party or for old family ties."

His steady gaze made her feel uncomfortable, so she gave her attention to the menu.

When the waiter had placed their quiche florentine and tomato bisque soup on the gleaming black lacquer tables before them, Stephanie looked at her slim gold watch and issued her challenge. "The caucus convenes at two o'clock. That gives you just over forty-five minutes to change my mind about that bill."

He shook his head. "I don't want to talk about the bill. I want to talk about the nature of man."

"That sounds like a reasonable topic to tackle in forty-five minutes."

"Sure, we'll solve the world's problems by the stop-watch method. Whatever we've decided on when the buzzer sounds will be the correct answer." He took a spoonful of his soup, then continued in more seriousness. "Our families have lived side-by-side for three generations. I know we're coming at this issue from similar backgrounds."

"Yes, that's why I couldn't believe it this morning when you opposed the bill to fund substandard housing clearance. You should be one of the first to say, 'As you've done it unto the least of these . . .'"

"Steph, I told you I don't want to talk about the bill right now. The premise you voiced in support of it is what concerns me. Do you really believe that better houses will make better people? You sound like those kids at the Farragut picnic. Do you really believe having free food, free drugs, free houses would make everyone beautiful?"

"I hope I'm not as simplistic as you make me sound, but I certainly believe that we have to try. I don't believe that just because Christ said, 'The poor you will always have with you,' He meant that He found it a laudable state of affairs. I know Idaho doesn't actually have ghettos or slums like the large urban areas, but that's all the more reason we have to do something now—before it gets out of hand here."

"But the evils you are trying to cure with legislation came into the world with the Fall—so for a real cure, you have to go to the root of the matter."

"I'm sure you're right—theologically speaking—but in the practical world we need practical answers."

"Like a Band-aid?"

"I thought you wanted to discuss the issues."

"I apologize. That was uncalled for." His quick, sincere apology was more disconcerting than his arguments.

"But," he went on, "if it's true, as you are saying, that man is innately good and all he needs is more education, a higher technology level, and a better environment to perfect him, then wouldn't history support that? Were there fewer atrocities in World War II and in Vietnam than in the wars of previous centuries?"

She opened her mouth to reply, but at that moment the waiter brought the check.

"Time." Carlton held up his hand.

"That's not fair, you had the last word," Stephanie protested.

"But it was a question, which means we haven't solved anything yet. The only recourse is for you to accept my invitation to the ballet Friday night so we can continue round two." He laid his American Express card on the check. "I'll do my half," Stephanie said.

"Certainly not. I consider you a mission project." Another flash of his warm, quirkish smile.

"Oh, well, in that case, how could I refuse? If I thought I were just being lobbied I'd never stand for it. If you take this much time over every legislator that opposes you, you must have a very full schedule."

"Only those I consider worth it—I predict a great future for you. I have to get your thinking straightened out for the sake of the party and the state."

No wonder this man was such a political success. He could say anything and get away with it when it came with that wonderful warm grin. He held Steph's chair for her and then, across the room, helped her with her coat.

She continued her surprised reflection at finding Carlton Sperlin to be a man of such deep insights—and such beautiful manners. A man who could easily charm the birds out of the trees and the votes out of the electorate—and that was what he was doing to her, even if she couldn't help feeling a bit flattered that he would bother. Was the bill that important? Certainly her support couldn't mean that much.

They were back in the capitol when he said, "Seven-thirty, Friday. Where do I pick you up?"

"What? I'm sorry, I was lost in thought."

"Yes, I noticed. Admirable depth of concentration. You'll find it a very useful quality trying to work in this madhouse. I asked where you're staying."

"Oh, I'm staying with my cousin. Her husband is in Argentina on an engineering project for Morrison-Knudsen."

"Oh, how convenient for you."

"Yes," Stephanie had to agree. "When my need for housing in Boise arose so suddenly, Susie's need for a roommate seemed like a godsend."

"Do I detect a note of ambivalence in your voice?"

Stephanie shrugged. "We're very different personalities, but we're managing to rub along well enough together."

"And her address is?"

"One seventy-five Curling Drive. Over the golf course. Why?"

"Because I'm picking you up at seven-thirty Friday to go to the ballet. We'll have dinner after."

114

Her thumb rubbed the ruby and diamond ring on her third finger, left hand. Even though it didn't look like an engagement ring, and the event was unannounced, the fact remained—she *was* an engaged woman. And yet, the evening did sound like fun. She hesitated.

"OK, Ms. Liberation, you can pay your own way if it'll make you feel better."

She smiled. Ah, not a date then. "More mission work?"

"You got it."

She went back to the caucus room, and he went to his office. His report to the meeting had been finished that morning. But she still couldn't figure out how it had all happened—or why. Or why she found herself looking forward so much to next Friday.

13

The second Monday in January 1973 dawned crisp and clear. The sun shone brightly, if coldly, on the fresh, white snow. The fact that the sun chose to shine on the official opening of the Forty-Second Legislature had to be a good omen.

Stephanie walked purposefully through the brightly lit, white marble rotunda of the capitol building. The high heels of her shiny black boots clicked on the patterned marble floor, and her soft, rust-colored suede skirt moved gracefully just above her knees. She was amazed that after only last weekend's series of meetings she was beginning to feel at home here already.

It was all so different from her life in Nampa and far more different still from the tiny farming community of Kuna where her roots grew deep. A small brass marker told her that the site for the capitol was acquired in 1905, and the building was completed in 1920. By the time the commission had purchased this ground for the state, her grandmother had already spent three years on her sagebrush homestead. And by the time this building was dedicated, Kathryn had married and borne four children.

The death of one child, the loss of another in war, and her widowhood had all occurred while laws were being debated and passed in these halls. In a strange sort of way, that made Stephanie's family a more historic part of Idaho than even this great building. With a genuine sense of pride she squared her shoulders and walked on.

In the House chambers the feeling of freshness continued. Not a spot on the royal blue carpet, not a scribble on the yellow notepads at each walnut desk, not a scratch on the freshly painted white balustrades around the rapidly filling galleries overhead.

Steph took her seat next to Fran. She had been happy to learn that legislators could choose their own seating arrangement, even if the newly elected ones did get last choice. She smiled at Fran, but before she could speak the gavel sounded through the chambers and the Speaker announced, "House be in order."

The air seemed to tingle with expectancy as the opening pageantry began. The report came from the chambers on the other side of the rotunda that "the Senate is in order." The committee from the Senate entered, returned the greetings that had been sent to them from the House, and then the senators were ushered in, formally welcomed, and seated on folding chairs down front.

Stephanie was surprised and impressed by the formal precision, which gave an added consequence to the occasion. She had always believed that happenings of importance should be marked with appropriate ceremony, so she was thoroughly enjoying the bit of pomp underlying this event.

Today was certainly one of the days that would live forever in her memory, although she wouldn't want any of the veteran members to know how impressed she was. She had witnessed the occasion before—once for her father's first swearing-in and later as a reporter—but it was far different being on the floor herself. The thought flashed through her mind that she was glad she wasn't in Scotland. That was quickly followed, however, by a stab of guilt over such disloyalty.

The gavel sounded. The joint session of the Forty-Second Legislature was open. Committees were dismissed to escort the dignitaries to the chambers. During the brief lull in the proceedings, the old-timers visited and read papers, but Stephanie sat quietly, not wanting to lose the sense of occasion.

The committee escorting the Supreme Court entered first, followed by the five dignified justices in their flowing black robes, who took seats at the Speaker's left. Next to be ushered in were the elected officials of the State of Idaho: lieutenant governor, secretary of state, attorney general —and suddenly to Stephanie's eyes there was no one else in the room.

That tall, slightly limping, dark-haired man in the three-piece black pinstripe suit, gleaming white shirt, and silvery gray tie and pocket handkerchief—that man whose quiet elegance could only be defined as class—that was the man she had sat with at a luncheon table and argued politics with only two days ago. Without thinking, her hand went to her throat to be sure the soft rust-colored silk bow was still lying smoothly over her gray jacket. As she did her ring caught a beam of light. What on earth was she doing looking at another man like that?

The committee to escort the governor entered, and the Speaker's voice brought her back to attention. "We have the distinct privilege of presenting to this body the governor of the great state of Idaho, Governor Nelson Chatburn." From the crowded gallery, press cameras flashed and TV cameras rolled to record the governor's annual State of the State message.

Stephanie tried to concentrate on the governor's words, but her eyes often strayed from the speaker back to the attorney general, no matter how much her mind scolded her. Afterward, she felt she could summarize the speech fairly by noting that Governor Chatburn was in favor of prosperity, clean air, and the future, but she couldn't recall what he wore. Now, Attorney General Sperlin—*no, you prefer tweeds. You're just missing David, or you wouldn't notice Carlton at all.*

Amid much political handshaking, the ceremonies ended, the committees escorted their assigned charges back to their offices and chambers, and the joint session adjourned.

"Well, tomorrow we get to work." Fran picked up a few papers from her desk and preceded Stephanie from the chambers. One advantage of being a freshman was that Stephanie was able to make her way around the rotunda and down the two flights of marble stairs to the basement coffee bar unimpeded by lobbyists, press, or constituents. She looked briefly at the tray of Danish pastries and decided the band on her skirt was just comfortable and should stay that way, so ordered only coffee.

"How about letting me buy that for you, and you can repay me by drinking it with me?" a cheerful masculine voice said.

Stephanie turned with a broad smile. "Jimmy. You do keep turning up like a bad penny. I haven't seen you since Farragut."

Jim carried their steaming styrofoam cups to a small table. "Welcome to the zoo. I hear your father's recovering apace. Clever of him to appoint you. You'll do a good job."

"Thanks. I sure hope so." She sipped her coffee. "Are you still with UPI? So why aren't you up in the press room filing your stories or something?"

He shrugged. "I got all the wires will be interested in—seems the guv is in favor of prosperity, clean air, and the future—what can I say?"

Stephanie laughed. "That's amazing! That was my summary, word-for-word!"

"Now, why don't you give me something worth writing about—as a freshman legislator, what do you see as the most important issues facing this legislature?" He pulled out notebook and pen.

"Besides prosperity, clean air, and the future, you mean?"

"Yeah." He returned her grin. "And besides the budget—that's all anybody ever talks about."

Stephanie thought for a moment. Jim was serious. What she gave him would go out on the wire service. Here was her chance to do something to promote her bill, to get her side out ahead of the detractors. "All right, I'd love to make a statement." She gathered her scattered thoughts—this had to be good.

"The governor today emphasized the need for a healthy economic environment and a high quality of life for all our citizens. I see these two issues as inseparably related—the higher quality of life all our citizens enjoy, the lower our crime rate, the better our social services—the more attractive our state will be to corporations and to those who can promote economic growth. That's why I think the most significant achievement this legislature could make would be the passage of the bill to finance construction of new housing for those living in substandard conditions."

The importance of the words she was speaking gripped Stephanie, and her voice rang with the warm emotion of her belief.

"This, I realize, presents an enormous challenge in administrative and financial terms, but Idahoans, true to our pioneer spirit, have always met and mastered challenges. We must create *now* the kind of future we want for ourselves and our children. If this legislature fails to accept this challenge and to seize the opportunity before us, the chance may not come again. If we fail to pass this bill, such an opportunity to bring increased prosperity to our state and improved quality of life to our people will be delayed and may be lost forever."

"Bravo!"

"Well spoken!"

"I'd vote for her even if she weren't beautiful!"

To Stephanie's amazement and embarrassment a group had gathered about their table to hear her speech. Now they burst into spontaneous applause.

Her cheeks colored, but like the politician she was, she met their cheers with a brilliant smile and words of thanks, and shook hands with those near her chair.

Jim's pencil stopped scribbling as he jumped to his feet and grabbed her arm. "Come on, we've got to get back upstairs before Sam leaves. I want photos to go with this story!" He pulled her through the spectators. "Excuse us, folks."

They found Sam packing the last of his equipment in a large leather shoulder bag, but he quickly reassembled to shoot the photos of Stephanie that Jim required.

A cameraman and reporter from a local TV station were just finishing an interview with the Speaker of the House and president pro tem of the Senate when the UPI activity attracted their attention.

"What ya got, Jimmy boy?"

"Have a heart, guys. This is an exclusive."

"News is news. Besides, you owe me one for that inside leak on the state hospital scandal last month."

Jim grinned and shrugged. "Calling in your markers this early in the session? OK, Steph, say your piece for the TV fellas."

Without so much as a chance to comb her hair, Stephanie found herself repeating her speech while the "News Beat" action camera focused its bright lights on her. Her interview with Jim had just been a warm-up. In front of the cameras she embellished and enlarged on her previous statement. Her voice glowed with conviction and authority, and the total effect was one of polish and poise.

"Not bad!" Jim grinned at her. "And besides, you're lots more photogenic than the governor."

But even successful media personalities have to buy toothpaste and keep gas in their cars, and, in spite of being a nine-minutes-wonder, Stephanie was no exception.

She had a long list of mundane errands to run, so it was getting dark and very cold by the time she could head her little green car up Bogus Basin Road toward her temporary home.

"Hurry! You're on the news!" Susie yelled before Stephanie even closed the door behind her.

Steph rushed into the living room just in time to catch a glimpse of herself smiling into the camera before they cut to another story.

Susie jumped up, scattering books and papers all over the thick umber carpet. "Great job, cuz! You looked and sounded so professional—like you've been at this for years."

Stephanie shrugged. "Guess I have been in a way. I always wanted a chance to do something like this." She still had trouble believing her chance had come so suddenly—and just when she had decided to give up on it all.

Susie laughed. "To the manor born, you might say. I remember you stirring up trouble over some pet cause of yours in college—Mother always thought you had an unfortunate attraction for controversy. She said it came from Uncle Eliot's side of the family." She snapped off the beginning sports news.

"Broncos lost again—we don't want to hear that. Hungry?"

Stephanie flopped in the nearest chair, her feet straight out in front of her. "Starved! I never even got to drink the coffee that news hound Jimmy bought me."

"Great! I've got a casserole in the oven. Don't even move. I'll throw another log on the fire, and we'll eat in here. When Bob's gone I always become a total slob—it's my only recompense for having to live without him."

"Can't I help?" Stephanie asked half-heartedly.

"Oh, no, I'm perfectly capable of becoming a slob on my own."

"Idiot! I mean with dinner."

"Yeah, I know you did," Sue called from the kitchen. "Not if you can put up with casserole and tomato juice, period. Its not really as unbalanced as it sounds—I put everything in the casserole." She placed the steamy dish on the raised Oakley stone hearth in front of a nicely blazing fire and ladled servings onto two plates before saying a brief grace.

"Oh, yum! I'm even hungrier than I thought." Stephanie swallowed her third mouthful. Having Susie Homemaker for a roommate wasn't all bad. And besides, she'd discovered her cousin wasn't nearly as compulsive as she had thought her to be—even if she did consider Stephanie "controversial."

"What's all this?" She indicated Susie's books and papers still scattered about the room.

"Mmm, didn't I tell you I guide a Bible study here on Tuesday evenings? The material is marvelous, but there's so much of it I don't know if I'll ever get it together before tomorrow night. We're doing First Corinthians thirteen. You know, you think you really know something you've heard all your life, but when you get into it . . ."

"Mmm." Stephanie nodded. "Have you read that part in Grammie's journal? Her papa made her memorize that passage when he thought her attitudes were wrong." For a moment her face softened with a faraway look. "It must have been nice—simpler times. Oh, I know, life was physically grueling—but not having to wrestle with great issues all the time."

Their conversation was cut short by the ringing phone. In a moment Sue returned from the kitchen. "For you—I didn't ask his name, but he has a very sexy voice."

Stephanie stuck out her tongue at her cousin and picked up the receiver.

"Congratulations. You represented your viewpoint very well—and yourself very effectively too, I might add," the indeed sexy voice of Carlton Sperlin said in her ear.

"Well, thank you. That's certainly a surprise coming from you." She hoped she didn't sound so stunned she'd lose any points her image might have accumulated for poise.

He laughed gently. "You shouldn't be too surprised. I've never taken any exception to your manner of presentation."

Then she realized the limitations he had placed on his compliment. "You mean you don't like what I said, but you like the way I said it." Her voice held a note of challenge.

"Stephanie." He sounded patient, with just a hint of warning underneath. "I called to give you a compliment, not a debate."

Then that unfortunate attraction to controversy that Susie had characterized her with took over. She goaded him. "I would never have picked you as one to back down." She managed to make her voice sound just the least bit provocative.

"I have no intention of backing down—from anything." He was firm, but still sounded amused. "But I see now what a worthy opponent you will be in the battle for public opinion. I've never known the public to be anything but impressed by shining rhetoric and glittering generalities."

Stephanie gasped.

And then, even more infuriating, he laughed—a chuckle of real amusement—and told her good night.

In spite of the fact that Susie's guest room boasted the latest in up-to-date comfort—a waterbed—it wasn't a good night. *Glittering generalities, indeed!* Stephanie fumed. And every time she flung herself from one side to the other, she would have to wait for the waves to subside under her before she could make another attempt to sleep.

Worthy opponent is right. He has no idea how worthy I can be. I'm on my way, and I have no intention of letting anyone get in my way. Mr. Attorney General Carlton Jules Sperlin hasn't seen anything yet.

14

But David Fraser, Carlton Sperlin, and the housing subsidy bill all had to take a backseat to the more immediate matters of Stephanie's week. Each day began with a brief session in chambers for roll call, prayer, and the first reading of a few bills before the members were dismissed to committee work. Then each evening had its schedule: a Chamber of Commerce banquet, a dinner hosted by the Idaho Commission for the Blind, a party given by the hospital association. Then she went home with a briefcase bulging with bills and reports to be studied before the next day's meetings.

And because she was determined to be not just adequate at her job but great, everything had to be studied in detail. Then a quick glance at what was going on in the rest of the world—investigation of the Watergate break-in taking top billing—before she could fall into bed.

Today was no different: a short night of sleep, a morning running from one meeting to the next, endless details and statistics to be sorted, juggled, and applied. Returning from a hasty lunch, which she had chosen to eat alone, she dashed past the replica of the liberty bell and up the broad sandstone steps to enter the capitol through the front portico.

There, breathless, she paused. Would she ever get over being impressed every time she entered the great four-storied marble rotunda? Two rows of enormous marble pillars circled the room. Graceful marble stairways curved upward on both sides of her.

Craning her neck backward, she viewed the skylit dome, more than two hundred feet overhead, and its centerpiece of star-spangled blue glass—forty-three stars representing the fact that Idaho was the forty-third state admitted to the Union.

She thought guiltily that she needed to be on her way. But she took just one more moment to pause before the gilt equestrian statue of George Washington. She really didn't have time to read the whole plaque, but the story captured her imagination: This life-size statue was carved by Charles Ostner, an Austrian immigrant, from a single yellow pine and hauled through drifted snow by hand sled. Most of the sculpting was done at night by the light of a pine torch held by the artist's son. Ostner's model for the head was a postage stamp of Washington. It took four years to complete and was presented to the Idaho Territory in 1869 in memory of Idaho's pioneers.

With a surge of pride in her state, her pioneer heritage, and her role in serving this state and preserving this heritage, Stephanie turned and hurried up the marble stairs she had admired a few minutes before. She put behind her any feelings of guilt over her stolen moments. They had produced a renewal of energy and vision. She could draw strength and vigor from these marble halls, be as stalwart as the massive columns that supported the dome.

Even after her brief respite of reflection in the rotunda, she was the first member to arrive at the Health and Welfare committee meeting. She smiled at the lobbyists, visitors, and press members seated around the room, then gave another smile as her favorite newsman entered.

"I see your housing bill had its first reading this morning." Jim sat in the brass-studded, leather and oak chair next to Stephanie's. "When do you expect it to get to committee?"

"In about a week, assuming the Printing Committee is expeditious."

"No worry there, with the kind of attention this bill is getting."

"Thanks to you." She grinned at him.

"I understand the attorney general's office is taking a large posture on it."

Stephanie's smile changed to a look of grim defiance. "It's going to be a battle."

"Well, stick with me, kid—the power of the press and all that, you know. We could make a pretty powerful team."

"I do appreciate your help, Jimmy."

He looked satisfied at the sincerity in her voice. "That's fine. I may find a way for you to return the favor. You know, if you could just come up with a method for creative financing with your bill you'd have a real coup on your hands—think about it."

Jim moved quickly from the table to one of the spectator's seats as Chairman Detweiler and several of the other committee members entered the room. The rest of the afternoon was spent listening to expert testimony, studying the fiscal impact report, and questioning the sponsor of House Bill 72 to require a mandatory minimum fine for conviction under the uniform controlled substance act.

The director of the state narcotics bureau testified, a law enforcement officer testified, and a house member presented a breakdown of the projected economic benefit to the state from such a law.

Stephanie was impressed by the incisive questions her fellow members leveled at the witnesses and the seriousness of this hard-working committee. But as the afternoon wore on, her frustration mounted. It seemed that all they talked about was money—the cost of enforcement versus revenue from the fines.

"What about the *people!*" she wanted to shout. They were all just like Carlton—cold, calculating, uncaring. All the bills could just be run through an adding machine, and if the bottom line showed a profit they could be declared law.

But that brought Jim's parting words to mind. Money was the bottom line on everything. If she could come up with a way to finance her housing bill without adding to the tax burden or taking away from other programs . . . If she could think of some way to satisfy their unfeeling, analytical balance sheets, then maybe she could beat them at their own game.

Tonight she had a meeting out with that great adding machine that sat in the attorney general's office. She shivered at the thought. She toyed with the idea of canceling it.

She could stay home and write a long letter in answer to the two brief notes she'd received from David since he arrived back in Scotland. She had been a bit disappointed at their brevity, but she knew he was busy settling into a new job.

She had almost determined to call the AG's office and leave a message that she wouldn't be available tonight when she had another thought—she needed to stay on good terms with her party leader. She would write to David before she met with Carlton. If she told David all about her plans, she wouldn't have to worry about feeling she was going out behind his back. Because, of course, she wasn't.

"If there is nothing further to come before the committee, the meeting is adjourned." Chairman Detweiler's voice penetrated Stephanie's consciousness, and she realized how lost she'd been in her own thoughts. That had always been a habit of hers. Intense powers of concentration could be a blessing, but as she often learned in school, they could also get you in trouble if you concentrated on the wrong thing.

When Carlton called for her that evening, however, wearing a dark blue/black suit with palest blue shirt and silk pocket handkerchief, Stephanie had to admit he was the best looking business appointment she'd ever had.

He raised his eyebrows in obvious appreciation at her emerald green, peau de soir evening suit that matched her eyes. The gesture made his forehead wrinkle in the most endearing way, and in spite of all her powers of concentration, she almost forgot that she didn't like this man. Well, she didn't like his political policies—well, *one* of his policies, at least.

Carlton helped her into the car, then went around and started the smooth engine. "I've been looking forward to this all week."

"You have?" She couldn't have suppressed her surprise if she'd tried. "Why?"

"Why?" He seemed as surprised by her question as she was by his statement.

"Yes, why? As in 'To what do I owe the honor?'"

Who had said, "Know your enemy"? Whoever it was, she was set on following his advice. She would get to know what made this man tick so she could emerge the victor in their battle.

He was quiet for a moment, then raised just one brow above a twinkling eye. "Well, we could say I'm looking out for an old family friend."

"Nonsense."

"OK, how about, as the leader of our party I believe we need more time to talk?"

"Right." He saw the evening just as she did, so she could relax.

The thought held her quiet all the way to the Boise High School Auditorium where Idaho's newly formed resident ballet company, The Ballet Folk, was performing. She kept trying to nudge herself. She had set her goal for the evening to get to know her opponent better. *Knowledge is power.* But she found it impossible to probe for the knowl-

129

edge she sought. It took all her effort to fight the anesthetizing sense of euphoria threatening her.

Stephanie looked around the ornate white and gold rococo auditorium built at the turn of the century. She sensed the excitement in the air over the opening performance of the new year. And when the curtain went up on *Carmina Burana*, the showpiece of the evening, she could see that the audience's expectations were not ill-founded.

In front of a medieval cathedral backdrop, the fifteen-part dance depicting the festive joie de vivre of a group of wandering students of the Middle Ages unfolded. The moods shifted dazzlingly from stately black-robed monks bearing candles and moving to a Gregorian chant, to a scene of tender young lovers, to a group of peasants just in from the fields, cavorting in wild merriment.

"Oh, bravo!" Stephanie cried in accompaniment to the enthusiastic applause when the curtain fell.

"Yes," Carlton agreed, "as one big city reviewer said, it's good to know that Idaho is producing more for the nation than just potatoes."

"Well put." Stephanie laughed, still applauding. Then as the applause quieted and the lights came on for intermission she added, "They really are marvelous, aren't they? So absolutely polished a company in such a—well, an obscure place."

"That's much of their reason for being—a dedication to taking dance to cities and rural areas alike. I'm glad you're enjoying it."

"Oh, I am! I think maybe I've been too focused for too long. Politics and news are important, but its easy to develop channel vision. Do you have time for things like this often?"

"I make time as often as I can. I brought Todd and Tessa to the *Nutcracker* the day after Christmas. It was really a first class performance, too—which is especially important when you bring children."

"Why especially for children?"

"Adults will make allowances; children are purists. But even more important, how are children going to learn if you don't do it right for them? They've got to have good models if they're going to develop sound aesthetic judgment. Living with shoddy entertainment can tear down all we've worked to build up in church and school."

The lights were dimming for the performance to continue, so she didn't reply, but she sat thinking deeply about Carlton's words. He never failed to amaze her—was there anything he didn't hold a philosophy on? Everybody had opinions, but this man's mind was so keen that he approached everything—including taking children to the ballet—like a course in systematic theology.

The last half of the program was a harlequinade entitled "The Comedians." Its sassy, carefree air came from a choreography based on acrobatics and balletic tricks that demonstrated the athletic abilities of the company. Stephanie and Carlton laughed with the rest of the audience as the clowns danced and pranced in the richly colorful frenzy and glitter of a carnival atmosphere.

Steph changed moods with the dance as a broken-hearted comedian laughed through his tears Pagliacci-style, until finally celebration reigned in a dazzling climax, ending with a delight of balloons falling from the ceiling.

Their late dinner at River Parke seemed to Stephanie a perfect finale to an evening of fantasy. The dining room glowed with rich burgundy carpet, pale golden wood furniture, and myriad tiny amber lights reflected and re-reflected from etched smoked glass around the walls. She leaned back in her chair and studied the infinity of lights as the reflections repeated and renewed endlessly.

She gave Carlton a slow smile.

"Hungry?" He surveyed his menu.

"Well, since they cleverly parked that sumptuous dessert cart right by the entrance, I think I'll just have the house salad and save room for really important things."

Carlton agreed, and in a few minutes the salad captain was before them, performing his mysterious rites. With the raw ingredients of salami, Parmesan cheese, cauliflower, mushrooms, sunflower seeds, a variety of lettuces, and other items Stephanie lost track of, he built a salad to gratify the most demanding gastronome. His activities held their interest without conversation, but after savoring her first bite she settled back with a satisfied "Mmm."

"Well, what do you think of life in the monkey house?"

She shrugged. "Too soon to tell. But I've always felt driven to accomplish something. Like they tell you when you go to a campground—'leave it better than you found it'—that's what I want to do for the state. That's why the housing bill is so important to me."

There, she'd done it—broken the tranquillity of the evening. Here was her chance to make some points with her opponent. "Carlton, I kept thinking tonight that you said you can't educate people into goodness—I grant you that, but you *can* educate them into an appreciation of the arts—like with Todd and Tessa—and I believe that *can* make them better people."

He finished his bite of salad and nodded thoughtfully. "Agreed—it broadens their horizons and gives them wider choices—like someone with a limited vocabulary who's left with swearing for want of a better means of expressing himself. People with an unlimited appreciation of activities can choose to spend their time in more elevating ways."

She moved in with a quick rapier thrust. "Precisely. So, if education can elevate people, why doesn't it follow that slum clearance can make them better people?"

A hint of amusement twinkled in his eyes, as if he were enjoying the tilt. "Moving people to what will amount to another tenement isn't culture—that won't accomplish anything."

"And you can't educate people to a better life?"

He gave a little half nod that was more just a ducking of his head. "You can, to some extent."

"So why aren't you supporting my bill? Why must you be such a bullheaded bigot?"

"Because your bill won't work."

"But you just agreed with me!" Stephanie hit the table with more force than she meant to, then looked up in deep embarrassment as she realized the waiter was standing there.

"May I take your plates?" he inquired with perfect passivity.

When the waiter departed with the dishes, Carlton grinned. "Just in time to rescue the china."

"I might have felt like throwing something at you, but I didn't forget myself quite that far." She rested her left hand on the table.

He glanced at the ring sparkling in the candlelight. "Beautiful ring."

"Thanks. It was a Christmas present."

He nodded and went on with the conversation, leaving Stephanie struggling to figure out why she'd said that. Why didn't she just tell him it was an engagement ring? If she had thought about it, she would have supposed her mother had told Grace, and that Grace's nephew would know. It was a measure of how upset Elizabeth was over Eliot's health that the family grapevine hadn't operated.

But it was just as well. She didn't really want to talk about David at a business meeting.

The dessert cart made its enticing appearance, and when they had been served rich slabs of banana cream cake and chocolate mint torte with steaming cups of coffee, the duel resumed.

"I *didn't* agree with you. Look, I'm not against everyone in the world having a better house complete with a garden—but when they move from the slums into that garden, they will take the same tempers, anxieties, and passions with them. Trying to change the world through government legislation is as useless as trying to change the individual through spiritual legalism."

"So you just give up?" She threw her hands into the air.

"Not at all. It's fine to do what we can—we must. But it's imperative to realize that we won't automatically reduce crime and make good people by doing so."

"Then why do it?"

"Because you love the people."

His answer was so unexpected and spoken so quietly it left her speechless. It occurred to her he might be putting her on for what he probably considered her bleeding-heart approach to politics. But his voice and manner held no hint of irony.

When his answer had made its full impression he added, "And it's important that any method adopted to improve people's circumstances be consistent with the other values of our society."

She set her coffee cup down with a clatter. "Are you trying to say that my bill is un-American?"

"No." He held up one hand in a calming gesture. "It's always a matter of balancing: a maximum of freedom, a minimum of coercion—a maximum of reinforcing reward, a minimum of stultifying charity—a maximum of opportunity for individual achievement, a minimum of government defined molds."

He spoke quietly, just to her, but the timbre with which the words were produced made her want to applaud.

"With rhetoric like that I can certainly see why you were elected."

"It's not just rhetoric. It's what I believe." His eyes held hers in the soft light of the room. "But it's not all I believe. I also believe you have the most beautiful green eyes I've ever seen."

If it was a technique to win a debate, it was brilliant. There was no possible reply to that.

Even more disturbing were the questions flooding her mind to which she found replies impossible. She had made success her goal. Did she love the underprivileged, or did she want to pass this bill for her own success? Would she be willing to put her success on the line with an unpopular stand, as Carlton had done in opposing this bill? She had accused him of being cold, calculating, an automaton—but which of them really was? The nation was scandalized with reports of the Watergate fiasco. But was it far easier than she realized to fall into the trap of believing the end justified the means?

They finished their coffee in mellow silence, and Stephanie found it impossible not to return the tiny smiles that played around the corners of his mouth.

It was when he was returning from the checkroom with her wrap that she noticed he was limping more than usual.

When they were in the car, she turned to him. "Tell me about your time in Nam."

He shrugged. "Maybe some time. It's a rather long story—"

"And you're tired?" she finished.

"I guess so, but I wasn't aware of it. I've had much better things to think about."

And Stephanie certainly had plenty to think about as she finished her letter to David later that night. She tried to share her thoughts and feelings of the evening honestly, but it was hard to do. Scotland was so very far away.

15

"Stimulating politics and an interesting personal life—must be an unbeatable mixture." Sue looked up as Stephanie entered the kitchen a few days later. "You look like you have the world on a string." Susie's voice held just a tinge of envy.

"You left 'getting to sleep in' off your list. No early meetings today!" Stephanie stretched and turned to brewing coffee and making whole wheat toast. She hummed softly to herself.

Unfortunately, the wrought-iron stand that held the coffee mugs was precariously balanced. When she took a mug off, the remaining three overbalanced and fell with a clatter, breaking the handle off one.

"Careful!" Sue snapped with irritation in her voice.

"Oh, I'm sorry!" Stephanie was appalled at her own clumsiness and at Sue's touchy response.

Then Sue gave a jerky laugh. "Oh, Steph, *I'm* sorry. Can you believe I was so deep in my study of love that I practically bit your head off!"

Stephanie handed her cousin a mug of coffee. "Here's your chance before I break the rest of the cups."

"Don't worry about that. They're perfectly expendable." She took a sip. "It seems it's easier to study about love than to live it—especially with my husband thousands of miles away for months on end. I'll have to confess this incident to my study group tonight. Believe it or not, this is what I was reading when I snapped at you: 'Courtesy is love in little, everyday things. The secret of politeness is to love. Love cannot be rude.'"

Stephanie smiled. "That's an excellent description of you most of the time, Susie. Don't be too hard on yourself for being human. What're you studying tonight?"

"Kindness. I found a good example from Great-grammie's book."

"Oh, read it to me."

Sue picked up the volume but didn't open it. "Can you imagine what it must have been like for those few brave souls that homesteaded in the desert on faith that water would come?"

Stephanie shook her head. "Unthinkable. I'll bet Grammie's papa found lots of good sermon material in stories of the forty years in the wilderness. I'm sure the one of Moses hitting the rock for water would have been my favorite."

Sue laughed. "I know you—you'd have been out there hitting every rock you could find."

"I probably would have, at that. But what about the story?"

"Oh, yeah. Well, even before they could grow crops they went ahead and prepared the land to farm—on faith that water would come. The first job was clearing the sagebrush."

Stephanie nodded. "Mmm, I remember how Grams hated sagebrush."

"Well, she hated it worse after weeks of helping her papa grub it off the land. It seems that some farmers had horse-drawn disks that made it a little easier. The ones that didn't have disks used rails from the railroad. When those without horses got too exhausted from attacking it with shovel and saw, they burned it. That was a pretty desperate measure, because they needed the sagebrush for fuel."

"And I remember how Grams said she hated the stink of burning sagebrush—it got in your hair and clothes and just never came out—like skunk, I guess," Stephanie added.

"That's right." Susie opened the book. "So you can imagine how she felt the morning she got up dreading the burning-off of the homestead next to theirs. 'When I opened the door I couldn't believe it—the air was clear and fresh. There were two men I'd never seen before pulling a disk behind a team of horses—and sagebrush lying flat everywhere. Papa said they were neighbors from across Indian Creek, but I think they were angels.'"

"That's great. I wonder if people would help each other like that now? Isn't that really what life should be all about—doing little things for people?"

Sue nodded. "That's exactly what I want to bring out in this study—that our natural inclinations are toward greed, anger, and lust, but God's love can make us behave with compassion and kindness. Can you imagine a world without love—with only lust?"

Stephanie stopped with her slice of buttery toast halfway to her mouth. "I never thought of it that way." Actually, she didn't think much about God at all—but it seemed He had been creeping into her thoughts more and more recently.

Her mind went back over her last conversation with Carlton, about the causes of crime. He'd certainly agree with Susie's analysis of the nature of man.

Another thought annoyed the edges of her consciousness. Her personal life and her political life were going full steam ahead, but what about her spiritual life? Raised in a Christian home, she'd been a believer since she responded to the message of a vacation Bible school teacher the summer after the first grade. But how much had she grown since then?

Had she only graduated from the first grade spiritually? She certainly believed the gospel (to the extent she understood it), and prayed (if she didn't fall into exhausted sleep first), and went to church (if political duties didn't interfere). But Sue with her Bible study, and Carlton with his penetrating understanding, seemed to have a depth she lacked. And for the first time she wondered—what about David? They had never discussed spiritual matters, and now it seemed an awkward topic to explore in a letter. A chime from the living room clock brought her to her feet.

"I've got to get ready." She took her dishes to the dishwasher. "Tell me more about it later—I'm intrigued."

In her room she quickly pulled her static-cling rollers from her bright hair. She made the ends flip out today. Then she slipped into a deep red silky blouse to go under her black and white glen plaid coatdress.

From long years of observation Stephanie had developed her own theories about how women in politics should dress. Candidates should stick to basic-colored, tailored clothes, but always brighten them with a spot of feminine color so as not to blend into the background as "one of the boys." Candidates' wives should dress in lovely rich colors that were never flashy but made them stand out from the crowd. Voters always wanted a touch of glamour as a reward for going to the effort of attending a political rally.

She smiled into the mirror. Whatever her philosophy, the results today pleased her.

Driving to the capitol, however, her mind was not on her appearance but back on her talk with Sue about the unloving, greedy, self-centeredness of man. As she seemed to do with everything, she applied that to her work. It did make sense that lust was largely at fault for the state the world was in: lust for money, for sex, for power. But that made it all so hopeless. If the problem was within people, as Carlton kept insisting, what could one do? And she simply refused to throw up her hands and admit defeat.

But she did want to talk to Carlton about it again. His well-reasoned answers seemed to give her a new avenue for thought—no matter how much she disagreed with them.

She parked in her slot in the garage behind the capitol and walked through the underground tunnel into the building. Glancing at her watch she saw that she still had twenty minutes before she had to be at her desk. She'd just stop in and say hello to Carlton. Maybe they could discuss her questions over lunch or something.

Going toward the attorney general's office, she passed along the corridor of doors lettered with names of the divisions he headed: Business Regulations, Natural Resources, Criminal Justice, Public Finance, Appeals. Her steps slowed. She was awed by the magnitude of responsibility resting on this one man. And she knew the activities listed on those doors didn't even include criminal investigation and serving as technical adviser to all state agencies, counties, and cities.

She hadn't really thought about it before, but now, as she neared the double glass doors leading into his offices, she did think about it. All those duties were incumbent on those perfectly tailored broad shoulders—and yet he had made time in his life for her.

It seemed that his time at lunch that day, however, was not to be hers. The receptionist very politely but very definitely informed her that Mr. Sperlin would be out all morning and wasn't expected back until after lunch. "The attorney general has a standing appointment on Tuesdays. Would you like to have him call you when he returns, Miss Hamilton?"

Steph was surprised at the use of her name, then realized she was wearing her name badge. "No. No, thank you. It wasn't anything pressing."

The morning business session moved expediciously, as they were not yet to the point of the lengthy floor debates. Those would come later in the session when more of the initial committee work was done.

"Do you have a luncheon meeting, or do you want to grab something quick in the lounge?" Fran asked as soon as the adjourning gavel fell.

"No meetings. Isn't that great! Let's grab a snack in the lounge." Stephanie stuffed a handful of papers into her briefcase.

But leaving the chambers, she was hailed by Jimmy's friendly voice. "How's my favorite bill-pusher? Got anything hot for me today?"

"How about, we need more money for education?" Stephanie laughed.

Jim made a face. "I had in mind something we don't hear more than fifty times a day. You lovely ladies going to lunch? How about brightening a poor reporter's drab world by eating with me?"

"What did you have in mind—tuna sandwiches in the janitor's room?" Fran asked.

"Ah, I see you know my style. But actually, today it's peanut butter. I could forgo the brown bag, however, for something swank like the Sweet Shoppe."

"Beats hot dogs in the Members' Lounge," Stephanie said.

"Right. I'll get my coat." Jim led them into the News Media Center and disappeared down a corridor.

Steph and Fran stood for a moment, observing the shabbily cluttered press room. They watched a cluster of reporters gathered around electronic equipment to edit a tape of some interview, and listened to the clackity-clack of typewriters from the row of small offices on the other side.

The effervescent Jimmy soon returned, wearing a slightly soiled trench coat. He was accompanied by a tall, thin man who wore his blond hair slicked back from his forehead and his black-framed glasses halfway down his nose.

"Ladies, this is Arnold Bartmess, my brother-in-law. Arnie, meet Fran and Steph."

Stephanie returned Arnie's slightly limp handshake.

"These are some of my powerful political contacts I was telling you about," Jim told his relative, and they all laughed.

Then with the conventional pleased-to-meet-yous, Arnold took his leave. "Give Sis my love," Jim called after him and ushered the ladies into the rotunda.

At that moment the doors of the attorney general's office swung open, and a stunning woman with sleek black hair and an equally sleek black "dress for success" suit over a crisp, white, high-necked linen blouse walked past them.

Jimmy's gaze followed her with unfeigned interest. "Whew! She must be an assertiveness training teacher— did you ever see anyone exude so much self-assurance?"

But Stephanie wasn't listening to Jim. She was watching the regal female approach an equally polished male. The woman reached out and kissed Carlton Sperlin. No wonder the attorney general wasn't expected back in his office.

"You ladies feel like walking?" Jimmy slipped a hand through each of his companions' arms and piloted them toward the door.

"James Linzler! Do you mean to say you asked us out to lunch, and you don't have a car?" Stephanie laughed with incredulity.

"I guess I didn't exactly think it through."

"Oh, come on, I've got mine." Stephanie was still shaking her head.

At the Sweet Shoppe they sat on old fashioned ice cream parlor chairs and ate crispy vegetarian sandwiches.

"By the way," Fran said, "she's not an assertiveness teacher. She's a lawyer—the woman back at the capitol," she added to Stephanie and Jim's blank stares. "From eastern Idaho. I think she's attached to the AG's office somehow."

"I'd say she looked plenty attached," Stephanie observed.

"Just a minute, I'll think of her name." After a moment Fran snapped her fingers. "Anne. Anne Smith."

"You're kidding. No one in the world is less plain Ann Smith than that woman!" Stephanie said.

"Well, I think she spells the Anne with an 'e'—if that's any help. But then I don't suppose her parents could know she'd turn out quite like that when they named her."

That seemed to be all anyone had to contribute on the Anne Smith issue, so Jim moved in. "Speaking of the attorney general—" he looked at Stephanie "—I hear you're getting to be rather good friends."

"Where did you hear that?"

"Basic bloodhound instincts. I keep my nose to the ground."

"That's guaranteed to get it dirty."

Jim ignored Fran's remark. "Has he said anything to you about his time in Vietnam?"

"I know he was there with JAG, and that he was wounded." She shrugged. "I'm sure you know about the Distinguished Service Medal. Why?"

"That's all anyone knows. I thought there might be a story there. You know, personality profile—good human interest stuff." He finished the last of his sandwich. "Let me know if you get a drift on it—the public just laps that sort of thing up. After all, they're paying the salaries. You can't blame them for being interested in the lives of their public servants."

"Being a public servant means you can't have a private life?" Stephanie didn't know why Jimmy seemed more irritating than usual.

"You ladies gonna let me treat you to a truffle? They're really an out of sight experience." He grinned broadly.

But Stephanie and Fran declined the delicacy and paid for their own sandwiches.

On the way back, Jim brought up the attorney general again. "He's really gonna get himself in hot water this time—clear over his head if he doesn't watch out. Its hard to imagine a politician with any savvy taking such an unpopular stand, but then, you never know . . .'

"What are you talking about?" Stephanie asked, more quickly than she meant to.

"This drinking age bill the youth vote is supporting."

"I haven't heard about anything like that in the hopper," Fran said.

"My goodness, don't tell me news doesn't travel across the hallowed marble halls of the rotunda. There's a move on to lower the drinking age to eighteen. The bill isn't printed yet, but word is it's set to have it's first reading in the Senate next week."

"Who's carrying it?" Fran asked.

"Not sure. But it'll be someone very powerful, you can count on that. The AG drafted it."

"What?" Stephanie couldn't believe that.

"Word is it's coming straight from Sperlin's office and that he's taking a very large stand on it—seems like the attorney general manages to come out on the wrong side of all the issues, huh?"

"I haven't seen anything in the papers." Stephanie struggled to make sense of it all.

"You will, baby, you will," Jim promised with a gleam in his eye.

"And Carlton is coming out on the wrong side of this? You're sure?" Steph insisted on a straight answer. She must know the truth.

"I told you. He drafted it himself. Wrong Way Corrigan rides again, just like he's on the wrong side of that fine piece of legislation you're carrying the banner for."

Fran and Jim continued visiting all the way back, but Stephanie was silent. Back in the office, she picked up her phone before she even sat down.

"I'm sorry, Mr. Sperlin is out. May I take a message?"

"Give me his secretary." She hadn't meant to sound so gruff, but it got results. Not the results she hoped for, however.

"Oh, yes. That bill came from our office. I typed it myself two days ago."

"But did the AG write it himself or one of his assistants?"

"Oh, no. Mr. Sperlin was very particular about drafting that one personally. He worked with a research assistant, but he stayed very close to it. He said he didn't want any loopholes."

Stephanie replaced the receiver without replying.

How could Carlton do this? How could he possibly favor a bill to lower the legal drinking age? She thought of the articles she'd read on teen alcoholism and the increased highway death and maiming of young people due to drinking. Surely she was mistaken. But no, Carlton had even written the bill. Jim was certainly right when he said the AG was on the wrong side of this issue. It was impossible to imagine an issue with more clearly defined black and white sides.

Was this his misguided idealism gone berserk? She wished she could recall his exact words—something about you can't make people good with laws—but if that were followed to its extreme the next step would be to legalize murder. And he had been strong for drug enforcement at Farragut. No, the answer had to lie elsewhere.

The liquor industry had a powerful lobby, and Carlton's campaign had received heavy support from college students—and yet it didn't seem possible that he would bow to that. She really had credited him with stronger moral fiber, even if she disagreed with many of his ideas. Was it possible she had been so swayed by his handsome looks that she had endowed him with integrity he didn't possess? With an almost physical ache she had to accept the possibility that Carlton Sperlin was just another slick, calculating politician, selling out for power.

16

"Steph! I'm so sorry, I thought we had that fixed, but when rain gets in around the garden light it flips the circuits in here."

Sue's voice penetrated Stephanie's consciousness. What *was* her cousin running on about? Stephanie sat up in bed. She'd just had the most awful dream. Carlton was serving drinks to a bunch of teenagers. She had tried to get to him to make him stop, but her feet wouldn't move.

"Stephanie!" Sue's voice cut in again. "What I'm saying is, your alarm didn't ring."

It was eight o'clock. She had a nine o'clock appointment. It was going to be "one of those days." She dressed hastily in her camel hair suit and jade blouse and pulled on her tan boots. She must find time to get that loose heel into the shoe shop soon. Hopefully it would hang together for just this one more time.

Susie stuck a granola bar in Stephanie's purse as she hurried toward the door. "Be careful. Last night's rain froze. These hills will be treacherous."

Somehow Stephanie managed to stay upright as she hurried to her car over a glaze of ice. Even without Sue's warning she would have driven very carefully, indeed. The roads were unbelievable. Even so, she arrived at the capitol five minutes before her scheduled appointment and

146

couldn't believe her luck when she spotted an empty parking space right by the back door—lots quicker than going into the parking garage. Well, it should have been, but that decision led to her downfall—literally.

She was three feet down the sidewalk when she stepped on a chunk of ice, slipped, and the loose heel came off her boot. She managed to grab a parking meter so was spared the ultimate humiliation of falling flat on the icy walk. But there was nothing for it but to go home and get another pair of shoes. That meant being abominably late. She tried calling her desk from Sue's, in case the people she was to meet were waiting for her there, but got no answer.

So back down those slick streets once more. And besides that, it was *cold.* Her heater, always a slow starter, still hadn't warmed up, and that bright, frozen sun just made the cold seem more penetrating. The tips of her ears were tingling by the time she reached the chambers doors.

There her progress was impeded as two lobbyists for the miners' union accosted her. After a quick shaking of hands and stretching of smiles all around, she excused herself. "I'm sorry, but I'm frightfully late for an appointment."

As it turned out, she wasn't just late for her appointment. Whether they got tired of waiting for her or were themselves held off by the icy roads, no one was there. "Oh, well, so much for the lobby to guard the Snake River water plain against dangerous waste disposal," she muttered, looking quickly over her desk calendar.

"Did you say something?" a pretty blonde high school girl serving as page asked.

"Oh, good morning, Pam. No, just mumbling to myself. Here you are." She handed the girl two ring binders from the side of her desk. The pages' first task each day was to put the newly printed bills in the desk books, color coded red for the Senate, blue for the House—which matched the carpets of the chambers. With the white marble walls, all looked very patriotic.

Fran entered in her breezy, friendly way. Other members offered brief, warm greetings, and everyone settled in for a new day.

Stephanie was discovering that one of the nicest things about being a legislator was the comradery that developed between the members. It was rather like summer camp—a world set apart where relationships could develop on the basis of interest without the restrictions usually set up by society.

Or maybe it was somewhat like it would be on a cruise—then her relationship with Carlton could be labeled a shipboard romance. Not in the sense of a love story but in the old-fashioned sense where the word meant adventure. Yes, that was it—knowing Carlton Jules Sperlin was definitely an adventure.

She began sorting papers into the three-level tray at the back of her desk: to do/read; constituent mail; appointments.

Her phone rang. A member of the Idaho Woolgrowers Association.

"I feel totally nonpartisan on this issue," she assured her caller. "You set up a meeting on it, and I'll sit in." She hung up smiling as she thought of the association's bumper sticker, which read, "Real Men Don't Wear Polyester."

And that made her think of David. He certainly was a real man in his tweeds and wool sweaters. She needed to see him again, to feel his arms around her, to hear his lovely Scots brogue, to share another of the kisses that were so rare in their relationship. She could count them on her fingers and have some left over. Perhaps it was partly their rarity that made them special.

Then her phone rang again. "No, I'm sorry, I won't be able to catch the four o'clock meeting on reapportionment because I have a meeting on higher education funding. Let me know what happens, though, will you?"

Ten o'clock. Time for her meeting with the Governor's Commission on Youth. She hurried up a flight of curving marble stairs and gratefully accepted a cup of coffee offered by the chairman of the commission. At that point her stomach reminded her of the granola bar, so she took it out and had breakfast while the two lawyers in the room battled over the technicalities of the proposed legislation. Not for the first time did she wish she had a law degree as well as her BA in political science.

By the time the last of the granola bar disappeared with a swallow of coffee, however, Stephanie felt it was time to get things into focus.

"Look," she said, "the issue here is that most runaways are picked up on Friday nights and can't see a judge until Monday. We don't want these kids sitting in jail. What we've got to do is come up with some plan so we can keep them in custody but not treat them like hardened criminals."

That seemed to get the committee working along more fruitful lines, but soon she felt her frustration level mounting as the exchange moved without direction.

Stephanie glanced at her watch. "Look, I've got to go, and I'm afraid we're really at a stalemate here. If we don't come up with a one-two-three plan of action nothing will get done. Now, can some of you stay here and hammer out a conclusion so we'll have something concrete?"

There were mumbled replies, which she took to be agreement. It should have been the chairman's place to make that request, but the committee was so completely rudderless—someone had to show some leadership.

She slipped into her seat in the chambers just in time to push her button for roll call.

The gavel fell resoundingly. "House be in order. We will now proceed to the second order of business, prayer by chaplain, the Reverend Edmund Robertson." The House rose.

"Our Father, let us today be sensitive to the needs of those around us. Let us not be so pressured or so hurried that we pass by one to whom we can give a cup of cold water in Your name. Guide us that those decisions that are made this day in these halls will not be our decisions only, but will have the guidance of Your hand upon them. In Your gracious and mighty name we pray. Amen."

Stephanie sat down with the others, but breathed her own silent *Thank You, Lord* for that one moment of sacred quiet in a day of hurry and hassle. She was thankful for their chaplain. It seemed that every day his brief prayer had something special to help get her day on the right track. If only she could carve more such times in her day. Every day lately it seemed her tracks were looser, and soon, she was afraid, the whole train would come clear off like the heel of her boot. Trouble was, there was never even time to figure out what the problem was, much less seek an answer, as the business of each day rushed ahead.

The gavel fell. "We will now move to the fifth order of business, report of standing committees. House Bill number eighty-two is assigned to the Judiciary and Rules committee."

"If there is nothing further in the fifth order of business, Mr. Speaker, I move we go to the ninth order of business, first reading of engrossed bills."

"Mr. Speaker, I ask unanimous consent that the bills be read by title and number only, and that the Journal show that they were read at length."

The breathless pace of the business caught Stephanie as she scrambled to keep up with the titles of the new bills being read.

The gavel fell again. "We will now move to the thirteenth order of business, miscellaneous and unfinished business."

Steph listened carefully to the announcements of various committee and caucus meetings, jotting down those pertaining to her.

The gavel fell once more, and they were adjourned until eleven-thirty the following morning. The formal session that day had lasted less than half an hour.

Stephanie and Fran grabbed a quick lunch in the Member's Lounge. They sat with two other representatives, who were deeply absorbed in the sensitive subject of reapportionment.

"I just don't know what it will do to my seat."

"Well, I think I'll be all right, but that new plan will play havoc with the party in my end of the state."

"But the other plan would make my campaigning a lot more arduous."

Stephanie bit hard on her pork chop to keep from flashing a hasty retort. What about policy, not personalities? Which plan will represent the people best? But there was no time to challenge the thinking of these seasoned campaigners.

Dashing down the stairs, Stephanie said breathlessly, "We just have time to make that meeting at the Y. You're coming too, aren't you?"

Fran nodded and laughed. "Sure. You know, I think our salary figures out at about two cents a mile."

Stephanie slowed, smiling. "The compensation comes in working with people like you—and in the satisfaction of making a contribution."

At the curve of the stairs they met, almost head-on, Stephanie's least favorite deputy attorney general.

Today Anne Smith was wearing a dark, wine-colored dress, almost shocking in the simplicity of its cut.

They passed without speaking, but as they left the building to dash across the capitol mall to the YWCA, Fran said, "Guess what I heard. Our Miss Smith used to be engaged to the attorney general. Rumor has it that she wouldn't be adverse to renewing old times—at least they say she canceled a full calendar at the drop when she was asked to come in to Boise as research assistant on this drinking age thing and some other legislation the AG is working on big time."

Stephanie stood stock-still in the middle of a puddle created by the melting of the morning's ice.

"What's the matter? Did you forget something?" Fran asked.

Worked with a research assistant—stayed very close to it . . .

"No, I just remembered something." She moved forward, but the hurry was gone from her step.

The women of the crisis center at the YWCA were already discussing their proposed legislation to toughen the statutory rape laws. Again, Stephanie thought of her conversation with Carlton about legislating morals. Problems you couldn't educate for you had to legislate for. This statutory rape bill wouldn't be a deterrent, but a means of punishment was better than nothing.

It would be a help to talk to Carlton about this, but Anne Smith was talking to him right now. Stephanie's head had begun to ache, and she carried no aspirin in her purse. She tried to concentrate on the issue before her. Everytime she closed her eyes in an attempt to suppress her headache, the image of Carlton was before her. In that case, she decided, she would just have to keep her eyes open.

After a few minutes of discussion, she saw a weakness in the proposal. "This doesn't set any minimum sentences," she said.

"We were advised not to," the chairman replied. "I wanted them, but everyone said—"

"I don't care what they said. This group doesn't want to sponsor a bill that will accomplish less than the one now on the books."

Soon after that they had to leave, but Stephanie felt she had made a substantial difference in her brief time there.

"If you have trouble getting the statistics you need," she told the group, "call the clerk and tell them you're doing research for me. You can get a lot more done through a legislator—it's a political world out there."

Back through the melting slush, up the steps to the caucus room. The atmosphere of easy comradery and relaxed joking was a pleasant change from the intense concentration of bill analysis. Here they were all comrades—no press, no opposition party, no constituents. For just a minute Stephanie gave in to closing her eyes and feeling the throb in her head. Then, somewhat reluctantly, she pulled herself back together and ignored it.

The caucus today was for the purpose of educating party members on the formula for financing higher education in the state. Soon Stephanie's head was swimming with figures. She struggled to follow the complicated mathematical processes being presented.

The Speaker passed out copies of a twenty-page bill and asked the legislators to read it that night—not just read it, but study and evaluate it. Stephanie sighed as she flipped one corner of the thick stack of papers before her.

"The skids are pretty well greased over there in the Senate to pass this thing," one legislator remarked.

"I need to be brought up to speed on this." Fran asked a question.

The answer included a reference to action proposed by a fellow legislator. "That makes him feel like a United States senator—sending everything to conference," and the caucus members laughed.

"We need to come to a consensus on this—prioritize our beefs," the assistant majority leader suggested.

The caucus ended. Steph now had a little time of her own before her next meeting. She went back to her desk in the House chambers. Working here was like working in the proverbial goldfish bowl. Her desk was in the middle of the floor, and everyone was moving around her. Anyone could come in the chambers when the House wasn't in session, and the place was crawling with lobbyists.

Maybe I can get up to the study room for a bit. I need to concentrate.

But first she had to meet with one of the interns, a political science major from Boise State who was working at the legislature for college credit. She drew out a fat manila folder.

"Let's go over these now, Alan, but I have to stop at three thirty to prepare for tonight."

Alan shook his long brown hair out of his face, took out his pen, and began taking notes.

"I want figures on the average per capita income of the six contiguous states and comparison figures of teachers' salaries." She gave him a newspaper clipping. "Find out what's happening on this issue—did the governor include it in his budget?"

The legislator at the desk behind her was talking loudly on his phone about launching a statewide campaign for the US Congress. "I'd want to have a good solid war chest behind me before I commit to this." He named a figure as being the least he could consider.

Stephanie forced her thoughts back to her own desk. "Now this is top priority. On this housing subsidy bill, I want all the statistics you can dig out relating crime to environmental conditions. And see what you can find in the way of sociological studies. But our real problem, Alan, is budgetary—if you get any brainstorms on financing the measure, I'd sure like to hear about it."

She handed him a letter from a constituent. "Call these women and find out what's happening with this bill. It started in the Senate. Ask them if there's something I can do to help."

Alan pushed his glasses back up on his nose with a quick jab of his left hand while the pencil in his right moved swiftly. The legislator behind her hung up his phone and began amusing several of the female pages gathered at his desk. A fellow legislator stopped by to solicit Stephanie's support on a bill he was carrying. It was 3:30. Time to go up to the study room.

But she still needed to make a phone call. She thanked Alan, then reached for a stack of unopened mail with one hand and her telephone with the other. While the phone rang on the other end of the line, she momentarily leaned back in her chair and looked up at the great etched, frosted glass dome overhead, supported by the marble columns encircling the room. Sometimes she needed to regain a sense of the significance of her task to keep from getting buried in the minutiae.

Voices swirled around her.

"We've got to get some action on this. Until something happens, I'm dead in the water."

"I'm not saying the state board of education is wrong, but . . ."

Her phone call ran on longer than she expected. Now it was too late to go to a quiet room to study. She just stuck her fingers in her ears, lowered her head over the document before her, and commanded her mind to concentrate.

A few minutes later she looked up. "Oh, no." She groaned. Four o'clock already.

This was to be a joint committee meeting, so it was held in the old Supreme Court chambers. Committee members sat on a raised dais like justices. A soft afternoon light fell through the domed skylight onto the blue and gold carpet woven with symbols of justice.

But not even the stately magnificence of the room could revive Stephanie's flagging energy level by now. The speaker presented his cause with the aid of an overhead projector focused on the white marble wall between torchlike lamps. The material was dull, but important, so she tried to follow it. In spite of the powers of concentration on which she had always prided herself, however, her mind kept wandering. She felt like a landscape in a surreal painting with clocks melting all over it.

It was dark by the time she got out to her car. The snow and ice that had melted earlier in the day were now freezing again. Traffic up Bogus Basin Road was a solid line on both sides. Weary executives were going home up the hill. Equally tired, but happy, day-pass skiers were coming down from the slopes just half an hour up the mountain.

Stephanie heaved a heavy sigh as she pulled into Susie's carport. She was desperately tired. No wonder they called it "the pressure cooker world of the legislature." All she wanted to do was take a hot bath and go to bed. But she had a dinner meeting at eight, and she still had to study the material that would be presented there.

She had tried so hard, and she knew she had made a difference on a few things—but probably no more than anyone else in her position would have. Was it worth it? And if a man like Carlton could be corrupted by political considerations, what hope was there for anyone? She shivered. She had brought the cold winter night in with her, and it had touched her heart.

The dinner was a grueling endurance test. Somehow she managed to get through it with smiles at all the right places and apparently acceptable, if vague, comments on the issue being lobbied. Of course she agreed that Idaho's wild rivers were a sacred trust. Certainly she didn't want to see them polluted. She tried to walk a narrow line between agreeing as much as possible without actually promising to vote for something she hadn't studied yet.

Even when her dinner partner drank too much, put his arm around her, and declared loudly, "You mark my words, this little lady has a brilliant future—brilliant," she managed to handle the situation gracefully, all the time asking herself why was she doing this? Why didn't she just pack her bags and escape to the calm, green world Scotland and David offered her?

When she got home she hadn't even had time to hang up her coat before Sue's phone rang. "For you," her cousin called.

"Some people have no sense of decency. The body isn't even cold yet," Stephanie muttered on her way to the phone.

Sue held her hand over the mouthpiece. "You look beat. Shall I tell him you're not available?"

"The only thing I'm available for is a slab at the morgue, but as long as there's breath in me, I'll talk." Steph took the receiver. At the sound of the voice in her ear the slump unconsciously left her back. "David! What a surprise. How are you?"

"I'm not well at all, Steph. I'm verry angry as a matter of fact."

Then she noticed the slur to his speech. "David, are you drunk?"

"Just a wee bit, but it's no wonder, is it?"

She was too confused to reply, and he went on. "I got your letter. All about this Carlton fellow ye're dating. How do you think that makes me feel?"

"Dating? I'm not dating anyone. That's why I told you about my meetings—so everything would be aboveboard. After all, I'm an engaged woman—aren't I?"

"I don't know. Are you?"

"Look, my relationship with the attorney general is a purely working one—and it doesn't seem to be working very well right now."

"Oh, well, that's a pity. And he's a fine handsome fellow, is he?"

Because David's insinuations so irritated her, she said, "He's *very* handsome—and he's sober."

Her hand was still on the receiver when the phone rang again.

"Carlton!" She was right. He did sound sober. Sober and very tired.

"It's this drinking age bill, Steph. We knew it'd be a hot issue, but things are really getting out of hand. It's to have its first reading in the Senate tomorrow, and there's going to be a big demonstration on the capitol steps. The BSC student body president—who was also campus coordinator for my campaign—is leading the thing and . . . well, you can see it's looking rather heavy."

157

He paused, whether from weariness, or in expectation of a comment from her, or just to catch his breath she didn't know. But when she remained silent, he continued.

"Stephanie, I know it's getting on toward the middle of the night, but could you possibly help me? I really need a sounding board—this thing is sure to get top media billing and I—"

Stephanie cut in. "Really, Carlton! I don't see how even you could be so crass as to ask that. And what's more, there are still a few of us around who won't sell out to the highest bidder."

She didn't hang up on him in anger so much as simply replace the receiver because there was nothing more to be said.

David drunk. Carlton working for the liquor interests. She had been right in the first place—she would be better off without any men in her life.

This time she got halfway across the room before the phone rang again. She walked on to the closet, deliberately hung up her coat, and turned again in resignation as the ringing continued. Sue would come down to answer it if she didn't, and there was no sense in that.

"Look, I said *no!*"

Before she could replace the receiver, she heard a chuckle. "Wait a minute, baby, you haven't heard the proposition yet."

"Jimmy! I'm sorry. It's been such a long day I don't really know what I'm doing."

"Not to worry. I won't quote you on a thing. What I have in mind is really a very straightforward business proposition."

"Are you sure you even know what straightforward means?"

"Ouch! No fair. This is straight *quid pro quo.* You get me some background info on the AG, and I'll get you an editorial favoring your housing bill."

"You don't write the editorials, Jimmy."

"Friends in high places, baby. That's what makes the world go round."

"What kind of information? He fought an intensive statewide campaign. Surely there isn't anything about him that isn't public record."

"Public record is public enough but incomplete, and I quote from my own quite brilliant but necessarily incomplete notes: 'After a brilliant career at Harvard Law School, where he attained the heady status of Law Review, he began an equally brilliant and soon-to-be-lucrative law practice, which he then patriotically abandoned to join the army to serve in the Judge Advocate General, which should have been safe as houses, but during the TET offensive in 1968 —which you, my chick, may barely remember—"

"What do you mean not remember? I remember vividly following the events blow-by-blow."

"Blow is right. The American embassy and all Saigon was blown very nearly to bits, our friend Carlton apparently with it."

"During which he apparently saved several people and received wounds for which he was later rewarded. Jimmy, it's after midnight. I have an appointment at eight-thirty in the morning. I don't need a course in not-so-current events."

"Right, I shall summarize. In 1970, Carlton Jules Sperlin returns home a decorated war hero. He joins a prestigious law firm, makes a big splash over the law and order issue following that rock festival thing, and gets himself elected attorney general, the second youngest ever to attain so auspicious an office in the history of our state."

"I told you it was an open book."

"Some detective you'd make—what about the two-year gap?"

"You just said yourself that he was terribly wounded. Jim, he still limps—it's hardly a sinister secret. If you want to prove he's unfit to serve, get him on the issues. This is a dead end. Besides, all you'll do is arouse public sympathy by bringing up the war hero stuff again."

"Aha! You're beginning to see my point. Why the big secret there? Every other candidate speaks of his war record with pride—if he has a good one. Why is there never a reference to this brave, self-sacrificing act in any of his campaign materials? What is he covering up?"

"Jim, you're imagining things."

"Not a chance. I got a good nose—I can smell a cover-up at a hundred yards."

"Idaho's own Jack Anderson?"

"You got it."

"Look, Jimmy, if you want to know what happened to wounded veterans between '68 and '70, I've got two suggestions. Go to the library and ask one of their reference librarians on the second floor—which Alan assures me are excellent—to teach you how to use a *Reader's Guide to Periodical Literature*, a skill your high school English teacher apparently overlooked. Or call the Veterans' Administration, which you will find listed in the telephone directory."

"Listen, smart lady, you think I'd be groveling to you if those methods had worked? Now, all I'm asking—"

"Jimmy! OK, OK! I'll do anything. Just let me get to bed. I think you're delirious, but I'll let you know if I learn anything. Now, good night."

Her waterbed felt delicious, but she lay long, shivering in the black and the cold. In her mind she walked through the marble rotunda, up the curving, balustraded stairs, past the picture of Senator Borah—Idaho's "Lion in the Senate."

Could she be as strong as the marble without being as cold and impersonal? Could she follow the path of the great leaders who had gone before her without giving in to personal considerations? Was she drawing her strength from the wrong source? She needed strength from some-where, because she was quickly depleting her own re-sources. What had the chaplain said that morning? Something about asking the Lord to be our guide. That was it. *Lord, I do need Your guidance.*

17

"US AND NORTH VIET ANNOUNCE CEASE-FIRE."

The announcement the world had awaited with held breath for months splashed across the top of newspapers covering the table outside the chamber door. Stephanie had heard the eight o'clock headline news driving to the capitol. Now, as then, she paused briefly to sigh. *Thank You, Lord. It's over at last. Thank You.*

Then she rushed on. An unusually fat stack of mail in her box at the Legislative Information Center sent her hurrying to her desk for her letter opener. She was still tired from yesterday, but today's schedule was less demanding. She had no doubt that adrenaline, coffee, and grit would carry her through.

The adrenaline started flowing as soon as she caught the impact of her mail. She had first heard of the drinking age bill only two days ago, and already constituent mail was pouring in. If she had held any doubts whatsoever about her stance on the issue, this morning's mail would certainly have resolved it. A letter from a mother whose seventeen-year-old daughter was killed in a car wreck when her boyfriend had been drinking and driving. A letter from a college professor telling of problems in the dorms caused by drinking. A letter from a young man now permanently in a wheelchair after a DWI accident.

Her righteous indignation rose apace. She read through example after example of heartaches that would only be increased if a lower drinking age became legal. In spite of all she had heard about the strength of the other side, not one letter favored the bill. But then, these were just from people—hurting people—not from powerful special interest groups who didn't have to write letters because *they* could buy their support. Buy people like Carlton Sperlin. The agonizing war in Southeast Asia might have finally ended, but Stephanie had only begun to fight.

She gathered up the bundle and marched with it into the office of the attorney general.

"Good morning, Representative Hamilton. I'll be happy to announce you, but I think he—"

Stephanie stormed right past the receptionist's desk, oblivious to any objection Mrs. Stadler might raise.

The scene inside the office caused second thoughts about such hasty action. Attorney General Sperlin and Special Deputy Attorney Smith sat on either side of the desk, their heads bent toward each other, deep in concentration on the notes on the yellow legal pads before them.

But Stephanie wasn't to be put off by mere second thoughts. "I brought you some reading material." She dumped her letters on the desk. "I don't expect it to affect your position, but now maybe you'll see why I feel as strongly as I do on this issue."

And she turned on her heel and walked out, aware of the two pair of eyes looking at her in amazement.

The rapid-fire floor session was racing toward adjournment when the phone on her desk rang. "Representative Hamilton."

"Stephanie." She gasped to hear Carlton's voice. "Thank you for the letters. I may not have time to use them today, but will you come to the rally? Twelve-thirty out front."

"Use them! I didn't intend for you to—"

The Speaker was calling for a vote.

"I've got to go now. OK, I'll come." She hung up, wondering where she could get a big bag of nice rotten eggs or squishy tomatoes on such short notice.

The chill in the air had done nothing to cool the fervor of the crowd of students gathered on the capitol steps and spilling back across the street to Steunenberg Mall. They stood chanting, "Old enough to fight—old enough to drink." They waved banners and placards proclaiming "WE'RE ADULTS WE DON'T NEED BABY-SITTERS" (with a picture of a baby nipple on a beer bottle), "WE WANT A FIFTH OF THE ACTION," and "NO WHOLESALE APPROACHES—PARTICULARIZE!" Tension was in the air. Some of the student leaders looked really angry.

Stephanie glanced around uneasily at the few policemen there for crowd control and hoped events wouldn't get out of hand. She thought briefly about her unintentional involvement in the antiwar protest a few years ago.

"Old enough to fight; Old enough to drink!" The chant grew louder and louder as it bounced back from the stone walls of the capitol. "Old enough to fight . . ."

The double glass doors of the capitol's ceremonial entrance opened then, and Carlton Sperlin stepped out. Stephanie was probably the only person in that great crowd who noticed the increased drag to his limp. Looking white and drawn, he lacked his usual air of amused savoir faire. In spite of the opposition she felt toward his policies, her heart went out to him. For a brief moment she even wished she had helped him last night.

Then to her amazement the most vociferous of the student leaders turned toward Carlton. He punched a fist in the air and shouted above the others an angry *"Et tu, Brute!"* The throng began shouting, "Judas!" "Stab in the back!" "One vote; one drink!"

Stephanie felt suspended in time as the full impact of the student reaction to Carlton's appearance registered in her mind. He *wasn't* on their side. What awful mistake

164

had she made? With her heart in her throat, she watched him standing there, facing that angry mob alone—calmly, never flinching.

He held up his arms for quiet. Amazing as it seemed, the stormy sea of demonstrators obeyed him.

He spoke in a voice of such calm authority that Steph felt that even without the battery powered microphone he held, his voice would have carried on the crisp air to the back of the crowd. He acknowledged them as his friends. Many of them were among his most faithful organizers and precinct workers. Several of them he called by name—including the boy who had shouted first, a tall fellow named Brett in a dark brown coat and with hair just brushing his shoulders.

Then Carlton got down to the issues. "'Old enough to fight; old enough to drink'" —he pointed to a bright orange banner— "is a slogan, not an argument. There is no rationale to it. The activities aren't parallel."

"Why?" one of the boys holding the banner shouted.

"For one thing, being in the military doesn't have an adverse effect on society. Statistics show a lowered drinking age does. As a matter of fact, young people shouldn't be killed and maimed in war either—" he was interrupted by a shout of agreement "—but we can't necessarily control that. Drinking is something we *can* control."

"You're treating us like babies!" a young woman yelled from the center of the crowd.

"The age of adulthood *is* an arbitrary age set by society. But the fact that a person is an adult for one purpose doesn't automatically mean that he or she is an adult for all purposes. How many of you are bearing adult responsibilities yet? How many of you have full-time jobs? How many are self-supporting? How many bear the responsibility of a family?"

An undertone of muttering showed the students couldn't reply to that.

"Let's suppose lowering the drinking age would cost twenty lives a year in Idaho. Would the pleasure of the majority be worth sacrificing those lives? Suppose it were something other than drink—a pill that resulted in some users' death. It would be taken off the market for everybody, and you would favor the action. But you're up in arms because your pleasure is threatened!"

He's splendid! Stephanie's mind repeated over and over. *Valiant. Steadfast. Undaunted.* Disconnected adjectives came to her as she looked at him. *But he looks so tired. I wish I could do something to ease the strain for him.* And with that thought she felt herself blushing with shame to realize how she must have added to the load by her mistaken attitude. How could she have been so wrong? She tried desperately to recall her conversation with Jim—what had been said that she could have gotten her wires crossed so badly?

Brett was now beside Carlton, speaking into the microphone which the AG still held. The boy made a brief but impassioned speech for the students to fight for their rights.

When Carlton obviously felt it had gone on long enough, he shook hands with his somewhat nonplussed opponent, then turned back to the discontented crowd. "Brett is right. You must go on working for the right as you see it and speaking out on issues you believe in. But be sure you have your facts straight first, so you will always be speaking from information, not emotion."

He paused and the crowd was unusually quiet, waiting. "I realize you came here today hoping to change my view. The fact that you have not accomplished that should not disillusion you—the fact that you were allowed to speak your piece proves that the system works. But as you are allowed the freedom of your convictions, so I must be allowed mine, and on this issue, 'Here I stand. I can do no other, so help me God.'"

There was even a scattering of reluctant applause as the demonstrators dispersed, but Stephanie hardly noted it. Her heart was full of what she had just heard. Here was a man of fidelity and honor, a man with the courage of his convictions, a man who could say with Luther, "Here I stand," or with Moses, "Let my people go," or with Joshua, "As for me and for my house, we will serve the Lord." A man who could stand beside the great men of history.

She went to him, holding out both hands, which he grasped firmly in his own. "Oh, Carlton, I'm so proud! I had no idea . . . I thought . . . that is, Jimmy said . . . I mean, didn't you draft the bill?"

He looked at her intently, as if the several hundred people milling about—many of them waiting to speak to him—didn't exist. "My office did, yes. That's part of our job when the administration requests it. And I kept a close eye on it to be sure it was as tight as possible in case it passed. But that doesn't mean that I support the measure. That's one of the reasons I felt it was so important to speak out on the issue."

She felt her face turning red. "What a muddle I made. Please forgive me. I'll do anything to help you on this."

He brightened visibly. "I have personal reasons for fighting this, Steph, and I'd like you to understand—you'd better if you really mean you'll help. Do you have any meetings tonight?"

She shook her head.

"OK, dinner at my place." He gave her the address. "Eight o'clock, OK?"

"Perfect." One tiny corner of her mind told her David wouldn't agree that the arrangement was perfect.

"Absolutely perfect, Carl." Anne Smith arrived beside him, and for a giddy instant, Stephanie thought Carlton's deputy was going to say, 'I couldn't have done better myself.' Instead she called his attention to the newsmen waiting for interviews and accompanied him into the fray.

Still feeling dazed, Stephanie turned to go back to her desk. Then, giving in to a desperate need to be alone, she went instead upstairs to the study room. As always, it was deserted, simply because in the rush of legislative life one seldom had time for quiet study.

Stephanie had to think this through. She felt completely washed out, yet at the same time strangely elated. She wondered briefly if she were feverish—coming down with the flu or something—but she dismissed that as ridiculous. Her problem, she feared, was far deeper seated than a simple virus.

She replayed in her mind the whole scene on the capitol steps, facing it as honestly as she could. The fact that seemed now to stand out, even more than Carlton's courage, which had so overwhelmed her at first, was his courtesy to the students. She blushed to recall her own lack of courtesy to him in the sharp words she had used. If she had listened to him as openly, as politely, as he listened to the dissident students, all that harsh unpleasantness could have been avoided.

The picture of Carlton that developed in her mind was that of a true gentleman. It seemed impossible for him to be inconsiderate. She knew she had never met anyone like him. But then, she had never met anyone like David, either, she added hurriedly before she could accuse herself of being disloyal.

18

Because her new life in the fast track had taught her to do everything in half her normal time, Stephanie was ready for dinner early that evening. So she treated herself to a brief reading from her grandmother's journal. She skimmed passage after passage where the young Kathryn talked about her confused feelings for the dashing Merrick Allen—and about the conflicts that rose when she misjudged him.

Stephanie noted with considerable irony Kathryn's tender feelings for Carlton's grandfather as well.

Suddenly she longed to talk to the woman who had recorded those experiences and insights. She longed for the wisdom her grandmother could share. She missed her with a physical ache. Then she realized—it wasn't just her grandmother she was missing but a part of herself—a gentler, more contemplative self that had gotten lost in political hassles. But there was no time for deeper thought. She must be moving.

At the address Carlton had given her on Warm Springs Avenue was a big, white, pillared house that looked almost antebellum.

"Carlton, this is gorgeous! Is it really your home?"

"Someone has to keep up the old family place." He helped her out of her coat. "It's been in Mother's family for three generations. The ranch is home to the folks, but they can't bear to part with all this history—even if the plumbing is abominable."

From the entry floor of black and white terrazzo squares she looked up the sweeping, red-carpeted stairway. "It's practically as magnificent as the capitol."

"Hardly. But one thing they do have in common is a lot of stairs to climb. This is the only true Georgian house in Boise. It was built soon after the turn of the century by a Southern planter who came here to live but was homesick for his native style. Would you like a tour?"

"I'd love it."

To their right he took her through a music room complete with a collection of antique musical instruments, Persian rugs, and grand piano. "Do you play?" She wondered what other hidden talents this man possessed.

He shrugged. "Julia does. The only thing I play well is a stereo, but I am a consummate appreciator."

"Me too." She laughed. "When I think of the money my parents wasted on piano lessons for me—but I don't suppose it was really wasted. I did absorb a little background. Enough to help my kids through lessons, I suppose." Then she added hastily, "If I should ever have any, that is."

He gave her his heart-stopping, one-sided grin and led on into the sun room.

"What a welcoming room! The yellow and coral look sunny even at night."

"Kitchen's back that way." He pointed. "Bedrooms upstairs aren't exactly decent for public consumption. I really must have them redone someday. I moved into the master suite and left Julia's and mine still looking like our teenage days. The folks didn't move to the ranch full time until we were out of high school."

"This must have been a marvelous house to grow up in! Did you slide down the banister as a child?"

"Of course. What else are banisters for? Julia tried it too—unfortunately she fell off and broke her arm. It rather dampened the sport for both of us after that. But this was a wonderful place for Christmas. We always had the tree in the entry, and it reached clear up to the second floor. Mother put real candles on it for Christmas Eve—it was incredible."

For a moment a little boy with wonder in his eyes stood before Stephanie in place of her suave host. She felt a tightening around her heart.

He led her through the parlor, beautifully furnished in Sheraton mahogany on an Aubusson carpet, on to the likewise eighteenth-century style dining room. Here, French doors looked out on the back lawn. Even in the darkness, Stephanie could tell it was overgrown with evergreens and bare-branched deciduous bushes.

"Don't you rattle around, living in such an enormous place by yourself?"

"I have a live-in housekeeper. But I do rattle a bit. Know any volunteers to rectify the situation?"

She managed to ignore the question by turning to admire the Steif silver on the sideboard.

Then Carlton brought her a stemmed glass of ruby red cranapple juice, lighted the tall white tapers on the table, and held her chair out for her. To her surprise he served their dinner himself.

"Where's the worthy housekeeper?"

"Ada has her own apartment upstairs. I think 'Mary Hartman' or something like that is on tonight. The fact that she's been here for more than twenty years would bear little weight if I trespassed on that."

The plate of fetuccini with creamy clam sauce he set before her was delectable. "Carlton, this is fabulous! Did you really cook it yourself?"

He gave her an almost sheepish grin. "Louie's Italiana does take-out."

"That's great—you get just as many points in my book for getting it together."

"I can, however, take credit for having tossed the salad myself."

She took a bite of the fresh greens dressed with a light, tangy vinaigrette. "Obviously the work of a genius."

Later, when Ada's chocolate mousse was only a fond memory to their tongues and they sat before the parlor fire sipping their second or third cups of coffee, Carlton turned to her. His eyes, which seemed always to hold a smile, were now grave. He took the coffee cup from her hands.

For a moment she thought he was going to embrace her. And the worst part was that she started to let him. *David. Remember David,* she told herself.

But before she could draw away, she felt herself being pushed back against the sofa.

Carlton thrust her cup back into her hands so roughly the coffee spilled. "Sorry. After you hear my story you can decide if you still want to do that."

"Carl—?"

"I hate to disrupt the evening with anything sordid, but I did invite you here on the pretext of doing business, so perhaps we'd better get on with it."

"I don't think anything sordid could intrude here."

He paused, as if gathering courage for what he had to say. That was odd indeed, since just a few hours before he had faced an angry mob without hesitation of any kind. "There's no way to ease into this or to gloss it over." He stared at his cup. "I said my reasons for fighting the drinking bill were personal as well as philosophical." He raised his eyes to look directly at her. "I'm a recovered alcoholic."

Her cup found its way to her saucer with a clank, but she said in a perfectly steady voice. "Tell me about it."

"Of course I was above the age this bill would cover when it happened, but having been there myself, I'll do anything I can to keep it from happening to anyone else.

172

I'll try not to bore you with details, but I want to tell you enough that you can understand."

She set her cup and saucer on the low table in front of the sofa and turned sideways to face him.

"You know I was in Saigon when the Vietcong came in. Just before they had the embassy completely surrounded I managed to get all our office staff out—including Lam Son, a civilian who did clerical work for us." He closed his eyes as if seeing it all again in vivid detail.

"I was out in the street when four North Vietnamese planes flew over and dumped out a dozen five-hundred pound bombs. The place erupted in panic. It was pitch dark, except for the light from fires started by the bombs. People were running everywhere, screaming and crying. Everyone who had a gun was firing at the sky like they could bring the planes down.

"I had been lying in the street for some time before I even realized I'd been wounded at all seriously. People actually ran right over me—one man swore at me when he slipped in my blood." He laughed grimly. "I suppose I blanked out for a while. Then along toward morning Lam Son, my friend, found me and literally dragged me to what was left of his house. His wife had been killed.

"Absolute mayhem reigned—the streets were barricaded and jammed with people begging to be evacuated. There was no possibility of medical help. Lam Son had a rudimentary first-aid kit that probably saved my life and a good supply of saki that dulled the pain and kept me from worrying."

He got up and paced about the room. The flames from the fireplace flickered on his smooth black hair and one lock that had fallen on his forehead.

"Three days later Lam Son smuggled me aboard a junk loaded with refugees. He chose to remain with his ancestors, but he sent all his saki with me. I suppose we would have floated clear across the South China Sea to the

Philippines if a navy cruiser hadn't picked us up and taken us to Clark Air Base."

They were both quiet for several moments. Stephanie had been sailing in that junk with him, imagining the stink, the hunger, the crowding, the pain. Finally, she asked quietly, "How long did you drift?"

"I don't know—Lam Son had a lot of saki. That is the point of this ignoble tale—it was long enough that by the time I was in decent medical facilities I was thoroughly hooked. The rest of the story is somewhat worse. But don't worry—I have no intention of putting you through that." The humor returned to his eyes, showing that the retelling, as well as the actual experience, was behind him. He refilled their coffee cups.

But Stephanie was still under the spell of what she had heard and experienced vicariously. "Thank you for telling me. Does anyone else know about this?"

"Just family. It's—uh—not very good dinner party conversation. Oh—" he added as an afterthought "—and Anne."

"Anne?"

He took his seat on the sofa again. "Anne Smith. You've seen her around the office. There was some consideration of her—uh—becoming family at one time, so she knows."

"I see." Stephanie could think of nothing else to say— nothing that could be said. What she was thinking was, *I wish I could have been there.* She would have pillowed his head in that junk, sat beside him and held his hand through the long hours in the hospital, gone with him through whatever horrors of withdrawal there must have been. *If only I could have been with him.* In the strength of her empathy she reached out to him without even realizing it.

But he didn't take her hand. "Stephanie, I want to be very clear about this. You understand the phrase 'recovered alcoholic'—it means there's no cure. I'm recovered, and with the help of God there'll never be a recurrence. A simple chemical dependency like mine is a lot easier to deal with than a problem springing from psychological compulsions. But the disease, the susceptibility, is there."

Her closed throat would allow no words. She leaned toward him.

Now he took her hand, then pulled her into his arms almost fiercely. She felt so right in his embrace, and she responded to his kiss with all the warmth of what she wanted to tell him she was feeling—a strange mixture of compassion and pride and longing.

But above all was the image of warmth—the warmth of the fire, the warmth his personality had brought to her life, the warmth that gave meaning to the cold, calculating political world that she found herself in.

It wasn't until she was back at Sue's house and saw David's picture in its silver frame by her bed that she felt guilty confusion.

19

Susie sat at the breakfast table reading a letter from Bob when Steph came down the next morning.

"Mail so early?"

Sue gave her a dreamy smile over the top of the stationery. Her saucer-round eyes were soft. "It came yesterday, but reading it again gets my day off to a good start. He'll be home in less than two months now, so I'm beginning to think I'll make it. If he gets another overseas assignment this long I'm going with him no matter what."

"I'm not a very good substitute, am I?"

"Thank goodness you're here! Without you and my study group I don't know what I'd have done. I suppose I should get a job, but then I wouldn't be free to go with Bob on his shorter trips."

"How is the study going?" Stephanie found herself suddenly interested in the subject of love.

"Oh, it's great! But all that studying about love makes me just ache to put my arms around Bob." Still in her fuzzy mood, Sue hugged herself a little forlornly. "One reason I'm especially missing Bob right now is that we're still studying 'Love is kind, and love is courteous.' They were supposed to be separate lessons, only I can't separate the two. It seems that everything we talk about so exactly describes Bob that it just makes me ache for him. Here, listen to this."

She picked up her study book. "'Good manners are a demonstration of God's love for those around us. Divine love should spill over in courteousness, politeness, gallantry.' Isn't that great? I never thought of that before."

Stephanie put her coat on, still thinking of what Sue had read. "Gallantry. I love that. It's such an old-fashioned word, but something we could do with so much more of in this world."

"Not much in keeping with today's vogue of 'let it all hang out,' and 'do your own thing,' is it?" Sue laughed. "By the way, that persimmon blouse is great with your brown skirt."

Stephanie grabbed her briefcase and went out with a wave, but all the way driving down the hill and along Harrison Boulevard, lined with its stately homes and likewise stately, if leafless, elm trees, she was thinking how Sue's description of Bob was equally applicable to both David and Carlton. But did Sue's description of her feelings toward Bob apply best to her own for David or for Carlton? She felt disloyal even asking the question, but she had to know.

On her way into chambers, wanting to see what kind of press yesterday's rally had received, Stephanie picked up several newspapers from around the state that were provided for legislators.

She knew better than to expect a lot of media support for Carlton's stand, but she was shocked at the scathing satire of their personal attack on the attorney general. One showed him in a high pulpit, wearing clerical collar and robe, preaching the necessity of legislating morality. Another labeled him a teetotaler and showed him as a little old lady presiding at a tea table telling her cronies, "We must do something about these young whippersnappers drinking spirits." Another showed him as Carrie Nation taking an ax to a college dormitory.

Stephanie felt physically sick, knowing, as did the papers, that the surest way to destroy a political opponent was not with logic and statistics but with ridicule. Her first impulse was to rush to him, but that was silly. Carlton was a big boy. He didn't need his hand held over a spot of political heat. And besides, what could she say?

On the contrary, what she was required to do was marshal more forces against him. After her media splash over the housing bill, Representative Harding, its sponsor in the House, had asked her to help him carry it. She had agreed enthusiastically and recruited Fran to assist them. This morning they were getting their heads together in a strategy meeting.

"Considering the strength of the opposition to this bill, we've got to be on our mettle. There's considerable chance we could die in committee." Harding was a good-looking man in his late fifties, short and stocky with silvery hair and a collection of tweed jackets that Stephanie very much admired.

"Who do we have lined up to testify for us?" Her pen was poised for action.

"From the Department of Health and Welfare we have the head of the child health bureau."

"Not the director of the agency?" Stephanie was surprised they wouldn't pull in the chief on this.

"There's no love lost between the director of the agency and the chairman of our committee. The head of child welfare will go over better."

Stephanie shook her head. "Tell me I've got a lot to learn!"

"How about someone from academia? Maybe a sociologist from the college?" Fran suggested.

Harding frowned. "We don't want too many social types for this committee. I think an economist would be better. We'll need support for our fiscal analysis—any way you look at this, cost is our major bugaboo."

"I'm still working on that one. I know it's the biggest hurdle, but there has to be an answer. And when we solve the money problems we'll have it made."

"Any ideas?" Fran asked.

Stephanie shook her head. "I've got Alan, my intern, on it—I'll come up with something. Now, about testimonials . . . "

"What about some man-on-the street-types? A mother from the River Street area, maybe?" Fran asked.

"Yes—with a baby in her arms! I can just see it!" Stephanie cried. "And then a social worker right after her! That's really a powerful package!"

The bill's sponsor shook his silvered head. "Save the dog and pony show for the media."

"What about out-of-state support?" Stephanie didn't want to leave any stone unturned.

"Sure, if you want to kill it fast. If there's anything Idahoans don't cotton to it's outsiders telling them how to run their state. Last thing we want is a demonstration by the National Urban League."

"Pioneers had to be hard-headed independents." Stephanie nodded. "I agree."

She spent the rest of her day squeezing phone calls into every spare minute. "We're going to have a tough time on this one, and your support is really essential. We want to do the strongest sales job we can. So when the bill gets out of committee, get your people to contact their legislators." By the time she'd been through that about a dozen times she began to feel like a tape recorder—one with its batteries running down. But she got some affirmative reactions—enough to keep her going.

At the back of her mind, buzzing like a mosquito in the dark, was a prickling thought: how good this would be for her career if she were successful. She kept swatting at it. She was not doing this for any reasons of personal glory. She believed in the bill—wanted to help the people, wanted to fight crime and injustice—she told the mosquito every-time it buzzed. And then the lone mosquito was joined by a whole storm. "What career? In a few months you won't even be living in this country."

By late afternoon she completed the last call and turned her attention to what Representative Harding termed her dog and pony show for the media. She hadn't talked to Jim for a couple of days, not since he'd offered his quid pro quo deal—her information for his help.

Suddenly it dawned on Stephanie that she had the in-formation Jim was digging for. She couldn't help being im-pressed with Jim—he said he had a good nose for news. No one else had noticed that gap in the attorney general's biography and suspected a story there.

But what would Jim do with the story if she gave it to him? Of course it had been given to her in the strictest confidence. But if she dropped a hint that could allow Jim to unearth the story himself, would it be justified by the public sympathy he said he wanted to create to help Carl-ton? Even if it would help him, did she have the right? He was, as the much-abused phrase went, a public servant. But how much did the public have a right to know just because they paid his salary?

She glanced at the newspapers still on her desk, now buried under the mass of the day's documents and scrib-bles. She winced as she thought of the caustic tone of the editorial cartoons. Would they really print a human inter-est story favorable to someone they seemed bent on cruci-fying?

Her fear of the answer to that left a ring around her heart as icy as the streets outside.

Well, she didn't have to decide right now. Jimmy didn't know she knew anything yet, and he had offered to help her. After all, he believed in her bill too.

She found him at his desk in the media center.

"Well, how's our friend of the homeless?" He greeted her with his audacious smile.

"Tired. Championing the homeless, hungry, and hurting is a lot of work." She sank into a metal chair by his desk. "I hope that didn't sound too flippant. You know how committed I am to this, but I'm exhausted."

"Go ahead and flip. It relieves pressure. You don't have to convince me of your dedication. I was thinking of ordering you a suit of armor, Joan of Arc style."

She laughed. "Somehow Stephanie of Nampa just doesn't have the same ring. Maybe you could simply order me a cup of coffee instead?"

"Righto." He left the room and returned in a minute bearing two rather grubby looking mugs.

"Are these ever washed?" Stephanie eyed hers suspiciously.

He shrugged. "Why? Coffee is boiling. It'll kill anything growing in there."

"I think you really mean that!" She drank anyway. "Oh, thank you. You just saved my life. Probably infected me with something incurable and unpronounceable too."

"I predict you'll live to fight another day."

"Oh, yes, fight—that's what I came to talk to you about."

"Things warming up on the housing issue?"

"Its slated for committee next Wednesday."

"OK, what do you want?"

"I think we've got a strong enough case to get it out of committee—in spite of the size of the opposition's arsenal. I'm looking ahead to floor votes now. Jimmy—" For some reason she felt suddenly nervous as she came to the point of asking for his help. She took a sip of coffee and spilled a drop on her skirt, which fortunately was coffee brown anyway. "I need your help to put together a really powerful layout, maybe even a series, on people living in substandard housing around the state—you know, with pictures of mothers holding babies in their arms, statements from social workers, that kind of thing."

"Uh-huh, I can see it." He held up his hands in a framing gesture as a movie producer might do. "Tear-jerking, get-you-in-the-gut, voter-level stuff—just what we need to put this puppy over."

Her reaction was something between a gasp and a laugh. "Well, that was a bit more crudely put than I would have, but I think you got the germ of my meaning."

"Germs. Right—we'll do a medical angle too. Got any doctors testifying before the committee?—get somebody from public health." He stood and walked around his desk, then leaned back on it right next to Stephanie, and folded his arms over his chest. "But we do understand each other, don't we? I don't work for free."

"I was under the impression United Press International paid your salary."

"Baby, in this business there are more important things than money—or maybe I should say, things that lead to more money—like information. Information is power. If you've seen today's papers you know your boyfriend's image is flagging a bit. What we need is to come in big now with the other side of the story. I mean, I'm talking front page."

She remembered the pain in Carlton's eyes last night and the sense that he trusted her completely, too completely even to bother asking her to keep what he told her confidential. "He's not my boyfriend. Not in the least." Then she remembered the kiss and felt herself flush.

Jim noticed, of course. "Anything you want to tell me?"

"No. I don't know yet." It was probably a lie to let him misunderstand deliberately, but she let it stand.

"Well, that's OK. We won't have this story together for a week at least. It'll be strongest if we can make it really state-wide. That'll take longer, but it'll be worth it. When do you expect the floor debate?"

"I would think we have two weeks yet anyway."

"Fine. We'll have it all sewn up by then. See how simple it is? You got a problem—you just bring it to Uncle Jimmy." And he leaned forward and gave her a kiss that wasn't the least bit avuncular.

It was getting late, but Stephanie returned to her desk for a meeting with Alan. She must have dozed off, because when the phone rang her head came up with a start. "This is Stephanie Hamilton."

"Hello, dear. How are you?"

"Mother!" For a glorious moment she closed her eyes and felt herself transported back home. "I'm fine. How are you and Dad? How's Palm Desert?"

"Wonderful! I've never felt so lazy and pampered in my life."

"And Daddy?"

"He's loving it here too. The doctor is really pleased with his checkups, and now that I finally got him to relax he's discovered what he's been missing all his life."

They talked on for a while about other family members. Then Elizabeth let a note of worry creep into her voice. "Steph, I don't suppose you've heard from Boyd, have you?"

"No." With a stab of guilt, Stephanie realized she hadn't even thought about her brother for weeks.

"Well, he never was much at writing, of course, but I always assumed he got my letters. Yesterday, though, I got one returned unclaimed."

Stephanie mouthed soothing phrases to her mother. "He probably just got a new job and forgot to have his mail forwarded, Mom. You know how casual cowboys can be."

At last she rang off. "Love you, Mom." And she knew she meant it.

Alan hurried in, and Stephanie did one of those quick gear shifts she was getting so good at. "What have you got, Alan?"

Alan brushed his shaggy hair off his forehead and adjusted his glasses before spreading the contents of his file over her desk. "Here's the figures you asked for on education funding comparisons of the contiguous states."

Stephanie scanned the neat column of figures. "Good. Now did you find anything really creative in formulas for resource development?"

"Well, most states are raising sales taxes. But it's unpopular. New Hampshire has a state lottery. I've got the stats here. Best way seems to be to increase the tax base—promote tourism—something like that."

"Thank you, Alan. You've done a great job. I'll study these. Can you have those other answers for me in three days?"

Alan assured her he could, but Stephanie was already so deep in study she didn't even hear him leave.

The figures from the New Hampshire lottery were impressive at first glance, but she didn't want to make any mistakes about this. She worked her way down each column carefully. Trouble was, a lottery was a major undertaking, one that would dwarf the proposal it was meant to prop up. If she could just think of something simpler.

Finally she dropped the papers on her desk and leaned back, tapping a rhythm on the file folder with the eraser end of her pencil. Any legislator who voted for a tax hike would be run out of office. But voting to boost the economy—to increase tourism and the amount of money the state could earn from resorts. That was the ticket.

She sat a long time, thinking deeply, rocking gently in her chair. Then she leaned forward once more and read carefully through the entire report. She had to battle down the sense of excitement she felt rising inside her. If she got carried away too soon she might miss some vital point that required clear-minded thinking.

But in the end it was impossible to suppress the exaltation. This could be it—the answer she had been seeking for weeks. The answer to all the economic arguments against her bill. The answer to all her problems.

20

Stephanie stood on the capitol steps two days later holding both hands out to catch giant white flakes on her red mittens.

"Oh, what gorgeous snow!"

Carlton held a large, black-gloved hand next to hers, and they stood a moment watching the frosting pile up. Childhood memories of snowball fights were irresistible. Stephanie clapped her handful of snow on the back of his neck, then moved away smartly before he could retaliate.

"Unfair. You know I can't do a thing with half of Boise looking on." He offered his arm to escort her down the steps as if nothing had happened. "I shall, however, extract my revenge. How about Sun Valley this weekend?"

She stopped in her tracks, staring to be sure she'd heard him right. She couldn't decide which to ask first: Weekend with you? or, In the middle of the session?

Political considerations won precedence. "Leave town in the middle of the session?" The question came out on a gasp of incredulity.

"What's the matter? You think they have roadblocks set up outside town to be sure legislators don't escape until they've done their work? Might not be such a bad idea, at that. But we could always make it over the mountains on snowshoes."

185

"Carlton, be serious. I have mountains of work to do that can't be climbed over in snowshoes. And there could be an emergency committee meeting, or something. The idea sounds positively irresponsible."

He laughed, tossing his head back so that the drifting flakes landed on his face. "Intense lady. Look, we won't leave until after the session on Friday. I have to make a speech to the Idaho Bar Association that night. We'll play in the snow Saturday, and I'll bring you home after church Sunday. You'll have plenty of time to study up for roll call Monday morning. I know you don't believe this—but the break will do you good."

If I say no will you invite Anne? flitted through her mind. Then she remembered that she didn't care. "What an example of 'give an inch, and they'll take a mile.' I agree to lunch, and you plan a weekend."

"Great, I'll book our rooms."

It was enough to take most of the conviction out of her protest. "I haven't said I'd go."

Tell him about David, her conscience ordered. But she didn't.

They crossed the little mall in front of the capitol, and Carlton paused to look up at the statue of Governor Steunenberg. "As a kid I asked my folks the story of the Steunenberg assassination every time we drove by here. I think they finally started going blocks out of the way just to avoid it."

"Oh, my grandmother wrote about that in her journal. She actually attended the assassin's trial."

"I'd have loved to have been there. William Borah prosecuted, and Clarence Darrow defended. I have a photograph of the trial in my office. Remind me to show you sometime."

"I will. What happened to the union boss who hired Orchard? Grammie didn't say."

"He fled to Russia, apparently expecting to be made a hero. But I don't think he was. Anyway, he died there."

They walked on to a little sandwich shop a few blocks from the capitol. "Hungry?" he asked when they were seated.

"Am I! I—uh—sort of forgot to eat today."

"See why they call it a rat race? What rat were you racing today?"

She laughed. "You!"

He looked puzzled for a moment with that endearing way he had of wrinkling his forehead. "Oh, yes. Housing subsidy debate in committee."

"Right. And I can warn you right now, we're going to be formidable."

"I never doubted it."

Talk of the bill they were to debate that afternoon created a barrier that resulted in the most extraordinarily formal restraint in their relationship. They didn't verbally resort to "Yes, Miss Hamilton" and "Please, Mr. Sperlin," but the atmosphere felt as if they had. They concentrated for a few moments on their salads and flaky croissants.

Stephanie glanced at the clock on the wall and thought it didn't seem possible that in less than two hours this man would be her worst enemy. "I wonder if croissants count?"

"Count for what?" He raised an eyebrow at her non sequitur.

"Wasn't there something in the old days about not breaking bread with your enemy?"

"Oh, the committee. I think it was taking salt." He moved the salt shaker to the edge of the table against the wall. "But, no matter what you think, I have no intention of becoming your enemy."

No, just an enemy of the people, she thought but suppressed the urge to voice the words.

"At least I'm quite sure there's no prohibition against sharing chocolate." He signaled the waiter, and two eclairs instantly appeared. A Mozart cello concerto played somewhere in the background. "How is it?" he asked after her first bite.

"Music to my tongue." She felt as if she could sit there all afternoon just listening to the mellow sounds of the music and sipping espresso in the best French manner. But that wasn't the American manner, especially for an American caught in the onrush of legislative life. "You almost did it, you know."

"Did what?" He gave her his most innocent look.

"Lulled me into complacency. As it is, I should run all the way back, but after that lunch I'll be lucky if I can roll."

Out on the street, her flippant words almost became prophetic. An elderly man came toward them with a rolling gait, then suddenly staggered and fell against Carlton so heavily he jarred into Stephanie.

"Steady there." Carlton gripped the man's arm. "Are you OK?" he asked Stephanie over his shoulder. "Sorry about that—he caught me off balance."

"I'm fine. What's wrong with him? Drunk?"

The man was still on his feet but wouldn't have been without Carlton's support. He was mumbling something unintelligible.

Carlton shook his head. "I don't think so. He doesn't smell like it—much," he added as the man raised his face, and Carlton turned his head away in reflex.

"What are you going to do with him? Call the police?"

He thought a moment. "No, there's a fire station less than a block from here. I think that'd be better. Come on, try to walk a little, buddy."

Carlton was almost dragging the man. They garnered some very strange looks from passers-by, but Carlton seemed undisturbed by the fact, if he even noticed at all. His whole attention was focused on his human burden.

Although the distance was little more than half a block, it seemed interminable to Stephanie. She wanted to help, but she didn't have any idea what to do. Worst of all was the conflict she was battling inside—pity for the rumpled, unshaven old man and disgust at the state he was in.

The fact that he was drooling slightly on Carlton's shoulder didn't help her a bit in fighting the revulsion she felt.

Inside the station, the firemen instantly put into action their quick response training. They laid the man on a mat, pulled support equipment off the nearest fire truck, administered oxygen, took his pulse.

Stephanie sat heavily on a folding chair in a corner, watching the proceedings as if they were on TV. As soon as the patient was breathing regularly, the fireman in charge ordered a younger man near the desk, "Call dispatch to send the paramedics."

Carlton spoke briefly to the captain and handed him his business card, then turned to Stephanie and held out his hand. "Emergency is over. Shall we go?"

She still felt a bit weak at the knees. Something like this might be an everyday experience in San Francisco or New York, but not in Boise. "Do they know what was wrong?"

"No, but they'll take care of him whatever it is: stroke, senility, liquor . . ."

"I wonder if he passed a priest and a Levite first?"

Carlton laughed at the allusion. "I doubt it. Anyone would have done the same thing."

"I'm not so sure. Why did you give the captain your card?"

"Just in case he needed anything else."

"Like expensive treatment?"

"Well . . ." He shrugged.

"You *are* a softie!" She laughed.

But he didn't return her smile. "I guess one can't help thinking, 'but for the grace of God . . .'"

She felt suddenly very subdued. "I see what you mean."

"Oh, I don't mean just that he might have been drunk. Although I guess that fits too. What I meant is, I know so many people—old college friends, even—that life has turned out really rotten for. Divorces, sickness, out of work, real soap opera stuff. And I realize that I haven't done a thing to earn my good fortune."

She started to protest.

"Sure, I've worked hard, always tried to play fair, do the right thing—but so have a lot of other people that things just haven't turned out so good for. It makes you feel very humble."

"Yes, I do see what you mean. Grace is the only word for it, isn't it?"

They were now at the capitol steps, hurrying because the snow was coming even heavier now.

She was barely through the doors onto the marble floor when her feet flew out from under her.

"Careful." Carlton's strong grasp saved her from disaster. "These marble floors are treacherous when your feet are wet." He held her against him for a second until she could get back her equilibrium.

"That's two, in about fifteen minutes," she said. "Do you make playing Boy Scout a habit?"

"Notch my belt every night." Still holding her arm he started down the stairway to the lower level.

Just then Carlton, also with wet shoes on smooth marble stairs—and an injured leg undoubtedly weakened from his recent exertion—slipped and fell heavily, his foot caught under him. This time there was no Boy Scout rescue.

For an instant Stephanie stood suspended in horror—horror at the wrench of pain on his face and horror at her own desire to throw her arms round him. Fortunately they were at a curve of the stairs that was relatively hidden from view. Even if she had given way to such revealing behavior, no one would have seen.

But Carlton left no time for her to react. Holding to the marble balustrade, he pulled himself up, then winced as he tried to put weight on his foot. "Blast! I've got to get to a committee meeting to defeat a bill in a few minutes!" In spite of everything, he grinned at her.

"Wretch! I should leave you here in your misery—it's probably better than you deserve at that."

"But you won't, will you?"

When he grinned at her with that twinkle in those brown eyes, she was utterly hopeless. She sighed. "No, I won't. Shall I call in the paramedics, or do you wish to lean on me and hop the distance to your office?"

"That sounds dauntingly arduous. I believe I shall simply wait here, if you would be so good as to run up to my office and tell Mrs. Stadler I require the services of my briefcase and my walking stick."

It was a moment before the implication of that soaked in. "You mean this sort of thing happens frequently enough that you're equipped for it?"

"What makes you think I want the stick for walking? I want it to beat you with in case I can't out-debate you in committee."

"Oh, well, in that case, I'll certainly hurry right back." She turned with a small giggle. But two steps up she stopped and looked back, just in time to see Carlton, leaning against the railing, give a jaunty salute to two newsmen passing him on the stairs. "I must admit, I admire a sense of humor that can rear its head at a time like this," she said.

"That's the only time it matters—anyone can have a sense of humor when they're just sitting around telling jokes."

"Of course, but the grandstander in you has to have an audience—what else are good qualities in a politician for?" In spite of the banter, however, she could see signs of strain in his face, so she didn't waste any more time.

So it was that a few minutes later, Representative Hamilton entered the committee room, holding the door for her opponent and carrying his briefcase. All of which she would have rather enjoyed, except for the fact that in the process she also wound up holding the door for Anne Smith. She had insisted on accompanying them when she overheard Stephanie telling Mrs. Stadler what happened.

Carlton took a chair at the end of the table near the door, and it was Anne who solicitously pulled over a smaller one for him to put his aching foot on.

"Are you sure it's just a sprain?" she asked.

"Yes," he growled. "I've done it often enough, for pete's sake. Don't fuss."

"I'm not fussing," she returned in tones that said, I never fuss. "But you should have ice on it, you know."

"Later." And then he turned to greet several committee members who were entering the room with Chairman Detweiller. "Afraid I'll have to ask your indulgence to let me speak sitting down, Dick. I got my feet tangled up on the stairway."

"That marble's a hazard. They'll put runners on the stairs after someone breaks their neck."

"You suggesting I should make the sacrifice? I know at least one of your committee members who would volunteer to give me a push." He winked at Stephanie, sitting halfway down the table.

The intimacy of the gesture embarrassed her, but before she could return a scathing look the chairman called the meeting to order.

"Representative Harding, would you like to present your bill?"

The bill's sponsor took the podium and checked to see that everyone had a copy of the bill before him. Then he briefly outlined the major provisions of the proposal to create an agency that would be authorized to condemn substandard, slum-area housing and oversee contracting out projects to builders to construct low rent, but more adequate, housing in its place. Each project was to meet certain minimum standards, including a playground.

As he spoke, a model neighborhood took shape in Stephanie's mind: clean, neat apartment buildings; tree-lined, uncracked sidewalks; a well-fenced playground filled with happy children. And Carlton had the nerve to maintain that such an environment wouldn't produce better citizens. She aimed a searing look his direction. All her tender feelings for him were suppressed by the immediacy of the issue before them.

But his rather pale face was expressionless as he listened to the speaker.

The chairman next called on the attorney general to present his analysis of the bill.

Carlton greeted the committee members and thanked Chairman Detweiller for allowing him to speak sitting down. "I've heard it said our vice president can't walk and chew gum at the same time—since I wasn't chewing gum, I'm not sure what my excuse is."

There was a ripple of laughter, then the attorney general got down to business. "I must congratulate Representative Harding on his foresight in getting this bill started in Health and Welfare, because I can almost assure you it would never get out of Finance committee. If it passes the House, however, it will be assigned to Finance in the Senate and will be in real trouble."

Stephanie glowed with secret pride. She couldn't wait to spring her secret weapon.

"This afternoon, however, I am more concerned about the ambiguities in the drafting of this proposed legislation. First of all, it creates an agency authorized to condemn substandard housing, a vague term at best. This means that every house in the state below average, whatever average is, is subject to being condemned."

Her heart pounding, Stephanie sturdily kept her eyes on the papers before her. She simply didn't trust herself even to look at the speaker at the end of the table. *If Carlton were really my friend, he couldn't fight so hard to destroy something I care so deeply about.*

"Then, when the new homes are built, will the people who have been displaced be able to afford to live there? A better house doesn't provide a better job to go with it. If this were the answer, we could condemn substandard shoes and socks."

The others laughed, and only by a great force of will could Stephanie remain in her seat. She wanted to run from the room with her hands over her ears. *This can't be the same man I had lunch with, the man who only a few minutes ago was helping a sick stranger on the street, the man I wanted to hold in my arms when he slipped on the stairs. This hard, arrogant, critical creature is someone I don't know at all—someone I don't want to know.*

There were a few questions on some technical points from committee members, then the attorney general was excused, with the thanks of the committee for taking time to give them the benefit of his expertise. Leaning heavily on his walking stick, Carlton left the room attended by Anne.

Stephanie tried to force her mind to follow the next witnesses: the official from the Department of Health and Welfare, an officer from the Department of Law Enforcement, The United Way Chairman—all those they had selected at their strategy meeting. The testimonies went well, their statements were questioned little, and there were no surprises.

But Stephanie knew the attorney general's impact was powerful. There was little they could do to counteract it.

And what made her angriest of all was her fear that his arguments were sound. They were cold-hearted and hard-headed, but they could be sound. There really were no words for the conflicts this man aroused in her.

From across the room, Jimmy caught her eye and sketched a small wave. His happy-go-lucky friendship and the knowledge of his support were a balm she sorely needed. She waved back, with a weak smile.

After the last witness, Stephanie sensed an uneasiness in the room. The shuffling of papers, clearing of throats, and fidgeting with pencils told her the committee was out of patience.

Representative Harding apparently picked up the same signals, because he asked the chairman if the committee could continue its consideration of this matter at the next meeting due to the lateness of the hour.

Stephanie was relieved by this strategy. There was little doubt in her mind that if the vote were taken at that moment the bill would die in committee. She had to get her finance proposal together fast. That was it—she would have to spend the weekend on it. Now she had an ironclad answer to Carlton's Sun Valley Serenade scheme.

Chairman Detweiller studied his calendar. "Our next regularly scheduled meeting is next Tuesday. If there are no objections, we will adjourn until then."

The speed with which committee members and visitors alike gathered their belongings and cleared the room demonstrated their desire to get on to their next committee, appointment, or meeting.

But Stephanie was still slowly gathering her materials when Fran came in.

"Sorry I couldn't be here, but I had a conflict. How did it go?"

Stephanie shook her head. "I don't know if we can pull it out or not. There wasn't much left by the time the attorney general finished with his big guns. It won't come to a vote until next week."

"That's good. Harding probably has some favors he can call in if he has a little time to work. Don't look so stricken, Steph. We haven't lost yet."

Stephanie nodded, but a terrible void inside her told her she had lost more than support for her bill.

"What's this? Two fair maidens in distress? Sir James, Dragonslayer, at your service."

"I think slaying the attorney general might be a bit extreme, but it is the most practical suggestion I've heard for a while." Stephanie's accompanying smile was bitter, but at least it was a smile. Jimmy could always be counted on to raise her spirits.

"He did pack quite a wallop, didn't he? But we haven't played all our cards yet." People were filing into the room for the next meeting. "Come on down to my desk," Jim said. "I want you to see some of the pictures we got for that series. I showed them to the editor this morning. He's really turned on to it."

"I've got to run," Fran said. "Can I see them later, Jim?"

"Sure thing, Bright Eyes. Any excuse to get a woman in my office."

Fran laughed. "You're indecent. I'm old enough to be your mother—well, your aunt maybe."

"I've got some very foxy aunts."

A few minutes later Jim's desktop was covered with glossy black and white photos that told their own story: an old woman heating beans still in the can on a wood-burning stove, a small girl's face peering out a broken window, a heavily pregnant woman doing laundry with an old wringer-type washer and a two-year-old tugging at her skirt.

"Well, did I promise you impact—drama—or did I not?"

"They're wonderful, Jim." Stephanie picked up one for a better look. "They're just what we wanted."

But the more she looked at the human side of the problem the more furious she became with a man who could sit in a comfortable chair and talk callously about budgets and drafting ambiguities and administrative red tape. There was no way she could care for a man who could turn his back on needs like the ones in these pictures. "When will they be run?"

"We're ready to go as soon as the bill gets out of committee. How was it left? I was out in the hall clarifying a statement from a witness at the end."

"We'll vote next Tuesday."

Jim glanced at his desk calendar, "Aha—which brings us to February, with President's Day and Valentine's

Day coming up. Nothing like a good dose of patriotism and love to hang a series like this on."

Stephanie laughed. "Is nothing sacred to you?"

"Hey, what can I say? You gotta have an angle."

"If this doesn't do it, it can't be done." Stephanie examined another photo. "I simply can't imagine anyone turning their back on these."

"Anyone?"

Jim's question, loaded with emphasis, stabbed her.

"Anyone with a decent social conscience, that is," she replied crisply.

"Right you are. And that brings us to the little piece of business we need to conclude, hmm?"

"I don't think I want to be a party to any favorable publicity for the attorney general." She dropped a picture on the desk and picked up another at random.

For once Jim didn't have one of his incorrigible remarks handy. He seemed to be giving her a very calculating look. "It's all in the angle you take. Why don't you just supply the facts and let me worry about public reaction?"

Stephanie was about to stall him again. The words were in her mouth, and then she looked at the picture in her hand: a family of seven Mexican-American children were gathered around a one-room hut that was apparently their home. The appeal in their big, dark eyes was heart-wrenching. What chance did they have to grow up into stable citizens—to grow up without falling into the traps of juvenile delinquency, drug abuse, or teenage prostitution?

"I'll do better than that. I'll assign my intern to do the background research we need, and I'll give it all to you in black and white—just as clear and shiny as these pictures! I'll even write up my own special report for you—you might call it an exclusive interview. You can count on it—the report will be complete."

And to insure herself against another attack of cold feet, she shook hands with Jimmy.

21

The first thing the next morning Stephanie asked Alan to stop by her desk. She told herself she was being efficient in fulfilling her promise and gave herself no chance to question whether she was pushing ahead before she could lose her nerve.

"I want anything you can find on the '68 TET offensive in Saigon. Your friend at the public library can probably get all you'll need on that."

"Sure, I'll give Marilyn a call this morning." Alan's words were unquestioning, but the look on his face wasn't.

"No, this doesn't relate directly to any legislation. More to strategy, but you're here to learn all the ins and outs of how the system works, so it's a perfectly valid assignment."

"Right." Alan held his pen poised for the next item.

"This next one will be a little harder, but see what you can nose out about conditions at the hospital at Clark Air Base in the Philippines at that time and for a year or so after. Military hospital records would be about impossible to get access to. But see what you can learn about any—er—about any Idahoans that may have been there at the time."

She thought of adding something about the possibility of having constituents that weren't receiving their proper benefits, but couldn't think of any way to phrase it that wouldn't be an outright lie.

"Maybe you can get a line on their treatment for alcoholism." That was as close as she dared come to her real target.

"Oh, does this relate to the drinking age bill?"

"In a way."

Alan seemed satisfied with her vague reply.

"Now, what do you have for me on the tourist trade scheme? We have to be ready to go with it Tuesday, because if we don't have answers to the fiscal question the whole bill will go down in committee. It was just the shortness of time that kept it from happening today. And I didn't dare mention what we had waiting in the wings, because I didn't want to introduce the idea without proper preparation."

"Right." Alan drew a thick stack of papers from his briefcase. "Now you can be plenty prepared. I got all the answers you asked for and quite a bit beside. The stats look good."

"Wonderful! Thanks, Alan."

The rest of the day she concentrated furiously on the tasks before her and sturdily refused to allow herself to think about what she had promised Jim—after all, she hadn't done anything yet. Asking Alan for information on a subject that should interest any history student wasn't being party to an exposé.

Only when the chaplain's prayer made reference to not betraying "the trust that has been placed in us" did she allow herself a moment of remorse. But then she thought of the faces in Jim's pictures and told herself that helping those people was a sacred trust too.

The next thing she had to deal with was extricating herself from Carlton's weekend plans. The resort gaming proposal had to be drafted, and that was all there was to it. Fortunately, she didn't have to draft the formal bill. The legislative council did that. But she had to have all the facts and figures at the tip of her tongue and her fingers for the debate, as well as having a document written to distribute to committee members, a formal press release to go with it, and . . .

She punched out the phone number for the AG's office. But Mr. Sperlin had gone to the doctor to have his ankle wrapped.

Steph smiled as she hung up. Of course. Why hadn't she thought of that sooner? Sun Valley would take care of itself. Carlton couldn't have a snow bunny weekend on a sprained ankle. For the first time in days, she felt the gods were smiling on her.

But when she finally reached Carlton late Thursday, the gods were frowning again—or at least Stephanie was when she hung up the phone without having succeeded in changing the plan.

Her first tack of blaming the change of plan on his ankle didn't get her to first base.

"All the more reason for you to come with me." He used his most appealing voice. "You can't desert a poor old cripple who needs your help."

"Oh, don't worry, Carlton. With all the skiing accidents they must have, I'm sure dealing with cripples is a routine Sun Valley service. You can probably rent a motorized wheelchair with your room." Before he could protest at her heartlessness, she rushed on. "Besides, I honestly do have to work this weekend. Something has come up, and I must have a memorandum prepared by the first of the week."

"Well, why didn't you say so? If that's your only problem, bring the work with you. Do you have a good portable typewriter? Never mind, I'll bring mine. It's even electric."

"What? Go to a resort to work?"

"Best of both possible worlds for a workaholic like you, huh? Seriously, think how much more you can get done without any phone interruptions—you can even have meals room service if you want. No guilt over time out helping Sue with the dishes that way."

"Are you sure you can handle such exciting company?"

"Might be a bit much for an old cripple, but as you pointed out, they'll be well-equipped with emergency services. I'll ask to have a respirator standing by."

"You're an idiot."

"Well, you can't have everything. But seriously, that does solve a problem. My speech to the bar is really in-house shop talk. It would bore you to death. So you'll be well occupied Friday night while I do my bit for fair laws and friendly juries, and I promise not to interrupt you until you're through. Fairer than that I cannot say."

It was hopeless. Her bulging file case went in the maroon-carpeted trunk next to his portable typewriter.

"I knew your 'I need help on the snowy paths' was a put-on. You're not even using your stick." Stephanie gave him her best hand-in-the-cookie-jar scold.

He slammed the trunk lid and grinned at her sheepishly. "Ah, but we want to keep it that way, don't we? What would I do without a warm hand to support me on those treacherous trails?" He faked his foot slipping and threw both arms around her in mock desperation.

"I said you were an idiot." She unwound his arms from her neck. "It would have served you right if you'd really fallen." She jumped in her side of the car without giving him time to open the door for her.

The small jet from the Boise airport landed them at the foot of Baldy Mountain. They were the only passengers who collected briefcases rather than long thin cardboard boxes of skis from the baggage claim. Stephanie, after a busy day at work and with hours of it ahead of her, was relieved to find they were met by a private car and driver rather than having to crowd into the shuttle bus with the ski weekenders.

"I suppose it's terribly unfashionable of me," she confessed, "but I always liked Sun Valley as a summer resort better than at its more celebrated skiing time. But then, I suppose the fact that I don't ski has something to do with that." She looked out her window as the last streaks of the pink and purple winter sunset faded across the snow fields and lights came on in the scattered ranches and vacation homes around them. "Do you ski, Carlton?"

"Loved it in my wild, foolhardy youth. Was on the racing team in high school. Haven't done much in recent years."

Stephanie wondered if that was because of his injury.

"I've been thinking of taking up cross-country," he went on. "They say it's great exercise, and you really get to enjoy the scenery more. Maybe I could talk you into taking lessons with me sometime." His raised eyebrow put the question mark on the end of his sentence.

"Well, like I said, I've always gone in more for summer resorts. We used to come here at least once a year when Dad had a political meeting or something. My brother thought it was pretty boring and usually spent most of his time at the stables or fishing in Wood River. But Mom and I loved lounging in deck chairs by the ponds, poking around in the little shops, swimming in the glassed-in pools."

"Miss Hamilton, you're painting a picture of yourself as a lady of leisure—I can't imagine."

"Well, I was a teenager then. Of course, I always had a book with me when I lounged, and I went to a lot of the party functions with Dad too."

Carlton's hearty laugh filled the limousine. "I thought it was a delightful image—not a subversive idea you had to defend against."

Carlton was making her very conscious of how compulsive she really was.

"OK, I'll make you a deal. I'll finish up that work I absolutely *have* to do by noon tomorrow. Then I *will* relax the rest of the weekend."

"I'll believe it when I see it."

"Just a minute there. I'm not one of your opportunist politicians who goes back on her word."

Carlton put his hand over hers briefly. "That I do believe."

At Ketchum they turned off the highway. In a few minutes the big black car swept into the little Swiss village nestled at the foot of the ruggedly majestic Sawtooth Mountains. They pulled under the covered entrance of the massive, golden Sun Valley Lodge.

Stephanie shook her head as she got out with the help of the doorman's extended hand. "I have to touch those beams everytime I come here. I lost a bet with my brother when I was eleven years old, and I still can't believe that anything that looks so thoroughly wooden as this building is really cement. With all the railroad ties the Union Pacific Railroad must have owned, why do you suppose they manufactured ones out of concrete?"

"You've got me. Lower upkeep, maybe?" Carlton observed the building with a furrowed brow. "Can you satisfy the lady's curiosity, Franklin?" He read the doorman's name badge and addressed him like a lifelong friend.

"Not off the top of my head, I can't, sir. But I do keep a reference book handy." He pulled a rather dog-eared volume called *Guide to Sun Valley: Past, Present and Future* from behind the porter's desk. "I'll be glad to loan it to you."

Stephanie thanked him, then followed the porter to her room.

When Carlton came with her she wondered if she was going to have a hard time getting rid of him. But he merely tipped the bellboy for her, looked around to see if everything was all right, and said, "My room is upstairs. Call if you need anything. And don't forget to send down for dinner—that's an order. Shall I call you after the banquet, or would you rather not be disturbed?"

She really would rather not be interrupted, but he was being so nice . . . "Well, you did promise a weekend away from the phone, but if you want to just give me a quick ring to let me know how brilliant your speech was, I could probably handle it."

"That's a deal. So if you don't hear from me, you'll know I was booed."

The room was quiet and empty when he was gone. Stephanie put her briefcase on the table in front of the window, but she left it unopened and turned to the Sun Valley biography. Almost an hour later she glanced at the bedside clock and gasped. She had become so absorbed in the story of the building of America's original ski resort— the first resort in the world created purely for winter sports—that she had lost track of time.

She had been visiting here all her life but never knew that this now world-famous spot was the brainchild of Mrs. Averell Harriman, who wanted a place to ski without having to go all the way to Europe—skiing had been an almost unheard of sport in America in the '30s. Her husband, heir to the Union Pacific Railroad, hired an Austrian count to comb the American West and find a perfect spot for a ski resort. He had searched California, Colorado, Utah, and Nevada before discovering this wind-protected basin with its treeless slopes and its pine-covered Baldy Mountain standing sentinel at the valley's western side.

Stephanie allowed herself to read just one more page —which extended to two and a half. Then she saw that would finish the chapter. "Sun Valley boasted the world's first ski slope with a chair lift, designed by the Union Pacific engineer who didn't know anything about skiing, but had invented a system for loading bananas on a freight train and figured hauling people up a snow-covered mountain couldn't be much different." With great force of will she closed the book and opened her briefcase.

She hated leaving the history book, but the future was what was important. Besides, she had found in this brief study of history great inspiration for building her dreams of the future. Marie Harriman's vision of building America's first ski resort had been spurred by her own desire for a place to ski. But it had also fulfilled her husband's business goals of bringing tourist money to the West—more specifically to the Union Pacific Railroad. If Marie Harriman could inspire building a whole new resort, Stephanie Hamilton could inspire a slum clearance.

She began writing on the sheet in front of her. "The gaming commission shall consist of five members appointed by the Governor, with the director . . ." Her pen flew across the lines of her yellow legal pad, filling page after page. "The commission and director are required to report immediately to the Governor and legislature any matters . . ." She had nearly finished outlining the administration of her brainchild when the phone rang.

"Sorry if I woke you, but the meeting just broke up, and I did want to say good night."

Stephanie blinked at the clock that told her it was 1:00 A.M. She almost said, "What meeting?" Then she came back to her surroundings enough to realize what Carlton was talking about. "Oh, no, no, I wasn't asleep. Daydreaming, I guess, but not asleep."

"Daydreaming?"

"In a very practical way. Carlton, I'm going to build my dream, too—only not a playground for the wealthy like Mrs. Harriman built—mine will be a playground for poor kids. And since I don't have the Union Pacific millions to work with, I've got my own scheme. I wasn't going to tell you yet, but I'm so excited—it's going to be *great*. And even you'll have to agree I've got the ultimate answer."

"Stephanie, what are you babbling about? Did you forget to order dinner? Do you always hallucinate on an empty stomach?"

"Of course I forgot dinner. Do you think I have nothing better to think about than my stomach? And your clever ploy to put me off my work by handing me that fascinating history book did not work." She refused to admit that it almost had. "Quite to the contrary, I've seen what one woman of vision could build with money, and it's been a great inspiration."

"You are raving. Stay away from open windows and sharp objects. I'll be right there."

... duties of the commission and director are to put into action the rules and regulations ... Stephanie was immediately back into her work and didn't look up until a knock at the door startled her into running a line of ink across the page.

Carlton, white towel folded waiterlike over his arm, wheeled in a linen-covered room service table and began lifting lids from steaming dishes. "They were out of strait jackets, but the chef recommended fried zucchini sticks, hot cheese puffs, and shrimp egg roll." He dipped a zucchini stick into a spicy dressing and popped it into his mouth, then held one out to her. "Here, this will have you back to sanity in no time."

"I thought you'd agreed to stay away until tomorrow."

"Number one, it is tomorrow; number two, *you* promised to order dinner. I'm merely seeing you keep your campaign promises, if belatedly."

She surrendered to the seductive aroma of the cheese puffs.

"Now, what was all that about how you're going to become a millionairess and build another Sun Valley or something? You get a telegram from a rich uncle's lawyer while I was out?"

"Honestly! I don't think you heard a word I said. I was merely drawing a historic parallel to the fact that one woman with a desire for recreation was able to spark the building of Sun Valley, while I, a quite different woman with a thoroughly different desire for building, am inspired anew to carry out my vision."

"I know I'm going to be sorry I asked, but are you talking about the housing subsidy bill by any chance?"

"Well, of course. What did you *think* I was talking about?"

"And you're going to finance it by building a ski resort?"

"What a ridiculous idea! If I could finance a ski resort, I wouldn't need to propose resort gaming to finance the housing subsidy."

The room went silent.

Carlton ran a hand through his already tumbled hair. "I can only hope I'm losing my mind, or at least my hearing. Tell me you didn't say you're proposing to legalize gambling at Idaho's resorts to finance your housing bill."

Stephanie gave a crow of triumph. "Flabbergasted, aren't you! I *knew* that's the effect it would have! That's my ultimate weapon. I didn't mean to reveal it until next week, but I've got it almost all worked out." She held up the pages she had filled that evening. "At least the administrative angle. I won't do the statistical sheets until morning when I'm fresher, but I just couldn't wait any longer to tell you. I'm so excited! You about had us beat on the cost issue—I realize that. The budget really couldn't stretch anymore—I saw that." She paused at his stony look. "Oh, Carlton, I know we're on opposite sides on this, but it means so much to me—can't you be happy for me, if not for the bill itself?"

He rose slowly to his feet and crossed to the door. "It's too late to get into this tonight. I'll see you tomorrow, Steph." He shut the door behind him.

"Isn't that just like the male ego," she said to the empty room. "I suppose he's miffed because I forgot to ask him how his speech went."

In spite of working into the wee hours, Stephanie was up bright and early the next morning. An energizing flow of adrenaline and a pot of good, strong, room service coffee fueled her attack on the statement of projected earnings she would attach to her proposal.

Let's see, if 45 percent of the take is paid to prize winners and 55 percent allocated to administrative costs and the state budget... She pulled a leaf out of

207

Alan's report. She ran her eye down the column of figures and added it up. Stephanie was good at math, but she found it tiring.

At almost the precise moment she stood to stretch, the sun came out from behind its winter clouds, and Sun Valley beyond her window sprang, glistening, to the romance of its name. She stepped out onto the balcony and took deep gulps of the crisp air. What a great way to clear her head! Why hadn't she thought of that before?

She grabbed her red fur-lined parka, jammed her feet into boots, and went out the closest exit.

Stephanie took the trail that led to the Challenger Inn, named for the Union Pacific's streamliner. The snow-packed paths bustled with people clad in colorful ski wear, most of them carrying skis and poles over their shoulders. All were making for one of the many lifts on Dollar Mountain or on Baldy, depending on the degree of their skill.

Stephanie was just about to enter the inn, thinking she might get a sandwich in the cafeteria for an early lunch, when a familiar voice hailed her from the veranda.

In spite of the crisp winter air, which kept the snow in peak condition, the sun warmed this south-facing balcony sufficiently for comfortable outdoor sitting. Happy to see that a night of sleep seemed to have restored Carlton's spirits, Stephanie joined him. "I read about this last night." She waved her arm in an arc at the golden ball in the sky.

"About what?"

"The sun. About how Harriman hired Steve Hannagan, the publicity man who promoted a desolate Florida sandbar into Miami Beach, to promote his new, unnamed resort. The book said Hannagan threw up his hands over the forsaken snow field—until the sun came out. He named it Sun Valley and promoted it with posters of a girl skiing in a swimming suit."

Carlton nodded and pushed his sunglasses on top of his head. "They still have those posters up in the Lodge. But it must have been cold work for the model, even if the sun was shining."

They sat in silence for several moments, looking out on the snowy lawns crisscrossed with winding, tree-lined walkways and circled with quaint, chalet-styled shops. The sound of sleigh bells rang in the distance above the murmur of tourists' voices.

Stephanie sighed and smiled. "I'm so glad you talked me into coming. I love it here. I suppose its a bit old-fashioned compared to Vail or Aspen, but that's what I love about it. It still has a lot of the charm and elegance it had in the '30s and '40s when it was a playground for movie stars and socialites, doesn't it?" There was no response. "Carlton? Am I boring you?"

"No. You're worrying me."

Stephanie's puzzled mind replayed what she'd just said. What was there in that to worry about? "You're *worried* because I like a resort with old-fashioned charm?" She laughed.

Carlton took his feet down from the balcony rail and sat up straight to face her. "Sorry. I wasn't listening to what you were saying just now. I've been thinking about what you told me last night."

"Oh." She caught her breath at the austere look on his face.

"Stephanie, I've thought about this most of the night. I've been hoping—praying—we could come out on the same side on this housing thing. I hate having it—or anything—between us."

She caught her breath again, this time at his look of pained intensity and at the pressure with which he grasped her gloved hands. "But, Carlton, that's what's so wonderful—what I was trying to tell you. Now we *can*. I'm not sure you're right on the philosophical/theological part about better houses not making better people, but that doesn't really matter. What matters is that I've solved the practical consideration—now we *can* afford it. You don't have to fight me on the grounds that the state can't finance my program. I suppose you were too sleepy to get what I was saying last night."

He shook his head. "I got it—loud and clear. Stephanie, I can't morally take your side. And if I can't persuade you to my side, we're going to wind up farther apart than ever. Maybe too far apart to be bridged even by—" He dropped her hands and looked away.

"Morally? You oppose this *morally?"*

"If it were just the economic problems with the scheme, I might—"

She cut him off. "Carlton, I'm not talking about casinos—opening the state up to card sharks and organized crime and whatever else. I'm talking about state operated bingo games and punch boards. Like we had when I was a kid. I remember seeing them around—it wasn't a big deal. Now, I spent most of the night drafting administrative procedures. Of course its just a skeletal outline for the committee to work from. But the operations will be as tight as any state agency. What could be wrong with that?"

He took a deep breath before starting. "Increased crime, increased property tax, decreased work incentive." He ticked them off on his fingers. "Besides, there's the immorality of the state government treating its citizens as suckers."

He paused to give her time to think, but she was quiet, so he went on. "When you know that the state will keep fifty-five percent of the take, it amounts to nothing more than a rip-off. Even in the casinos in Nevada the odds are much better than that."

Suddenly the realization of what he'd said hit her, and she flared. "How do you know I proposed fifty-five percent for the state? Have you been through my papers? Has

210

Alan—?" She swallowed the rest of her words as she saw people giving them curious stares.

"Of course not." His voice was quiet. "That's about standard. Don't think this is the first time this idea has been around the track. I studied it ten years ago when a candidate ran for governor on a pro-gambling ticket. And lost, I might remind you."

"But this is different. I'm just proposing it for resorts—to boost tourist trade. The argument that gambling preys on the poor doesn't apply here." The fact that there were people around them forced her to keep her voice low, but her temper was rising to a boil.

"That argument applies perfectly because it's true. Compulsive gamblers will go wherever the action is—if they have to hitchhike. Statistics show that people gamble more when they become unemployed. Gambling is a habit-forming vice no matter who operates it. The false hope of getting something for nothing, or almost nothing, gets hold of them, and at the time they can least afford it they spend more."

"Giving people *hope* is immoral? Remember, someone *does* win."

"Yes, at the expense of all the others. At the expense of kids who can't eat bingo cards for lunch."

Stephanie jumped to her feet, her hands clenched in tight fists.

Carlton stood beside her. "I know you don't want to hear any more, but before you stalk off in a temper, let me give you just one more thing to think about. Statistics also show that when a state increases chances for legal gambling, illegal gambling also increases. How can people who look to the government for guidance see anything wrong in an activity the government is guiding—even pushing—them into doing?"

Then Stephanie did stalk off in anger. She had thought him pig-headed, close-minded, hardheaded, hidebound, intractable, mulish, and maddening before, but this was beyond anything. That he could accuse *her* of being immoral, or preying on the poor, of wanting to open the state up to organized crime . . . She kicked at a lump of snow by the side of the road—it shattered satisfyingly— just as she'd like to do to the infuriating Carlton Sperlin.

22

Without really paying much attention to what she was doing, Stephanie joined a group of skiers waiting for the shuttle to Baldy. She was the only one in the crowd not clutching ski equipment and talking in an earnest voice about powder, runs, moguls, and other terms she found only vaguely familiar. But she didn't have the least interest in the conversations around her. She continued to fume at Carlton's words.

When the shuttle arrived, she followed the crowd aboard. A few minutes later, when she followed them off and stood staring up at majestic Bald Mountain, her first thought was to wonder what she was doing there. Then she knew. Knew what she wanted to do at least.

On a long ago summer day she and her mother had ridden the River Run lift to the top of the mountain, a favorite viewpoint for tourists. Now she wanted to see the mountain in its icy splendor, bejeweled with colorful skiers darting down the long white runs. She wanted to go to the very top. And the fact that that was the farthest she could get away from Carlton Jules Sperlin had nothing whatsoever to do with it.

She wasn't sure they would sell a lift ticket for tourist purposes at the height of the serious ski season. So she was delighted when the lady in front of her asked her to hold her poles for a moment while she checked a map of the runs. Stephanie managed to look as if she belonged at least long enough to get her pass.

She did get some funny looks as she trudged along while everyone else slipped by in smooth streaks. But at least no one stopped her, and she was soon snapped into the little metal chair that would take her to the top of Exhibition Run, one of the steepest and toughest ski runs in the world.

From her perch above the mountain, however, the terrain seemed to flatten below her. Only when the lift jerked before grinding the cable yet higher did she have much sensation of steep elevation. The sun was warm on her back, and a fresh breeze blew off the mountain ahead. Even with people before and behind her on the lift, and others skiing directly beneath, she felt an exhilarating sense of isolation. The freshness, the simplicity, the purity of flying through crystal air and dark green pines heavy with pristine snow was a heady experience. Her anger at Carlton, her worries over legislation, could all be rolled into a giant snowball and sent to the bottom of the mountain.

Suddenly the lift jerked, and she realized the rider in front of her had deplaned. She was next. She got a rather strange look when she jumped off without skis, but she hurried around the side of the maintenance hut, and the attendant was claimed by the next chair.

Stephanie headed up the mountain. When she was well away from the mechanical sounds of the lift equipment, she made her way to a nice flat boulder that offered easy footing and turned around for her first forward view from Baldy.

It was astounding. The ground fell away almost vertically at her feet. For miles on every side, the world stretched dark green and white. She took a step backward and was thankful for the rock under her feet. She had heard stories of Eastern skiers, unprepared for an almost vertical trail, who freaked out completely at the sight and had to be carried down blindfolded. She had never believed such accounts before. But now . . . She took another step backward and found that was as far as the ledge went, so she stood with her legs pressed against the mountain.

It took her some time to get her equilibrium back and be willing to leave the security of her ledge. The thought of the humiliation of having the ski patrol pry her clutching fingers from the frozen granite spurred her into action. The glare of the sun on the snow was beginning to cause eyestrain even through her sunglasses, so she decided to follow a trail of packed snow around to the left where some darker clouds seemed to be forming. Maybe she'd find another lift to ride down on that side of the mountain. After all, Baldy had something like sixteen lifts. She shouldn't have to go far to find another one.

At first the going was easy. She walked along a trail probably used by the ski patrol or maintenance employees. Then she got into a more wooded area. Here the going was harder, and suddenly she was sinking to her knees with almost every step. She recalled sketches she'd seen of skiers in the early days of Sun Valley who routinely walked up the mountains, carrying their skis on their shoulders. It must have taken hours of labor for the few minutes of pleasure on the downhill run. No wonder skiers had flocked to the mechanized lifts.

Soon her jeans were wet through to her thighs, and her boots filled with bits of snow that worked in around the tops. When a chill wind turned her wet pants to ice she knew she'd made a mistake in choosing the cloudy side of Baldy.

Only last night she had read that Sun Valley boasts three days of storm to twenty of sun. Even then, it seldom stormed on all sides of the mountain at once. If skiing should be closed on one side, sport would be unhindered for the rest.

Clever of you to choose the one dark spot for miles around, she told herself and huddled deeper in her parka.

She gritted her teeth and struggled toward a small open area a few feet ahead. If she could spot some shelter . . . Surely the quickly gathering storm wouldn't last too long.

A rumbling in the branches overhead made her look up. She lunged back just as a huge mound of snow dumped on the spot where she'd been standing a fraction of a second before. She looked at what could have been her burial mound. The shivers that shook her body weren't just from the cold.

How stupid she'd been to take off into the wilderness alone. Even the thought of Carlton, whom an hour earlier she was sure she never wanted to see again in her life, was suddenly a very welcome thought.

But she knew that unless it was to be one of the last thoughts she ever had, she must keep moving—and keep out from under snow-laden pines. The open spot that had looked so near a short time ago seemed to stretch ever farther away. Deep snow sucked at her feet, gale winds pushed at her, and her frozen limbs refused to respond to her brain's orders to move.

Which direction should she go? She had assumed she could see some shelter from the clearing. But what if she was wrong? Maybe she should turn around, go back the way she came. She wrenched her body around a quarter turn in the deep snow. A blast of wind, more furious than before, spun her back to her former direction. The wind, which had seemed to be coming from every side at once, would be even more fully in her face if she tried to return. She must go on.

Her legs felt she must have covered miles when she looked behind her. The mound of fallen snow from the tree was still visible—ten feet away. She peered through the swirling snow, trying to judge her progress toward the open patch.

Then a fresh blast of wind blew a whirl of snow in her face. She realized the futility of struggling to an open spot anyway. Even if she made it to a view area, the blizzard conditions would prevent her sighting what shelter might be close at hand. She had heard stories of farmers who froze to death in blizzards when they got lost between the barn and their home.

Fear gripped her more icily than the physical cold. If she didn't move, find some kind of shelter in a few minutes, she would never move again. Her mind knew this, but she couldn't find the force of will to break the bonds of fear and cold. She couldn't move.

And then, for one brief moment, Carlton was before her. Carlton, as he had been that morning on the sun-warmed balcony. At first he smiled and raised an eyebrow in greeting. Then he looked at her with deep concern—and something else. And she knew. Carlton was thinking of her. He was worried about her. He cared.

She staggered forward into the whirling whiteness. For the first time that day, in many days, she prayed. *Help me. Please. Help me.*

Leaning into the wind so sharply that if it had stopped suddenly she would have fallen face-first down the mountain, Stephanie pulled one stiff, heavy foot out of the snow and set it down before her. Laboriously she repeated the process with the left foot, then the right.

Finally, the absence of dark forms on either side told her she had reached the clearing. She was fully aware of the danger of staggering down the mountain when she could see only a few inches in front of her. Only too well she realized that one false step could send her plummeting hundreds of feet. Nevertheless, she inched forward, choosing the dangers of activity to the certain death of freezing if she stood still.

It seemed she had been struggling for hours—days—when all movement stopped. The impact came so suddenly it didn't occur to her to question what she had hit. It was as white as the snow, but hard. A new panic gripped her. Had she become so disorientated she was heading back up the mountain and had come against an ice-covered boulder? If her senses were so confused she couldn't even tell which way was up or down, she had no hope at all of getting off the mountain.

She pounded her fists against the obstruction. The solid hammering sound that produced brought her back to reality. She was knocking on a wooden wall. She had found a cabin or lift maintenance hut—some building. She had found shelter. With a sob of joy she edged her way along the wall. When she reached the corner of the structure the wind howled more ferociously than before, as if making one last effort to drive her back. But she found her way forward, buoyed by hope.

The door was on the side of the hut. Wondering how she could ever manage to break the lock, she seized the knob and threw herself against it. Miraculously, it opened, and she fell into what appeared to be a tiny ski patrol hut. For a moment Stephanie was too dazed and overcome with relief to move. Then she realized the door was still wide open, and snow was gusting in.

She crawled on her hands and knees to slam it shut, still marveling at her rescue. Leaning against the closed door, she looked around. There was a wood stove and a pile of kindling in one corner, but the task of starting a fire was daunting at the moment. For now she opted to roll in all three thick blankets from the cot and tackle the box of Granola bars from the supply chest. Coffee making was a high tech job that could come later.

Halfway through her third bar, she relaxed enough to be able to think. The wind raged around the hut and flung angry handfuls of snow at its one tiny window. Stephanie thought of the fury outside—the fury she had been rescued from. And appropriately, in view of the name of the mountain, she thought of *Fantasia* and its "Night on Bald Mountain" scene. In her mind the whirling white snow transformed into the swarming demons of the animator's imagination. She knew the true significance of her rescue and this safe haven.

For the first time in recent memory she was alone. Truly alone. On the top of a mountain, isolated from politicians, public, press—everything that had filled her life and kept her isolated from herself and her soul. Now they were there alone together. Stephanie and her soul. She thought of the brief prayer she had prayed in desperation and realized that even those five words had been effective. He had helped her. How much more effective could a life of prayer prove.

Her recent conversations with Sue and Carlton had been waking in Stephanie the realization that something was lacking in her life. Now she knew what it was. She had never made a true commitment to God—a real "anything You ask of me, Lord" dedication of her life. Now she knew that a childhood prayer of "I want You in my heart, Jesus" was a good beginning, but it wasn't enough. She needed to go on from there.

She glanced out the window again. Everywhere was blinding, swirling snow. Whiteness as impenetrable outside as the darkness of her heart inside. She bowed her head.

When Stephanie looked up, smiling and relaxed, she knew that if she got down from Bald Mountain she would be a new person. And if not—she would go to heaven.

But that was silly. She jumped to her feet—well, more stumbled, as she was still stiff with cold. There was no danger of her not making it now. She might have quite a wait before the storm blew itself out, but she had everything she needed for survival—both internally and externally.

She fumbled with sticks and matches, directing her slow fingers to build a fire, and thought of the irony that the greatest need in her life had been to make a commitment. She was the most fully committed person she knew. But she had been committed to the wrong things.

She thought about that. No, the causes she'd been committed to hadn't necessarily been wrong. But her priorities had been. God had always been in her life, but at the bottom of her list. Now she saw that Bible reading needed to come before bill reading; praying before debating.

Then she looked at her other priorities. David. What of the commitment she had made to him? Was he the right man for the rest of her life? She really knew so little about him. They had never discussed spiritual things. Did they have enough in common to build a life together? And what about her very confused feelings for Carlton? Which man meant most to her?

The storm outside showed no signs of letting up, but the storms that had raged for so long inside Stephanie responded to the voice of the Master, "Peace, be still."

In her new stillness she thought, too, of her family. Especially of her grandmother, whose calm courage had always been an inspiration to Stephanie. She recalled the passage she had recently read from Kathryn's journal. Kathryn had been overcome by panic inside the Kuna Cave. God's voice had come to her too, with a reminder that He was with her—always. To the end of the world.

The water in the coffeepot had just come to a boil when Stephanie heard a new sound outside. At first she thought the wind had risen to even higher pitch and was flinging a tree branch against the hut. Then she realized someone was banging on the wall outside. *At last, the ski patrol.*

She ran to the door and shouted into the wind. "The door's here! Come on!"

Moments later a dark figure staggered into the hut, pulled off his ski mask, and she was in Carlton's arms. For a long time they just clung to each other, laughing and crying. Then they sank onto the cot, still locked in each other's arms.

His first words were "Thank God. Oh, thank God!"

He let go of her long enough to unsnap his snow-shoes and shrug out of his snow-packed parka, then took her in his arms again.

This time the swirling in Stephanie's head was neither memory of the biting, stinging flecks of ice she had battled nor the dark demons of "Night on Bald Mountain" but a glorious fantasia of a mountain sunrise after the storm.

The sizzling and popping sounds of water boiling over on the wood stove finally penetrated her consciousness, and she regretfully pulled away.

She handed Carlton a steaming mug of coffee. "How did you ever find me?'

He shook his head. "It was a miracle. I was so terrified I'd never see you again—or if I did, it would be too late." He took refuge behind his coffee cup. "At first it was easy. As soon as I realized you'd been gone too long I started asking around. Everyone remembered the smashing blonde in a red fur parka with no skis. I realized you'd taken the lift to the top of Exhibition and notified the ski patrol. They organized a search, but the storm made it almost impossible."

He set down his coffee and reached for her again. "I came up. I thought I saw smoke coming from the cabin, but in the storm it was impossible to tell. I was so afraid it was just the patrol or that I was hallucinating . . . Stephanie . . ."

Again they clung together. When they drew apart, he held her at arms' length and looked at her for a long time. "Stephanie, please don't ever walk out of my life like that again."

She couldn't promise. She hadn't settled that question yet. But there was one she had settled. "Oh, Carlton. I've got the most wonderful thing to tell you. When I was here alone—at first I was *really* alone—I realized how little time or place I'd made for God in my life. I got a lot of things straightened out, and the most important one is that, no matter what, now He's first."

Some day she would have to decide who was second. But this was enough for the moment.

23

When the alarm clock rang half an hour earlier than usual on Monday morning, Stephanie couldn't connect her thoughts. She'd been dreaming she was in a blizzard. Then Carlton came. Then, when the wind dropped, they'd been taken off the mountain in a helicopter. No. It wasn't a dream. It happened. And her life was changed.

With a rush of joy she remembered. She was back on the track she thought she'd lost. Funny—getting lost in the snow had helped her find her way in life. She had made the commitment. Now she had to live it. She knew the pattern—she had done it all her life until her college rebellion. But getting up early to read her Bible and pray would take some getting used to. "Help me, Lord."

She fumbled through a form of prayer and Bible reading. Then she managed to get ready for the day in spite of a sore throat. As she entered the capitol, the cold gray world outside seemed a perfect setting for the cold gray marble inside.

The feeling of glamour and excitement that had formerly carried her through her most hectic days was gone, leaving only the drudgery. She tried to analyze her feelings as she stared at her calendar. Old-timers had warned her about the midsession blahs. There was nothing overtly different about today's schedule from any other. She believed just as much in the issues she was fighting for—at least, she supposed she did—but she just felt as if someone had pulled the plug and all the fight had drained out of her. She sat with her head propped on one hand, staring blankly at her desk.

Then her vision cleared sufficiently for her to see that her desk wasn't clear. A memo in the attorney general's own handwriting stared up at her. "Reasons to Oppose Resort Gaming," the heading read. A regressive form of revenue that would repress, rather than stimulate, economic growth . . . escalation would occur once gambling interests had a foot in the door. She forced herself to read through all the statistics to the bottom of the page, even though her head pounded on every one of them. Why couldn't he let her alone? Things had been so lovely between them Saturday. Why couldn't he leave it at that?

And then her ringing phone made her head throb worse than ever.

"Representative Hamilton."

"Hello, Steph, I—"

"Oh, hello. Yes, I read your memo. No, I'm not convinced. Don't you ever quit?"

"We'll talk about that later. I need something else right now. I have to go out of town, and I was hoping you could take care of a few loose ends on this drinking bill for me. There are—"

"You've really got nerve, haven't you?" Her sore throat made her sound harsher than she meant.

"You offered to help. If I recall, the exact words were 'I'll do anything.'"

"Just what sort of one-way street is this supposed to be? We both work on the same bills, except I work *for* yours and you work *against* mine?"

"Steph, I would never ask you to work for something you didn't believe in. I thought you wanted to stop this measure."

"I do, but I also want the housing subsidy bill to pass."

"And I should support it, no matter what I really believe?"

"Couldn't you find *anything* good about it?"

"The only appeal that bill has is the sincerity of your belief in it. But I don't happen to be one of those who subscribe to the idea that it doesn't matter what you believe as long as you're sincere. I think you have to believe in the right things."

"And they're only right if *you* say they are?"

"I'm sorry I bothered you, Stephanie. See you when I get back." He sounded truly sorry and more than just a little tired.

She softened enough to ask, "Where are you going?"

"Pocatello. Speaking at a President's Day dinner. You haven't forgotten your promise to go to the one here with me?"

"I think I just lost my appetite."

"Your appetite to hear the speaker, you mean?"

"Hmm, he tells me he's brilliant."

"With a fan club like that, who needs an opposition party?"

The worst part of all was that she actually hung up laughing with him. Nothing could have made her more furious—betrayed by her own sense of humor.

She was now ten minutes late for her meeting. Her shoulders ached, and she considered skipping out, but a sense of duty prevailed. She jumped to her feet—too quickly apparently, because her head swam, and she had to sit back down momentarily.

She might as well have cut the meeting after all, because she couldn't concentrate on a thing that was happening. All she could think of was her aching back and her aching neck and how wonderful it would feel to be in bed. By the time people were leaving the room and she realized the meeting was over, she had come to another realization. She didn't have midsession blahs—she had the good old-fashioned flu.

She didn't even go back to the chambers for her papers —just headed straight around the rotunda for the closest door. It would have been a clean getaway if the attorney general hadn't chosen that moment to leave his office.

"Stephanie! You look awful."

"And here I thought you were limping from the snow-shoeing. Now I know its from putting your foot in your mouth. Bite harder next time."

"At least you can't be terminal if you can still get off cracks like that." And then he did a most surprising thing —he put his hand to her forehead, just as her mother had always done to see if she had a fever. His gesture of tenderness was her complete undoing.

His gesture and the way he looked at her—there was such caring, such—gentleness—that tears came to her eyes. For a moment she longed to be back up on the mountain with him, isolated in their white world, away from committees and speeches and bill debates—away from anything that would keep them apart.

He took a clean white handkerchief from his pocket and dabbed at the two tiny tears that squeezed out of the corners of her eyes. He took the briefcase from her hand. *Now if he'd just put his arm around me.* Instead, he said over his shoulder, "Anne, we're going to take Representative Hamilton home first."

"We'll miss our plane, Carlton."

"We've got time. Anyway she's in no condition to drive." And then, right there in front of the world and Anne Smith, he put his arm around Stephanie and all but carried her from the capitol.

She could feel the drag of his injured leg and was afraid she was hurting him. "Carlton, I'm too heavy. I can walk."

"Nonsense," he said in a tone that brooked no argument. Then he softened. "Well, maybe just one eclair too many."

"I hope you break your leg. After you deposit me, that is."

In a few minutes he had delivered her into Sue's capable hands, which in turn tucked her in bed and plied her with aspirin and cool drinks.

For hours Stephanie was so miserable she was glad Carlton had gone to Pocatello with Anne. It just seemed to round things out perfectly. The only sour note in all her delicious misery was when the florist arrived with a bouquet of daisies and jonquils from Carlton, forcing her to think nice thoughts about him and about how spring was coming. Why couldn't he leave her alone to enjoy her wretchedness?

And then the ultimate calamity occurred. In the muddle of feverish thoughts, one fact stood out with sharp coherence. Tomorrow was the final committee debate on her housing subsidy bill. Not just the debate—the vote. Without her financing plan, it didn't stand a chance.

The momentous task of presenting the idea and leading the committee debate was wholly hers. And she couldn't even lift her head off the pillow. There had to be something she could do. She had this hazy feeling that if she could just think more clearly, could make her mind focus, there was something she could do.

She struggled as long as she could, until, overcome by fever and exhaustion, she simply gave up. Her head limp on her pillow, she abandoned the fight.

Then the answer came, and she felt so ashamed. How could she have forgotten? Her new relationship with God was less than three days old, and already she had forgotten. She could commit the problem to Him.

Lord, You know how much this means to me. You know the vote is tomorrow. And I can't do anything about it. I can't cope. I commit it to You.

She was asleep before she could say amen.

It seemed hours later when Sue opened her door. "Sorry if you were asleep, Stephanie. But I thought you'd want to know right away. A Mr. Harding called. He said the Health and Welfare meeting has been postponed till Friday."

Stephanie didn't even reply. She just smiled and turned over before going back to sleep.

At noon Wednesday she sat up and ate a bowl of chicken soup—with three soda crackers.

"Ah, there's life in the old girl yet." Sue checked her over and pronounced her temperature to be normal. "But no ideas of going to the capitol tomorrow, young lady. You need several days away from that place."

Stephanie nodded wordlessly. In spite of the answer to prayer she'd experienced, and in spite of the fact that she was recovering, depression was growing on her. She tried to tell herself it was natural after being sick, or that she was just being silly about Carlton's going to Pocatello with Anne, but the real cause was deeper than that.

She simply had to sort out her feelings for David and Carlton. She couldn't stand the thought that, as things now stood, she was lying to both of them by not disclosing her feelings for the other. But the truth was, she didn't know the truth. Whom did she love? Whom did she want to spend the rest of her life with? She slumped down and pulled the blanket over her head . . . .

"You in there?" Sue's voice sounded a long way off.

And it was so dark. Then Stephanie realized she was sleeping under her blanket.

She looked out. "What's left of me is, but it's not worth bothering about."

"There's a man on the phone who would disagree with you. You feel up to having a visitor tonight?"

"Carlton?"

Sue nodded.

"No way. Tell him I died." Then she sighed. "No, he'd just insist on viewing the body—what a disgusting phrase. Can you bring the phone in here?"

Sue plugged it in beside her bed and plumped the pillows behind her back.

"Thanks for the flowers," Stephanie said into the receiver.

She wanted to talk about anything but tomorrow's conflict, but after they exhausted the topics of her health and his speech and what she had missed at the capitol this week, it couldn't be avoided.

"Steph, I know you've been sick and don't feel all that chipper yet, but have you been able to give any thought to what I said about the gaming issue?"

She sighed. She really didn't feel up to this. Besides, what could she say? They'd been over all the arguments on both sides. She just sat there, clinging to the phone.

"Steph, forgive me for bothering you about this when you're under the weather. Listen, don't even bother answering me. Will you just do one thing before that meeting tomorrow? Pray about your proposal. Please—for both our sakes."

A sharp intake of breath was her only answer.

"Sleep well now. And I'll be praying too."

The buzz on the line prodded her into replacing the receiver.

He was right. That was what she had to do. That's what total commitment meant. But what if Carlton was right, and the idea *was* morally wrong, and God asked her not to promote it? What if God told her to abandon her brilliant idea that she'd worked so hard on? Could she give it up? Was she willing to commit her housing bill and its financing problems to God? Even if He said no?

She realized she was facing one of the most important decisions of her life—maybe the most important. She could go right ahead, fighting this thing in her own strength and with her own ideas, or she could release it to God. But the real decision wasn't over the issue of the bill; the real decision was the validity of her commitment. Had it been a foxhole consecration, brought on by her fear of the moment? Or was it the confirmation and determination of a faith that she could build the rest of her life on?

24

"Couldn't you stay home one more day?" Sue asked at breakfast the next morning. "You still look pale. One more day could really get you on your feet. How much damage can they do down there in just one day without your watch-dogging?"

"No way. This is the day we vote my bill out of committee. And not just out of committee—but with a 'do pass' recommendation!" And on that confident note, Stephanie put just a dab of blusher on her cheeks to relieve Sue's very accurate diagnosis of paleness and went on her way.

The committee room with its beige walls, gold carpet, and brocade drapes was beginning to feel like home. Due to the attention this proposal had been getting, the room was filled with spectators and newsmen. Extra chairs filled every corner. Stephanie saw Fran come in and sit by Jim as the debate began.

At first the arguments seemed to be nothing more than a rehash of the attorney general's testimony.

"The fiscal impact statement is weak. If this thing is just going to die in the Senate finance committee, there's no sense in our going farther with it," an opponent said.

At the mention of financing problems, Stephanie had to bite her tongue. Her work on funding was in a file in her briefcase, less than twelve inches from her hand. But she was determined to leave it there. She had settled that much last night. She would leave the question before God and not do anything about it until she was *sure* what was right.

Today she would let the committee debate the housing bill on its own merits. She could still bring out the resort gaming proposal when it got to the finance committee. They were the proper ones to deal with that anyway.

And if her bill didn't get out of committee today? Well, she'd settled that with God last night. Her commitment was genuine, it was for life, and this bill was part of her life. So she would leave it in God's hands and accept the outcome. No matter what.

The debate continued.

"What about a more precise wording of this term *substandard?*" the representative from Melba asked. "Our farm isn't very fancy—my wife sure would be unhappy if it got declared substandard."

The committee laughed, but the bill's sponsor dealt with it seriously.

"We don't want to set monetary values, because those fluctuate too rapidly. But the present building codes define what's safe. Those guidelines can be followed. I assume, Chuck, you don't have broken windows or contaminated plumbing on the farm?"

"I've been kept so busy down here, I'm not even sure."

The committee laughed again, but it made Stephanie think. Her grandmother had lived in a homestead shack. Her mother and father had spent the first years of their married life—and she had spent the first few years of *her* life—in a tarpaper-covered, one-room house. They wouldn't have been better people if they'd had fancier houses. Could Carlton be right?

As the debate progressed, she kept mental track of the way the committee members seemed to be leaning. Judging by their comments, her best guess was that a "do pass" recommendation would be voted down five to seven. If they could just do something to get one more vote, she was pretty sure Chairman Detweiller would vote with them in a tie. She thought hard, trying to organize her strongest arguments.

"Mr. Chairman—" she was given the floor "—we have all come here with a heavy responsibility to represent the people of Idaho the best we can. This is an important bill. We can't let it die in committee. Since the committee apparently finds considerable division of opinion on this issue, perhaps it can be more fairly decided by the House as a whole. Therefore, Mr. Chairman, I move that House Bill 94 be reported from this committee without recommendation."

She tried not to feel that making that motion had been a defeat. Compromise wasn't defeat—it was good strategy. But she had so hoped for a "do pass" vote. And she couldn't suppress the fleeting question of whether she had been right to hold off on the funding proposal. Would that have made the difference in committee support? But then she thought again of the peace that had accompanied her decision last night, and she knew, with relief and gratitude, that she had been right to wait.

The next few minutes proved the wisdom of her present tactic. Her motion passed by a two-vote margin. Fran sent her a broad smile, and Jim looked up from his notepad long enough to make her an OK sign.

The committee adjourned, and Jim caught Stephanie just outside the room. "Congratulations, Emerald Eyes. Once again you're the heroine of the hour."

"I am?"

"No false modesty with me. You know perfectly well that your bill would never have gotten out of committee without your brilliant compromise motion. In honor of your brilliance, I propose you let me take you to a concert tonight."

"A concert? I didn't know Black Sabbath was in town."

"Hey, what is this—some kind of a put-down of my musical taste? I'll have you know I'm talking real uptown stuff—I've got two tickets to the Philharmonic."

231

"Jimmy! I can't imagine you as a classical music buff."

"OK, so I'll admit it—I've been assigned to do an arts story, and I need a classy companion to set the right tone."

"That I can believe—you'll need me to translate the program notes for you. Answer questions like, "Who's this Beethoven cat?'"

"And to think, I called a woman classy who could wound me like that."

"Never mind. You'll recover. I'd love to go to the concert."

A message on Stephanie's desk asked her to call the attorney general's office. Well, here it was—another test of the resolution she made before God last night. Just as she had determined not to force her political programs without an inner assurance that she was doing the right thing, so she had committed her relationships with David and Carlton. No matter how tangled her emotions were—or rather, especially since her emotions were so tangled—she had resolved to keep everything just as it was—working with Carlton, writing to David. Keep everything calm. She knew that had to be a temporary solution. Sooner or later she would have to end one of the relationships entirely. But this was all she could cope with for the moment.

She placed the call, then spoke rapidly, concentrating on her own words rather than on what the sound of his voice did to her metabolism. "Sorry I missed your call. You heard that my bill got out of committee?"

"I heard. But first, I want to know how you're feeling."

"Oh." She paused. "I must be fine. I haven't thought about it all day."

"Are you sufficiently recovered to go to the Philharmonic with me tonight? They're doing 'Zadok the Priest.' Should be a stirring program with all those 'God save the King's."

"I'm sorry, Carlton." And suddenly, in spite of all her resolution to keep her relationship with him a strictly working one for the time being, she *was* very sorry. "But I've already got a date tonight."

"I'm sorry too," he began. Then his intercom buzzed in the background. "Oops, have to go now. I'll talk to you later."

She sat there staring at the telephone. Well, so much for that.

Besides, what she really needed was just to have fun with a friend like Jimmy, who left her emotions untouched and her career unthreatened.

In spite of the uneasy impression that such thoughts were disloyal to her escort, Stephanie did feel her rich brown velvet suit with the draped gold silk blouse was wasted on Jimmy with his shaggy hair and wide psychedelic tie. But as a pair they represented a typical cross-section of the audience attire, which ranged from Levi's to tuxedos.

"Boise never fails to surprise me," Stephanie said when they were seated. "This looks like a sell-out." The two seats in front of them appeared to be the only vacancies in the house.

"According to my in-depth research—" Jim flipped back a few pages in his omnipresent notebook "—Boise has a long history of culture because it began as an army post rather than a rip-roaring gold rush town like so many Western cities."

"What difference does that make?"

"Officers' wives, my deah." He pantomimed drinking tea with his little finger extended.

Stephanie could almost hear the rustle of a sedate Victorian petticoat and the tiny clink of a fine bone china teacup on a saucer. "Yes, I see what you mean. They went to the ends of the earth, but they took civilization with them." She was silent for a moment, thinking what it must have been like for a lady from Philadelphia or Boston to come to a cavalry stockade in the Oregon Territory surrounded by sagebrush and Indians. That would have been even worse culture shock than her grandmother's move from Nebraska to Kuna.

"That must have taken true grit. Those ladies had more stiffening in them than just the whalebone in their corsets. How nice to think we're still reaping the benefits of their endeavors."

"For example"—Jim was still perusing his notes—"the Boise Orchestra was formed by a group of eight men who got together in 1887. And did you know Boise had the first Music Week in the nation?"

"Really?"

"Would I kid you? Don't answer that. But yes. Now it's an annual event across the nation, but it got its little ol' start right here."

"Hmm, the legacy of an officer's wife with a harpsichord?" Brought across the prairie in a wagon or train as her grandmother's organ had been, she thought. Kathryn had been a preacher's daughter, not an officer's wife, but she, too, had brought civilization to the desert.

The lights dimmed, the concertmistress sounded an A, followed by a cacophony of orchestral tuning, and the conductor took the podium to the accompaniment of audience applause. Before the applause faded, a slight rustle in the aisle signaled two latecomers slipping into seats in front of them. The conductor raised his baton, and Stephanie settled back, letting the rich strains of a Vivaldi air soar around her.

She even closed her eyes to concentrate more fully on the music. When she opened them, the newcomers turned to talk to each other. The light from the stage highlighted their profiles, and Stephanie gave an inward groan. Of all the seats in the auditorium, those had to be occupied by Carlton and Anne.

When the number ended, Stephanie applauded briefly. Then, as the house lights came up, she busied herself with reading her program notes on the Handel anthems that were to be the showpiece of the evening.

Her hope, however, that Jim's notetaking would keep him too occupied to notice their ironic situation was short-lived. He nudged her and pointed at the couple in front of them, mugging something between a grimace and a grin.

She nodded as if seeing them for the first time and went back to her reading, praying that Jim would have the social grace not to tap Carlton on the shoulder.

Any urges Jim might have had in that direction were stifled by the entrance of the fifty-voice Boise Master Chorale, the guest performers for the evening. Stephanie noted that their number was very near the original forty-seven that performed the premiere of the work for the coronation of King George II in Westminster Abbey in 1729. Of course, women were now singing the choir boys' parts.

As the strings began the lilting opening phrases, Stephanie could see the coronation procession making its majestic way down the long, red-carpeted aisle of the ancient abbey. And when the music reached a crescendo, the instruments were joined by the voices of the Chorale, "Zadok the Priest unto the people hath said, Rejoice, rejoice." Everything in her responded to the stirring Handelian chorus, written for moments of great national jubilation. "Rejoice and say, God save the King, long live the King, God save the King, may the King live forever! Forever, hallelujah, hallelujah, hallelujah! Amen."

It spoke to her of the tradition of orderly transfer of power, of protection of individual rights, of the inviolability of personal property, ideals that were deep in America's roots for hundreds of years before she was even a nation. As a lawmaker, Stephanie was part of that tradition—just as the harpsichordist on stage was part of the continuum from Handel through the officer's wife cherishing her harpsichord in the sand and heat of Fort Boise. At that moment Stephanie could easily have joined those on stage as they sang, "Rejoice! Rejoice! Hallelujah! Hallelujah! HALLELU-JAH! Amen."

She applauded until her hands hurt. "Oh, that was wonderful!" she almost shouted into Jim's ear to be heard above the applause.

Then the lights came on for intermission, and she was back in the real world. All too real. Carlton and Anne turned to go out and greeted them with surprised hellos. But before any more could be said, Anne linked her arm in Carlton's and in her accustomed positive manner led him up the aisle, leaving Stephanie feeling just slightly frumpy.

It infuriated Stephanie that anything, or anyone, could manage to make her suit appear that way. After all, the blouse was real silk and the jewelry was real gold and nothing about Stephanie had ever implied mousiness in her life. Who did that woman think she was, anyway?

"Glad you enjoyed it." Jim's voice came as if from a long way off.

"*Enjoyed* it? Oh, you mean the music. Yes, Yes. Remarkable—especially since the program notes say it's rarely performed today because of the level of vocal virtuosity the work demands."

"I like the reference to Handel's 'big bow wow manner.'"

"You would." There was no sense in trying to explain to Jim how that music had moved her, what it had meant to her. But Carlton would have understood.

25

Tuesday morning, the first of the housing stories appeared in the *Statesman*. At first Stephanie was thrilled. The three photos chosen to accompany the story were the most grippingly graphic statements of human need she could have imagined—on a par with something *Life* magazine might do on a famine in Africa. And the story was a powerful plea for the passage of her bill. It explained the proposed legislation in simple, readily understandable terms and presented the arguments against it in a way that made those in opposition look callous and insensitive.

But then, as Stephanie reread the article, it began to dawn on her that it didn't just make the opposition in general look callous and insensitive. It made the attorney general in particular look callous and insensitive.

Of course, that's exactly what she thought too. But she found she didn't particularly enjoy having Carlton made to look that way publicly—especially right now when he was taking so much heat on the drinking bill. It was rather like the way she could enjoy a good laugh over a bad picture of herself, but didn't want anyone else laughing at it.

It was becoming almost a reflex for her to reach for her phone.

He answered on the third ring. "UPI. Jim here."

"Jim, what's going on? These stories were supposed to raise public support for House Bill 94. They weren't supposed to be a personal vendetta against the attorney general."

"Hey, whatsa matter? You didn't think my piece was effective?"

"Oh, it was effective all right. A very effective smear of a very hard-working and dedicated man."

"With whom you happen to have a thing going. What's the skinny here? You're suddenly putting personal considerations ahead of public?"

"We do not have a 'thing going,' as you so crudely put it! But besmirching someone who is doing his job as he sees it—even if I happen to disagree with his personal vision—is my idea of yellow journalism."

"Whoa! Now you've gone too far. My journalism is not yellow, and neither am I. I told you, you gotta have an angle. My angle is to help the reader sense the struggle going on over this issue. I'm not interested in straight sob sister stuff about orphans with no roofs over their heads. I want conflict, drama, opposing forces locked in combat in the hallowed halls of the statehouse—"

"All right, Jim, I get the drift of what you're saying. You really should have gone into acting, though. Your talents are wasted in mere newsprint."

"I thought you'd see it my way, kid. Now, about our unfinished business . . ."

"Don't push me, Jimmy. I told you I'd get the information. As a matter of fact, Alan is coming in in a few minutes."

She hung up, then jumped at the voice at her elbow.

"Wrong. Alan is here now."

"Oh, good morning, Alan. What have you been able to find?"

"Haven't got onto the alcohol part yet, but here's what I found on the TET offensive—pretty grisly stuff."

She took the file folder from him and scanned his neatly written notes: destruction, danger, smoke, and flames . . . no security . . . too many people . . . the panic beginning around 3:00 P.M. . . . pushing and shoving . . . shots fired . . . madhouse . . . chaos . . .

She closed the folder, unable to take any more. "I think that's what's generally referred to as 'not a pretty picture,'" she said quietly.

"Do you want any more on this?"

"No, this is plenty. You've done a good job." She spoke calmly, but she was sick inside. She knew from what Carlton had said that it was bad, but she really had no idea. And in the middle of all this, he was lying somewhere in a bombed-out house, seriously wounded, with nothing but saki for medicine.

The ache she felt the night he told her returned. Her desire to hold him, to shelter him was so strong she actually moved her arms out in front of her on her desk.

She had determined she would have nothing more to do with him—nothing romantic, that is—so why did she still feel like this?

Was the marble lady losing her willpower?

She forced attention to the story material in front of her.

The guilt she felt made a bad taste in her mouth. Carlton hadn't made the story public, and yet she'd promised Jim she would. And she wasn't even sure she could trust Jim's 'story angle,' as he would call it. One thing was sure, she couldn't face Carlton feeling like this.

Aghast at the thought, she dropped her head in her hands for a moment. Tonight was the President's Day dinner. She had promised weeks ago to sit at the head table with Carlton. Without even thinking what kind of excuse she would give, she called his office.

"I'm sorry, Mr. Sperlin is out right now. Would you care to leave a message?"

239

She slammed down the phone. "Out right now! Of course he's out right now. He's always out when I need to talk to him!"

"Who's out?"

"Fran! I didn't see you come in. The attorney general is out. *Grrr.*"

"Yeah, he's out in the rotunda. I saw him just a minute ago as I was coming in."

"Oh, do you think I can catch him?" Stephanie was on her feet.

"I imagine so. He was talking to someone . . ."

But Stephanie was already out of the chambers.

She reached the rotunda just in time to see him going out the door. Then she realized this was Tuesday. Carlton was disappearing for another of his mysterious Tuesday absences.

She raced down the steps, intent on reaching him before he got to his car. Hers was a block away in the parking garage. There would be no hope of catching him if he drove off. She thought of calling his name but shrank from the idea of creating a scene. Besides, she wasn't absolutely sure he would stop for her if he did hear her shout his name.

She was close enough to hear the door close and his engine purr into life. Her shoulders slumped, and she started to turn back when a bright yellow taxi swung through the circle drive and deposited its fare at the foot of the steps in front of her.

In the best of the old movie traditions Stephanie jumped into the back seat and told the driver to "follow that car." She couldn't imagine where this melodramatic chase would take her—a secret political caucus, an exclusive health club, a meeting of Alcoholics Anonymous were all ideas that raced through her imagination. She even went so far as to think of—then rapidly dismiss—the possibility of a mistress.

But she didn't have long to wait. The taxi followed the sleek maroon car down State Street to Fort and pulled into the parking lot at the Elks' Rehabilitation Center.

"Carlton!" She thrust some bills at the driver, from the snack bar money she carried in her pocket, and ran across the lot.

Carlton turned to her, his face registering absolute amazement.

She cried, "So *this* is your secret hide-away?"

The surprise on his face turned to a flash of anger that made her stumble backward.

"What are *you* doing here?" But even as he spoke, he reached out a hand to steady her. Then the angry spark turned to a humorous twinkle. "Well, don't you dare breathe a word of it—if this got out and spoiled my tough guy image I'd be ruined for life."

"But I still don't understand what you're doing here."

He shrugged. "Come on. Now that you know the real me you might as well see the worst."

She followed him inside. "But why the big secret?"

"Because I don't believe in making political hay out of things I believe in—especially not out of crippled kids. Think how their families would feel. Because I limp a bit, the kids see me as someone from their world—if the older ones saw a spread on this on the six o'clock news and thought they were part of my political image . . ." He shuddered.

"I see."

"No, you haven't seen yet, but I'd like for you to." He held the door open for her.

Stephanie knew that her last defenses were crumbling fast.

"What do you do?"

"Just spend a little time with the kids—gives them and the teachers a break from their classroom routine—I guess you'd call it recess. Anyway, they tell me the children respond well to men volunteers, especially the boys."

241

They were walking down a shiny, beige-tiled, well-lighted hallway lined with colorful posters and large, lacy Valentines.

"I can understand that. I should also think the sense of strength a man projects is comforting. How many kids do you have?"

"Each class is limited to five, but absences are high in the winter. The flu epidemic has kept attendance way down the last few weeks." He opened a door off the hallway, and Stephanie walked into a bright, green-carpeted classroom with child-size furniture and shelves of appealing toys.

Carlton glanced at the clock on the wall. "They're still in therapy. The therapists will bring them down in a minute."

"How did you get started in this? I mean, of all the extracurricular activities I might have assigned to you, this would have been the last I'd ever think of."

"Still seeing me as cold and callous, aren't you? Maybe someday I can convince you that being a realist doesn't automatically make one uncaring." He gave her a flash of the smile that always made her catch her breath. "I really had in mind working with Vietnamese orphans or something like that, but when I inquired around I found out about the need for volunteers here. So I gave it a try. After a bit it—uh—sort of gets hold of you."

The door opened, and the teacher, a cute little blonde with curly hair and round, bright blue eyes, came in with her arms full of felt cutouts.

"This is Judy." Carlton held the door for her. "Judy, my friend Stephanie. No problem with her watching this morning, is there?"

"No problem at all. Glad to have you here, Stephanie. You didn't get us at a very active time, though." Her words were addressed to Stephanie, but her eyes sparkled at Carlton.

"Kids still sick?" he asked.

242

"Yeah, just Mandy and Doug here this morning."

"Tell me about them," Stephanie asked the teacher.

"Mandy is three. She has cerebral palsy. If she's in a good mood she'll really respond, if not . . ." She shrugged. "Doug is five. He has some paralysis from an auto accident. He's full of it all the time—but very loving. He'll want to hug you."

"How are they doing?"

"With Mandy it's hard to tell, because she's so erratic. Doug is recovering—it's slow, but he really wants to play soccer like his big brother. I think he will."

Judy turned to her young students as they were wheeled in by their therapists. "Well, it's about time. We were just talking about you."

Carlton got down on one knee to address Doug. "Hi, tiger. I want you to meet a friend of mine. This is Stephanie."

Just as Judy predicted, Doug held out his arms.

Stephanie responded with a big bear hug. "They warned me about you. You won't be too hard on me, will you?" Even if they hadn't told her, Stephanie would have spotted the mischief in those big dark eyes. She looked at Carlton's twinkling brown eyes on a level with Doug's. "I wonder who teaches whom the tricks."

Mandy's mother had come in with her, so she had been occupied, but now they turned to her. The little girl was apparently in one of her recalcitrant moods. She shook off her mother's attempt to replace a blue bow that had fallen off one of her pigtails.

Carlton grinned at her but didn't speak. "It's better to let her make the first move," he said in Steph's ear.

And then, quite unexpectedly, Mandy held out her little arms for a hug from Stephanie.

"Carlton likes pretty little girls. Shall I put your ribbon in for you?" Stephanie whispered to her.

Mandy nodded.

243

Stephanie and Carlton helped their charges into big yellow and green wagons— Mandy's had a seat belt for safety—and they set out for a tour of the hospital.

They had gone only a few yards down one of the long halls when Carlton stopped abruptly. "Hey, what's going on?" He turned to Doug.

A delighted giggle told them the prank had produced the desired results—Doug had set the brake on his wagon.

"Look, pardner, you do that again, and I ride and you pull." Carlton grinned at him.

Carlton suggested they could be a train and Doug could make the chug-chug engine noises. That kept their progress steady, and a few minutes later, a cheerful "Little Engine That Could" chugged, "I thought I could, I thought I could, I thought I could" all the way back to the class-room.

"OK, guys, time to get to work. You be good for Judy, or she might not let us out next time."

Judy smiled at her young charges, but again, Steph-anie noticed, it was Carlton she made eyes at.

Out in the hall again, Carlton glanced at his watch. "Short session this morning since there were only two. Shall we grab a cup of coffee before we head back to the treadmill?"

Stephanie was still in something of a state of shock at discovering this new side of Carlton Sperlin. "Carlton, that was great—those kids really responded to you."

"They responded to you too."

"Yes, but, I mean—you do this every week?"

"When I don't have to be out of town on business." He led her into the staff dining room—all beige and chrome with a mural of Idaho's mountain scenery painted on one wall. Another wall was all windows, looking out on the courtyard. Carlton brought them each a cup of coffee, and they sat at a long table with a couple of therapists who were also taking a break. Carlton introduced his guest, and they made her welcome.

"This work must take a staggering amount of patience," she observed.

"Not everyone can work with disabled children," a speech therapist said. "Some people want to do too much for them. We had one volunteer who couldn't take it when we withheld snacks until the children asked for them."

Carlton nodded. "These kids are cagey. They'll play you for all you're worth. Sometimes you have to be really —er—" he looked pointedly at Stephanie "—callous not to let them take advantage of their handicaps."

"You're saying the world needs more hard-headed realists and fewer bleeding hearts?" she returned from behind her coffee cup. Then she changed the course of the conversation by turning to one of the directors of the center who had taken a seat next to her. "How long has the hospital been here?"

"Since 1947. The Elks Association wanted to establish a convalescent home for crippled children in the '30s, but the plan was interrupted by the war. Then in the '40s Idaho had a severe polio epidemic, and they really pulled all the stops out to get the facility operational in a few months."

The conversation at the table became general. Stephanie responded when addressed, but all she could think was, *He does care about people; he really cares! He DOES!* She almost choked on a swallow of coffee when her throat tightened up over her thought of Carlton's unfailing gentleness with the children. A true gentleman—a man who did things gently in love. And humble—he worked with those children, really gave himself to them, then went on his way and never said anything about it. She finished her coffee with a gulp. She wanted to be alone so they could talk.

In a few minutes they were in his car, and she turned to him. "Carlton, I owe you an apology. I was so terribly wrong about you. I really don't know what to say, I—"

He cut her off by placing a finger on her lips. "Apology not required, but it's accepted anyway."

245

"But I just still don't understand. You do all this, and yet you denounce all my efforts at—at, well for want of a better term—at social gospel."

He started the car and backed out of the parking lot. "Personal gospel and social gospel are both provisions of the New Testament. You can't choose between doctrine and ethics, between inner experience and outer conduct, between faith and works. Although you'll notice which I put first each time. That would be like trying to choose between soul and body—if you separate them you're left with a ghost and a corpse."

"Well put."

He laughed. "Yes, it is. But its not quite original. E. Stanley Jones said something like that."

Her face must have shown she was still thinking, so he went on. "The danger comes if we substitute social work for evangelism. But love has to show itself in service. So, with the full realization that I'm not changing human nature, I help where I can."

When she thought of the newspaper series and the accusations subliminally leveled at him in it, she felt overcome with guilt. It was probably the last thing in the world she wanted to talk about, but she knew it would be a barrier between them until she did. "Carlton, the *Statesman* articles about the housing bill . . ." She couldn't go any further, but she didn't need to.

"Mmm." He nodded. "People—especially politicians—with my beliefs are often accused of being heartless. I won't say I'm blasé about it, but it's to be expected. The truth is, we care too much to try to give only superficial answers to the problems around us. I'm not going to support a bill I know won't work just because it sounds humanitarian."

"Like mine for example."

"That's it," he said with a little nod of his head and his look of amused concern.

They rode the rest of the way to the capitol in silence.

As they were walking up the steps he said, "By the way, what precipitated your wild goose chase this morning?"

Stephanie blinked. "It seemed so terribly important at the time, then I forgot all about it. I was going to tell you I couldn't go to the President's Day dinner tonight."

"Why?"

"I—well—I hadn't thought of an excuse yet."

"No, I don't want to know the excuse. I want to know the reason for trying to give me an excuse."

"Guilt, I guess. I couldn't face you."

"The newspaper article, you mean?"

She nodded.

"Well, that's all right then. We've already settled that. I'll pick you up at six-thirty."

"All right," he had said. But he didn't know the whole story. His absolving her of any part she might have played in the articles only made her feel more guilt for what Jimmy still expected of her. And no matter how much certainty he put into his statements that her bill wouldn't work, she still believed in it. And she was going to fight for it, God willing.

26

Sue's study group was gathered around the big coffee table in front of the fireplace, eating cheese and crackers and drinking coffee, when Stephanie came in.

"Can you join us?" Sue invited.

"I'd love to, but I have to change for dinner. Maybe if I leave my door open I can garner a few of your pearls of wisdom."

"We'll talk loud. It's a good lesson."

Stephanie did leave her door open, then crossed the room to survey the contents of her closet. The banquet committee had asked all the women who would be sitting at the head tables to dress in red, white, or blue. Stephanie couldn't think what she had that would be appropriate. Then her eyes fell on her dark red jacquard silk dress. She loved the long sleeves with deep cuffs. And the high ruffle and soft bow at the neck would look good in front of an audience.

As she moved about her room, Sue's voice floated in. "Man's deepest need is love, and since God is love, we can only learn of love as we learn of God."

But when she went into the little bath off her bedroom she couldn't hear the study, so she flipped on her radio for the evening news. "The president today announced Operation Homecoming. The first of 142 POWs released by North Vietnam are on their way home."

That joyful announcement, however, was the end of the good news. The announcer moved on to the next story. "An IRA terrorist bomb exploded in a crowded London department store today, killing six people. This was another in a series of terrorist bombings that began with a similar attack at Christmas."

Sickened by the thought, Stephanie crossed the room to sit on her bed and pull on her stockings. ". . . Love is not a feeling; it is doing. Love is a continuing response outward." At the sound of Sue's voice, she turned to look at the open doorway. It was hard to believe terrorist bombings and studies of God's love were happening in the same world.

She didn't want to leave Sue's voice, but her shoes were in the bathroom. " . . . And in Tel Aviv today a busload of schoolchildren was attacked by Lebanese terrorists. The number of deaths is uncertain."

". . . Maturity is the prime characteristic of being able to give love; immaturity will take, but is incapable of giving."

". . . The president ordered the marines . . . "

She switched off her radio and slipped out the side door to meet Carlton without disturbing the study.

Since Stephanie and Carlton were both exceedingly verbal people, the silence in the plush burgundy interior of his car was most unusual. Stephanie wasn't sure whether it was because she couldn't think of anything to say or because she had too many things she wanted to say, and they just sort of bottlenecked in her brain.

For one thing, she felt a strange—well—almost shyness with Carlton, now that she had seen him in this revealing new light. The old armor-plated stereotype of his being tough and insensitive had been such a comfortable protection against anything he could do to her feelings. Now that had been shattered, and she felt exposed and vulnerable. Knowing what a caring person he was made her care so much more. She knew she was on very dangerous ground. Especially since it had been more than a week since she'd had a letter from David.

And as if that weren't enough, she was feeling almost battered inside—as if the tug-of-war between good and evil she listened to while getting ready had pulled at her physically.

Carlton looked at her in the warm, dim glow of light from the instrument panel. Then he reached out and took her hand. He squeezed it tightly for a moment, as if he knew she needed reassurance, then held it warmly all the way to the Riverside Inn. It was strange that one could feel both vulnerable and secure, battered and protected, at the same time.

The inn's ballroom glowed with gold lights from the myriad square crystal chandeliers spanning the ceiling and from the tall white candles in the center of each round table. From the side room where the VIPs were gathered before making their entrance, Stephanie looked in at the double row of long head tables on an ascending dais. Each was decked with red, white, and blue floral arrangements and napkins alternating those colors, folded like flowers in long-stemmed glasses, all in front of a bunting-draped background.

Carlton pinned a white corsage backed with blue ribbon on her shoulder, and she helped him with his red boutonniere. It seemed no detail had been overlooked by the committee.

The band struck up a rousing number with a martial beat, the bank of spotlights came on over the head tables, and the introductions began. The MC announced their names.

Stephanie and the attorney general entered, waving and smiling to their many friends and political supporters. She felt a stirring of pride and pleasure accompanied with the flickering thought that she could get used to this. Being the companion of one of the most important men in the room was pleasant. Could being a politician's wife be more pleasant than being a politician herself? But what about being a Scottish veterinarian's wife?

"The sixty-second annual banquet meeting of the Idaho President's Day Association, the oldest active organization of its kind in America, will now be in order." The committee chairman rapped his gavel.

Local Boy Scouts trooped the colors, and, with everyone else in the great hall, Stephanie placed her hand over her heart and pledged her allegiance to "one nation, under God, indivisible, with liberty and justice for all." As always, she felt as if she should conclude with "Amen." And again, she felt a surge of pride and renewed dedication to her country and to her job.

Then, in perfect keeping with her mood, the invocation recalled great men of faith who had led the country, and thanked God for them. Almost against her will she thought of the man beside her.

As a veteran of many a political dinner, Stephanie expected the menu to consist of tired roast beef and limp green beans. As a matter of fact, one of her earliest memories was of eating potatoes and gravy off her father's plate at a party fund-raiser. So her serving of succulent pink salmon filet in a delicate sauce surrounded by an assortment of crisp vegetables that included the unique spaghetti squash was all the more delightful because of its unexpectedness.

But Stephanie had to leave the last of her potatoes in herb sauce and join members of Idaho's congressional delegation who had flown in from Washington, DC, for the dinner. Their presence had been requested in the corner of the room inhabited by television newsmen with their cameras and bright lights on tall tripods.

When the congressmen and senators had been interviewed, the questioner turned to Stephanie and Carlton. "As major spokesmen of two of the most controversial

251

bills before the legislature this session, what outcome do you predict?"

Both spoke optimistically about the strength of their support and the wisdom of adopting their positions. The interviewer then turned to Carlton. "Your opposition to the housing subsidy bill has drawn some scathing attacks on your position. Would you like to comment on the charge that you simply don't understand about such needs as those depicted here?" He held the pictures from the morning paper before the camera.

"I understand more about those pictures than you might think," Carlton replied in all seriousness and yet with obvious good humor in his approach. "There is often more to pictures than meets the eye."

"I believe that's what many of your detractors are saying—that there wouldn't be such a brouhaha if there weren't some real problems there." He turned to Stephanie. "Representative Hamilton, as one of the most outspoken supporters of this measure, how do you feel about the controversy it has aroused?"

Here was her chance to make a heartfelt appeal for the legislation, but suddenly she didn't want to fight anymore—not to fight Carlton, at least. "Opposition is a healthy thing in a matter like this. Those of us supporting the bill have to be continually refining our position to be sure we are doing our best job. It's what makes the system work."

In the folds of her skirt, Carlton squeezed her hand. She hoped the cameras didn't catch that—or her momentary blush.

The news crew thanked them, and they returned to their seats for the last course. Again, Stephanie's appetite had a pleasant surprise. The band struck up a stirring number, and the lights dimmed—leaving only a pale candle glow in the chandeliers across the great ceiling. Then a large flambé table was wheeled in. As lines of waiters stood bearing trays of long-stemmed dishes of ice cream above their shoulders, the chef prepared the sauce for cherries jubilee. The final fanfare was his throwing powdered sugar on the flames to make a shower of sparks fly to the ceiling.

The pyrotechnical display over, the program began with a tribute to great American presidents of the past. "Though we honor these men today, they were often scorned by those who opposed them in their own day," the speaker said. "But they were true leaders, men who took the hard road and stood for what they believed in. May we always be worthy of the trust of carrying on the legacy of those who have labored before us. May we rededicate ourselves to the principles that have bound us together."

And then Carlton was introduced: "The attorney general of the sovereign state of Idaho, a man of courage and conviction, a relevant leader for our times, Mr. Carlton Jules Sperlin."

With a lump in her throat and what she hoped wasn't a foolish smile on her face, Stephanie listened to his words. Rather than treating his hearers to mere party rhetoric, Carlton had chosen to discuss one of the most serious problems facing the nation and the world.

"As I was preparing to come here tonight, I was thrilled, as I am sure you were, to hear that our POWs are coming home." He paused and smiled with the cheers from the audience. Then he held up his hand, and his face sobered. "But I was also shocked at the new reports of international terrorism, of innocent victims being slain in struggles they can't even understand."

He went on to discuss the nature of the terrorist as one who places himself outside all internationally accepted rules of justice.

"This is a difficult, complex problem, and I don't pretend to have all the answers. But let me propose some possibilities which we, as a party, could support as national policy." He offered several suggestions so logical that

Stephanie wondered why they hadn't been put into effect long ago.

Thunderous applause hailed the speech when he finished. Stephanie couldn't tell whether she was applauding harder or smiling harder, but she knew that moment would be with her forever as one of the high points of her life.

What a mind! she thought. *To be able to define, analyze, and propose solutions to the stickiest problems facing the world. This man should be secretary of state —he should be president!*

Stephanie stood with the others as the evening concluded with the singing of the state song. "Here we have Idaho . . . Silver and gold in the sunlight blaze, and romance lies in her name." But as she mouthed the words, her heart was asking where she would be this time next year. Would she be far away from her home and country in a new life with David? Or would she be right here working for good government? What did she *really* want? And most important of all, what did God want?

27

On Wednesday morning, House Bill 94 had its second reading, putting it in line for a third reading and floor debate the next day.

Thursday morning, the last of Jim's articles ran, making a subtle but impassioned appeal for passage of the bill. The housing conditions chronicled by the accompanying photographs were unbelievable. It was simply intolerable that any human being should live in such squalor. Even Stephanie, as strongly as she believed the program was necessary, was shocked by this evidence of need. It was unthinkable, impossible, that such conditions could exist in their state.

Surely, even if there were quibbles over the propriety of gambling as a new tax base, in this case the end would justify the means. Again she battled over the question of what was right but could find no answer that satisfied her.

As she had learned to do weeks ago when she needed privacy in the middle of the goldfish bowl, she stuck her fingers in her ears and bowed her head. *Lord, please speak clearly to me on this. If bingo and punchboards are a moral issue as Carlton claims, You must have guidance for me.*

She took her fingers out of her ears but heard no voice from heaven. She looked up at the dome, but there was no writing on the wall there. She was alone in the forest without a map.

It was too late to have her funding proposal written into the bill. But maybe she could propose it as an amendment from the floor. She'd have to check the rules. Or she could break it as a news story, get the idea talked about before the final debate. She looked at the voting board. If only God would flash a red or green light at her.

Well, she had determined to hold off until she was sure what was right, and at the moment she wasn't sure of anything. So she would wait. No matter how strong the temptation to spring her secret weapon, she would wait for assurance.

She was still sitting at her desk, trying to dig her way out of a deluge of paperwork, when Alan came in.

"I've got your info on military alcohol treatment programs. Want to go over it now?"

"Did you—uh—get anything on anyone in particular?" She dreaded his answer but knew she had to face it.

"No. I guess that would be classified or something. But I learned that the treatment is first class. Most of the programs in use in private industry have been adopted from the military."

"Thanks, Alan. That sounds good. I'll look this over and let you know if I need anything else." She studiously kept any note of relief out of her voice.

Alan left, and she scanned his notes: transfer to alcohol ward while under medical treatment for wounds . . . shakes first . . . withdrawal syndrome after three days . . . Valium administered . . . multidiscipline therapy, small groups, psycho-drama, films . . . Alcoholics Anonymous basis of program . . . 78 percent recovery rate . . .

She closed her eyes. *Thank You, Lord, that Carlton was one of the 78 percent. Thank You for being there with him when I couldn't be. Thank You, thank You.*

Her meditations ended abruptly as the crash of the

gavel and the speaker's voice resounded in the chambers. "House be in order."

She pulled a single sheet of typewritten notes out of the bottom of her basket. The notes she had written after Carlton's revelation. She stuck it in the file and buried the whole thing under a stack of papers.

The business progressed rapidly to the eleventh order: third reading of bills. The overflow audience in the gallery seemed to lean forward as one body when Representative Harding, as the bill's sponsor, rose to open the debate.

"Mr. Speaker, I ask unanimous consent to dispense with further reading of the bill."

"You have heard the request for unanimous consent. Is there an objection?"

There were no objections. Representative Harding proceeded to talk his listeners through the bill. "You see that this is designed to interfere as little as possible with local programs. The agency is to be a facilitator, not to impose rigid rules and regulations. At page five, line twenty-seven, you see we provide criteria for evaluation.

"Moving on to page seven, line forty-four, the bill provides the umbrella of due process protection for participants in the program."

As Steph listened, she hoped her fellow legislators had really heard the chaplain's prayer that morning. "We lay before You the work we have done. Where we have been uncaring, forgive us; where we have been careful, we thank You. Help us, O Lord, to be instruments to build a better world." *Help them catch the vision,* she prayed.

"So that's pretty much a rundown of the bill," Harding concluded.

The speaker recognized a member on the front row.

"Mr. Speaker" —Representative Jackson launched the opposition debate— "having good, clean, housing for the poor is a very emotional issue. Now, I submit that the measure before us today would be good for the banker, good

257

for the builder, good for the landlord—but is it good public policy? Is it good for the taxpayer who has to pick up the tab? Is it good for education and other programs that would have funds taken from them to finance this program?

"It simply isn't possible to cut funds that are necessary to maintain the basic infrastructure—roads, water systems, sewers. That means we would have to cut monies to education, state hospitals, the aging.

"I submit that the burden this program would place on the state budget is one that simply cannot be borne. Therefore I urge you to vote against it."

Stephanie had to admit to the truth of his argument. As she had realized long ago at the Farragut festival, somebody had to pay when you handed out freebies.

Fran was next to speak in favor of the bill. "There are a few charges I should respond to as far as the fiscal impact of this measure. This will generate revenue! Builders will profit, then pay taxes on their profit. Improved property values will increase taxes for the landlord. Let me remind you that every dollar spent in the housing industry turns over seven times. This is the best stimulation our economy can receive."

Their side was putting up a valiant fight. But Stephanie could sense the sentiment of those in the room—both on the floor and in the gallery—swinging away from them as the next speaker continued the debate.

"Mr. Speaker, I oppose this bill on the grounds that in order to do much good, the size of the program must be enormous and, therefore, the cost staggering. By the time you buy the property and level what's there, the ground is far too expensive for low income housing. And I would remind you that the fact that this is low rent housing doesn't make it low cost building."

Stephanie felt herself sinking lower in her seat.

Then the Speaker was saying, "Is there further debate? Hearing none, will the lady from district eleven please close the debate?"

Taking a deep breath, Stephanie rose sturdily to her feet. Her hunter green ultrasuede dress glowed under the lights, and her emerald green eyes blazed with the strength of her belief. "Mr. Speaker, ladies and gentlemen of the House, I think this discussion has gotten far afield. I would like to bring us back again to focus on the purpose of this bill.

"Our most precious possession is our children. The future lies in their hands. We must keep their future bright if we are to keep our own future bright. Having to live in a house without adequate lighting is not conducive to bright futures for anyone."

She caught Jim's eye where he sat at the front desk reserved for print media. His smile urged her on, and her voice rang with conviction. "It is our sacred trust to work to improve the quality of life of our children, of all our citizens, and of our future. Therefore, I urge your support to pass this bill. Thank you, ladies and gentlemen."

When she sat down she realized her knees were trembling and her mouth was dry.

"Is there further debate?" the Speaker asked. "Hearing none, debate is closed. The question is, Shall House Bill 94 pass? The clerk will unlock the machine and members will record their vote."

Stephanie firmly pushed the aye button on her desk, as if a forceful vote could carry extra weight. A glance at the flashing red and green lights on the board told her this was to be a very close race.

"Has every member voted? Are there any members wishing to change their vote?" A few lights flashed, but Stephanie couldn't keep track of the count. It seemed that the red outshone the green, but she hoped that was her own nervousness making it appear that way. The secretary read the votes that were paired by legislators absent for good cause, and again lights flashed on the board.

"The clerk will lock the machine and record the vote.

Roll call shows twenty-eight aye, thirty-nine no. The majority having voted against, House Bill 94 fails to pass."

Stephanie heard the results as if through a haze, as if her own refusal to accept them could keep them from being final.

Then Representative Jackson, who had been first to speak against the bill, rose for a point of personal privilege and requested that the House be at ease. "In honor of a long-standing tradition in these chambers, when a member loses a hard-fought, high-profile bill—" laughter rippled from those who knew what was coming "—especially, I might add, when it is that member's maiden voyage with a bill that goes down to defeat, we think it appropriate that that member publicly eat crow."

At that he produced a cocky, wooden blackbird perched on a flower-decked roost.

To the accompaniment of laughter and applause the crow was hung on Representative Hamilton's microphone where it would stay until some other member proved himself worthy of such ignominy.

The last thing in the world Stephanie felt like doing at that moment was making jokes, but it wouldn't do to appear to be a poor sport. She rose with a forced smile, switched on her microphone, and patted the creature on his fat little head. "Mr. Speaker, ladies and gentlemen —caw, caw."

The House showed its approval of her good-natured response, and cameras recorded the event for the six o'clock news.

The House then moved on to the next order of business, but Stephanie, feeling a mixture of failure, chagrin, and frustration, didn't follow the proceedings. In the end, it hadn't been her strategy, Carlton's logic, or Jim's journalism that decided the matter. It had been simply a matter of dollars and cents—the state could not afford the program. And she had, by her own volition, held back the solution to the whole thing. She had been a traitor to her own, hard-fought cause.

Doubts assailed her with more force than the wind-driven snow on Baldy had. Had she held back on the funding proposal because it was God's leading to do so or because her feelings for Carlton had undermined her determination? Had she done the courageous thing, taken a bold step of faith? Or had she weakly abandoned people who needed her because in the final analysis she couldn't stand up against her heart?

Lord, You know I'm trying to do what's right. Please help me know. I feel so lost. I need assurance that I was acting in love—love for You above love for anyone or anything else.

The session was adjourned and House members moved all around her, rushing to the usual appointments and luncheons, but Stephanie just sat there. She would have liked to move too, but she was paralyzed with depression. She had worked so long, so hard for this. All her hopes for really accomplishing something worthwhile had been pinned on this bill. Now, in defeat, she understood glaringly how much this legislation really meant to her.

She thought of all the work that had gone into drafting and promoting the bill. She thought of all the phone calls and speeches she had made. Were all her words merely sounding brass or tinkling cymbal? she wondered. But surely she had spoken in love.

Or was it true, as Carlton kept telling her, that if she loved people she wouldn't want to change them? That love would help them just as they were—like the sick or drunken man Carlton helped on the street. She struggled with the idea that her motives had been at fault. The bill had failed, she had failed, but love hadn't failed. Love never failed.

She must choose the way of love: love for the whole world, love for those around her, love for one special man.

But love only as it flowed from Christ through her—not just sentimental do-gooding. Now, in defeat, she could see how in striving for her own definition of success she had failed to seek God's definition. She saw how much she needed to learn and grow. Her new commitment to God had been just the beginning.

Show me, Lord. Open me more and more to Your love and Your guidance—help me grow in You. Lord, I know I haven't spent enough time with You, listened to You, sought Your guidance. Forgive me for seeking my own goals in my own strength. Help me to seek Your kind of success, Your kind of love. Help me first of all to love You more.

Fran walked over and gave her a consoling hug. "Coming to lunch?"

Stephanie shook her head. And then, as she forced a smile at her friend, a little of the assurance she had prayed for came. She was still in the dark tunnel of stunning defeat, but she now saw the light ahead, and—most important of all—was sure of her contact with the Source of all light.

"Would it help any if I told you the first one you lose is the hardest?" Fran asked.

"Probably not, but thanks for trying."

"Don't you think something to eat would help restore your perspective, if not your spirits?"

"I'm OK, Fran. I just need to think a bit. I'll clear up some things here and then get some coffee or something."

Fran nodded and went out, leaving Stephanie in the empty chambers. Mechanically she started putting notes, clippings, studies, the results of weeks of research and planning into files. At the moment she couldn't bear the final defeat of putting them in the wastebasket.

At the bottom of the stack were her clippings of Jim's series. She spread them out before her. They covered the top of her desk. She looked at the faces of the people: children, elderly, middle-aged. She saw the fear and despair in their eyes, the blank look of utter hopelessness. In her own defeat she felt complete empathy with these people. She knew the hopelessness of wanting to help and being unable to; of having tried and failed. She closed her eyes. *Lord, show me the light again. It's flickering.*

The she realized she wasn't alone. She was aware of a spicy masculine scent. Her heart leaped at the thought that Carlton had come to her.

"Sorry about that, kid, but we did our best."

Jim. She opened her eyes. "You certainly did your part. No one could have produced a more powerful piece of journalism."

"Now, about our unfinished business . . ."

She nodded, unsmiling. "I haven't forgotten. Alan gave me the last of his research this morning."

Jim held out his hand.

"No, the rest of it's at home." Had she purposely left Alan's first report at Sue's? "Come up this evening after dinner. Sue has a meeting at church, so we can go over it privately."

He regarded her suspiciously for a moment. "No backpedaling. The drinking age bill had its second reading today. We're down to the wire for this story to make its impact."

She watched the back of his head disappear out the door. *If only I could be sure what kind of impact he wants to make.* Carlton had once said that it was fine for the press to be an adversary to get the truth but not an adversary to destroy. Which way would Jim use her information?

In a moment of weakness, she had once yielded to social pressure and ridden the giant roller coaster at the state fair. It was years ago, when she was only a teenager, but she could still recall vividly the absolute horror of that first awful drop—the panic when she realized that her commitment was past recall. She was on the ride, and there was no going back. Up and up and up the precipitous incline to the moment of cresting the peak. Then the world fell away beneath her with the terror of crashing to certain death . . . jerking around corners first to the right, then to the left . . . then another dread-filled climb to a summit even higher . . . on and on, rushing, falling, jerking around the endless track—her punishment for the choice she had made.

And in her promise to Jim she had committed to a track equally inexorable. Even if she could stop the roller coaster, the consequence could be falling backward to a fate more horrible than going on.

She tried to pray, but got no answers. Did her commitment to God alter her commitment to Jim? If so, which way? Did it now mean that she wouldn't consider divulging Carlton's information? Or that it was more important to keep her promise to Jim? If she had thought putting God first was going to make everything easy, she saw how wrong she'd been. The determination to do right was easy. Knowing *what* was right was another matter completely.

28

Stephanie spent the time between her TV dinner meal and Jim's arrival pacing the floor. In spite of the blazing fire on the hearth, her hands were icy with nerves. She simply didn't know how she was going to handle this situation. The more she prayed, *Help me,* the farther away the light at the end of the tunnel seemed.

Desperate to take her mind off her dilemma, she picked up Kathryn's journal from the coffee table. It fell open to the late 1930s. She skimmed several pages without taking much in. Then a story caught her attention. Her grandmother recounted Elizabeth's struggle with commitment and trust. She felt God was telling her to give a set of antique jewelry to the missionaries. It had been an audacious thing to do. It made no sense in human terms. Yet she had felt sure of God's guidance, so she followed in blind faith.

When Jim's ring sounded, she jumped in surprise. *Even when the doctor sets the date, a death in the family is always a shock.* She opened the door.

Jim's jaunty greeting died on his lips when he saw her face. "Who died?"

"If I knew, I might not be so worried." She picked up the manila folder on the coffee table and sat on the sofa. "Why do I feel as if I'm about to commit suicide?"

Jimmy gave a forced-sounding laugh. "You made a bargain, you got your part, now payment's due. What's so heavy about that?"

Almost without thinking Stephanie said, "Yes, I had my twenty-five years of pleasure. Now you've come for my soul."

"What?"

"*Faustus.* I wouldn't expect you to recognize it." But Stephanie recognized it. As clear as if the heavens had opened up she understood. She knew exactly how her mother must have felt when she placed the family jewels on the altar. The "good angel" and the "evil angel" had been struggling for Stephanie's soul—her future. But no more. Her English professor had said that the tragedy of Faustus was not that it was that way, but that it might have been otherwise. Faustus could have repented of his bargain even at the eleventh hour. So could she. One could always repent of evil. At last, she had her answer.

The folder in her hand was stained with dark spots of perspiration where she had been gripping it. Getting slowly to her feet without looking at Jim, she tore the file and its contents neatly in two and threw the papers on the fire, making it a kind of sacrificial altar. As the notes went up in flame and smoke, she felt redeemed.

"Wouldn't betray the boyfriend, huh?" Jim said in barely controlled anger.

She turned to him. "No. I wouldn't betray myself."

Then the full meaning of the word they had both used struck her. "So it would have been a betrayal if I'd given you the story! You were lying all along when you said you wanted to bolster his image. You're working *against* Carlton."

"Hey, news is news. I print it and let the chips fall where they may."

"No. I don't believe that. You purposely made Carlton look bad with that housing feature, and you wanted to do it again with this. Why? What do you have against him?"

266

"I haven't got anything against Carlton. I'm just doing my job."

"Like you were just doing your job when you printed that picture of me at the antiwar protest? That was no mistake, was it?"

Stephanie put her hands over her eyes at the thought of what Jim could have done with this story. "Alcoholic AG Battles Booze Law, Ex-Lush Calls for Tough Laws," and similar headlines swam in her head.

At the door, Jim turned back to her. "I figured you for having more savvy than that. Few politicians can afford to make an enemy of the press."

The chill of fear his words sent through her was short-lived. A surge of buoyancy washed everything else before it. She wanted to laugh and shout and dance about the room. She had lost the housing bill. She had made a dangerous enemy. She had turned her back on long-sought power when it was within her grasp. But she had done the right thing, the courageous thing. She had always sought to act with courage. Now she understood. Courage didn't necessarily mean pressing blindly on. Courage could mean being able to say, "I was wrong." And make amends for your mistake.

She was through the tunnel; she had reached the light. Her career might be in shambles, but her heart was aglow. She had to share this, or she'd burst. She was shaking so with excitement she could hardly punch out the numbers on the phone. *Be home, oh, please be home,* she pleaded.

"Sperlin residence." The cool voice of Anne Smith burst Stephanie's bubble. Wordlessly she replaced the receiver.

When the telephone rang some time later, Sue was home to answer it. "For you, Steph. Long distance."

"David!" She rushed to the phone. That was what she needed—to hear David's soft Scots brogue reminding her that there was a place of escape for her.

But it wasn't David. Her brother's voice greeted her. "Hi, sis."

"Boyd! It's so good to hear from you! Are you calling from Vegas? How are you?"

"Yes, I'm in Vegas." He paused. "No sense beating around the bush. I guess I'm not so good. I'm broke."

"Broke? What happened to your job? Did something go wrong on the ranch?"

"There was a little—uh—dispute over a card game, but I don't want to go into that over the phone. That's not really what I called about. Sis, can you loan me some money?"

"Of course I will, Boyd. But I don't understand. Mom's been worrying about you. She called a few days ago."

"Listen, don't tell the folks. It'll just upset them. I can get this all straightened out if you can loan me some money."

"How much do you need?"

"Three grand."

"Three thousand dollars!" Surely she had misunderstood him.

"Don't yell at me, sis. There's no one else I can call."

She did some rapid calculations. She had a little in the bank, but not that much. Maybe she could borrow from Sue. Or—yes, she knew Carlton would help her in an emergency, no matter what. "Yes, Boyd. I can raise the money, but I have to know what it's for."

"Yeah, that's fair. Like I said, there was a little trouble over a card game in the bunkhouse. I know it was a dumb thing to do, but I lost more than I could pay. So I thought I could make it at a craps table in Vegas. I didn't."

"But, Boyd, you've never been a gambler. You were always so careful with your money."

"Yeah, and believe me, I will be after this. But it sort of gets hold of you. I kept thinking I'd win next time. The less I could afford it, the more I wanted to play."

"But what will you do if I send you the money?"

"Pay my debts and get out of here. I said I'd learned my lesson. Three thousand will leave enough to buy a bus ticket home. I'll get a job. I should be able to swing going back to college next fall."

"A *bus* ticket! You mean you sold your car?"

He hesitated, and Stephanie could sense how much her brother hated telling her this. "No. I lost it in a game too."

"Boyd, I think you've lost more than your money and your car. How long has it been since you've prayed?"

"About five minutes. But before that, about five years. You hit the nail on the head, sis, but it's OK now."

Suddenly it was all too much. She started to cry.

"Hey, drippy eyes, I said it's OK now. Honest it is."

"Yes, I believe you. I'm just so relieved. So happy for you—and for me too. Boyd, I'd lost touch too, so I know exactly what you're talking about." She paused for a long sniff. "I'll send you the money. The folks will be so happy to have you home."

"Thanks. That's great. Now I can call Mom."

"Right. And we'll pray for each other, huh?"

"We sure will. Thanks, sis."

"I love you, Boyd."

She was still staring at the phone when Sue tapped on her door. "Bad news?"

Stephanie started to say yes, then broke into a broad smile. "No. It was good news. Terrific news. It was an answer to prayer, only I just now realized it."

She patted the bed for Sue to sit down. She told her as briefly as she could about her struggles over her funding scheme, her debates with Carlton, her decision to hold back until she was sure, and then her uncertainty when the bill failed over the economic issue.

"But it took my own brother being an object lesson to show me how really serious the gambling thing is. Boyd was always such a good kid—if it could get hold of him, think what could happen to someone who was weak anyway, or who didn't have a Christian background."

She thought a moment before she went on. The events of the day seemed to be forming a pattern. She told Sue how she had decided at the eleventh hour not to help Jim in what would have been a smear campaign against Carlton.

"But the thing is, Sue, on both of these issues, I didn't *know*. I prayed a lot, and I did what I thought—hoped—was right, but the answers didn't come until afterwards. I don't understand. Why were the answers so late? Why did God hold off?"

Sue smiled. "I know what you mean. It's hard, isn't it? But God wants to teach us to rely on His guidance. Sometimes you have to act in faith first. It would be too easy if you had all the answers first. The Bible's full of examples. Remember, the multitude sat down in groups for a picnic, and Jesus said the blessing *before* the loaves and fish multiplied. It wouldn't have required any faith for the disciples to direct the crowd or for the people to obey if Jesus had filled the baskets first."

Stephanie nodded. "I think I'm getting it, but it'll take a while."

Sue stood up and pushed Stephanie back on the bed. "Sleep on it. You look beat."

29

Steph, you've got to listen to this debate, she lectured herself for the third time in five minutes the next morning. *The fact that you hardly slept last night and that your head is splitting in two clear down to your navel doesn't alter your sworn duty.*

Then her eyes rested on the crested ecru paper on her desk once more: "The attorney general requests your presence at the press conference to be held on the capitol steps at twelve o'clock noon."

If the conference is about the drinking age bill, then it's all the more important that you listen to this, she told herself sternly. But her brain was in rebellion. Yesterday's events had been simply too much, and today was boding to be even worse.

"Representative Hamilton, will you please register your vote." The speaker's firm voice broke through her torpor.

Hot with humiliation at the reprimand in his voice, Stephanie pushed the nay button on her panel. That added the red light by her name on the voting board to the majority tally refusing to lower the minimum drinking age.

Congratulations, Carlton, she thought. *It's nice to see the good guys win once in a while.* She'd tell him that in person—if she ever saw him again. Well, of course she'd see him at the news conference in half an hour, but that wasn't exactly what she had in mind.

She didn't really understand why this vote added to her depression. It was a victory for the right—so she should be happy. But it just seemed to contribute to her sense of emptiness. Then she saw the look of satisfaction on the face of the representative who carried the debate, and she understood.

She hadn't worked for the side as she had promised to do. She had really funked this one. She could have had a sense of accomplishment to balance the void over the housing bill defeat if only she'd followed through on her promise to Carlton—if she'd acted in love. Instead she'd been petty—acted out of spite and a desire for revenge. It was her loss.

Woodenly she followed Fran to the press conference, still mystified over the purpose of the occasion. The media was there en masse—radio, television, newspaper—all with cameras, tape recorders, and notepads ready. Stephanie was relieved to notice that Jim was avoiding her as studiously as she wished to avoid him. When she saw Representative Harding, she knew the event must have something to do with the housing bill, but his baffled reply to her question showed her he knew as little as she did.

The bells of Saint Michael's Cathedral, a block away, tolled twelve o'clock, and the attorney general came out the ceremonial entrance, followed by Special Deputy Attorney Smith. For an awful moment Stephanie thought they might be going to announce their engagement, then realized the ridiculousness of that—it might be earth-shattering to her, but it was hardly something one called a press conference for.

Then the guilt that was almost a reflex struck her. *She* was engaged. Why shouldn't Carlton be? And she knew she had to sort things out. Simply running from one meeting to another so fast she couldn't think or feel was not an adequate way to deal with the question of love and marriage.

For the moment she turned back to the conference.

Carlton greeted everyone and thanked them for coming, then got to the issue. "It has been brought most forcefully to my attention, and to the attention of the public, that there are citizens of our state living in substandard housing." He paused and flashed his priceless smile in a way that made the foregoing statement sound like a bit of self-deprecating humor. His audience returned his smile.

"The problem, however, apparently goes beyond merely substandard housing to conditions of actual danger." From the slim leather case he carried he produced one of the newspaper photo stories and held it up. "Broken windows, crumbling flooring, decrepit plumbing—these things aren't merely unsafe. They are illegal.

"Conditions such as these existing in our state mean that someone isn't doing his job. As the chief law enforcement officer of the state of Idaho, I intend to see that the law is enforced."

The cameras rolled, and a number of spectators who had stopped by on their lunch hour applauded.

"Mr. Garson, the chief building inspector for Ada County, is here with us, as well as the Boise city attorney and the county prosecutor. These men are ready for action."

Stephanie glanced in Jim's direction and noticed he looked distinctly nervous.

At that moment a large Greyhound bus pulled through the circle drive and stopped at the foot of the steps.

"Ladies and gentlemen, it is my intention to launch a statewide campaign to see that building safety codes are strictly enforced. I invite you all to accompany us now to inspect these buildings that the newspaper has identified as being in the Boise valley. This afternoon my office will contact building inspectors around the state to initiate similar actions in other areas. If the inspectors are not doing their jobs, or if bribery is indicated, my office will launch an investigation.

"We will be led today by the individual who brought

all this to public attention by documenting the problems, James Linzler of United Press International."

Jim, who had been edging toward the back of the crowd, dropped his pencil and swore. All eyes, and several cameras, were on him as the attorney general stood with an arm extended in the newsman's direction.

"James, will you please tell the bus driver where to take us to find the first of these houses?" As if choreographed, the bus doors swung open.

Jim stood rooted to the cement.

"Well, Jim? We have a crowd of very busy people here. Let's not infringe on their good will by keeping them waiting." Carlton's voice was calm and pleasant, but it carried just the slightest edge of goading.

Jim looked about him like a trapped wild animal, then muttered something.

"I'm sorry, we couldn't hear what you said." Carlton walked over to Jim and held the microphone out to him.

"I can't."

"What do you mean, you can't?"

"I wasn't there."

"Weren't there? You wrote the stories. Your photographer took the pictures."

For the first time Jim brightened, as if he saw a crack in the door. "Sam, you here? Where'd you get these pictures?"

Sam, his camera over his shoulder, and his upper lip wiggling as if his mustache tickled his nose, nodded. "I took them." Then he shrugged. "I took them out of the morgue of wire service photos."

The spectators' gasp was thunderous.

It was a brilliant piece of angling, and Carlton had his fish hooked. "You mean these pictures aren't current photos? Aren't even necessarily from this state?"

Sam shrugged again.

Carlton turned to Jim. "You identified specific towns in your story."

Jim did his best to pass it off with his old nonchalance. "So I exaggerated. It was a good story angle."

Another reporter stepped up. "I've heard rumors that Arnold Bartmess, your brother-in-law, wants to run for attorney general in two years. Does that have anything to do with your particular choice of angle?"

"None whatsoever." But the voice lacked conviction.

As the media turned their mikes from the AG to Jim, Stephanie stepped over to Carlton with a sense of déjà vu. It seemed that she was always having revelations about him on the capitol steps. "Did you know all along?"

Carlton shook his head. "Only suspected. We did some checking, but couldn't get absolute proof."

"So you decided to call his bluff. But what if you'd been wrong?"

"I wasn't bluffing. I was prepared to follow through and deal with the situation just as I said."

"That was really brilliant." She said it as much to herself as to Carlton. "What will happen to Jim now?"

"His editor will probably give him a considerably different beat. One with new scope for his story angles."

They were still laughing when a reporter asked Carlton for an interview and Fran reminded Steph of a committee meeting. She looked back only once—just in time to see Anne walk up and put her arm through Carlton's.

So, after the high drama played out on the capitol steps it was all over. The drinking age bill had failed, the housing subsidy had failed, and resort gaming hadn't seen the light of day. Carlton had been right on every issue. She felt as if it were Christmas night—all the presents opened, all the food eaten—just torn paper and dirty dishes everywhere as evidence of the past joy.

Several weeks of work still faced the legislature. Then Stephanie would put all this behind her and move to Scotland. Why did the thought make her feel so empty? She decided to go home and write David a long letter. That would make her feel better.

30

Stephanie got up late the next morning and found Sue ecstatic over a bouquet Bob had wired her. It was their anniversary, and Sue was starry-eyed with romance.

Stephanie could think of nothing more unromantic than studying proposed legislation, but that was the job that had to be done. Oddly enough, she soon found the very tedium of the task to be a solace after the drama of the past few days. There was something so down-to-earth about studying fish and game laws. Stephanie found herself completely absorbed in the question of how best to protect the spawning grounds of the chinook salmon when the phone rang several hours later.

"Hello, Steph." Carlton's voice right in her ear sounded so intimate that she pulled away from the phone. "I hope I didn't catch you at a really busy time, but Anne and I have something to tell you—well—show you, really."

She froze, at the excitement in his voice even more than at his words.

"Oh?"

"Could we drop by to see you for a minute?"

She started to refuse. She was studying a bill. She needed to wash her hair. Any old excuse would do—or maybe just a simple no. With all her heart she wanted to run from this moment, but it had to be met. "You sound like a celebration. I'll put the teakettle on." The only problem now was deciding which cup should have the arsenic in it.

Sue stuck her head around the corner. "I'm going shopping and then out to dinner with some friends. Want to come too?"

"No, thanks, Sue. I have some friends coming over." Friends, lovers, enemies—it seemed to be all the same. At least she could comb her hair and put on some lipstick. She had no intention of receiving her death blow looking like a corpse. When she committed her life and her relationships to God, she hadn't expected increased closeness between Carlton and Anne to result, nor for it to upset her so.

Sooner than she could have thought possible, she was opening the front door.

Radiant and flushed from the crisp air, Anne swept into the room. "Well, congratulate me. I finally talked him around."

Carlton grinned at Anne and raised his eyebrow in a way that made Stephanie decide to put the arsenic in her own cup. "But it took her long enough to do it." With a flourish he presented Stephanie with a stack of neatly typed papers. "Here you are, with love. You may consider it a Valentine's present."

Stephanie automatically held out her hands for the papers. "But I don't understand."

"Of course you don't." Anne spoke in her most no nonsense manner. "Carlton, you aren't making any sense at all. It's no wonder I had to argue with you over every word in the thing. It's high time this state had a woman attorney general so we could get some efficiency back in the office."

As if it were her own home, Anne led the way to the dining table. "Come here and let me explain." Taking the papers from Stephanie, she spread them out. "This is a substitute bill to provide for the building of low income housing through rehabilitation tax credits. It's a simple procedure to implement, because it merely requires passing the provision in the tax code. It requires no bunglesome state agencies because it is done entirely through the private sector. It results in no cost to the state because any revenue lost through the tax credits will later be made up as the rehabilitated structures increase in value. You will undoubtedly want to sponsor the bill—but it can't come through your committee because we are now past the thirty-fifth legislative day, and bills may only be introduced by State Affairs, Finance, or Judiciary and Rules. I recommend you take it to Finance."

With a toss of her head that said as clearly as the spoken word, "The defense rests," Anne placed a copy of the bill in Stephanie's hands.

Stephanie looked from the papers to Carlton. "You did this? But why?"

He wrinkled his forehead. "We can't have people living in ghettos. And if we don't propose something sensible, some neophyte bleeding heart may come along next session and stir up a lot of trouble with some harebrained idea of taking a bulldozer to substandard buildings."

Speechless, Stephanie sat at the table and read through the document in her hands. "Let me get this straight. This is a bill providing for a tax credit for any private builder who wants to fix up old houses or apartment buildings. And there's an added tax credit for the landlord if the rents are kept in the low income bracket?"

Anne nodded with satisfaction. "She's got it. Want a place on my staff when I become attorney general?"

Stephanie grinned. "I like this. I never really did want to demolish historic buildings. Now all the hand-hewn masonry and carved cornices and moldings—things like that—can be preserved, but safe plumbing and wiring and sound roofing installed too."

She was still reading when she realized Carlton had crossed the room to Anne. Stephanie looked up just in time to see him put his arm around Anne and kiss her.

"Thanks for everything, Anne. You've been a great help."

Anne moved toward the door. "Anytime, Carlton. Just call. I can always use an excuse to get out of the rut."

"You're sure you won't accept a permanent post?"

"Not on your life. But don't you forget my offer, Steph."

Grinning, Carlton held the door for her. "Not on *your* life. I plan to make her a better offer."

"And I have a plane to catch." Anne left with a wave.

Stephanie was still open-mouthed when Carlton turned to her. "What was that?"

"That was Anne Smith making an exit. Couldn't you tell?"

"But I thought . . . that is, it looked like . . . well . . . you and Anne . . ."

He crossed the room, took her hands, and led her to the sofa before the fire. "Yes, I rather thought you might think that. As a matter of fact, I think Anne might have thought something like that too, until she got a second look at things and decided she'd rather have my office than my name."

"That must have been a blow to your ego."

"I seem to have survived intact."

"I've often wondered how you've managed to survive intact—intact and unattached, that is."

"Ah, yes, well, you've heard no doubt that the law is a jealous mistress. It takes a very special lady to be willing to put up with a man who must submit to the demands of my job."

"And Anne couldn't?"

"Anne is a lovely lady, but we really don't have anything important in common."

"Nothing in common? You're both lawyers—"

"That's what I do, not what I am. I said anything important."

"Like what?"

279

He pursued his lips for a moment, considering. "Like teamwork. Working together—praying together, because you believe in something—like the kids at the Elks or low income housing." He pointed to the bill on the table. "I think we work much better as colleagues than as opponents." He drew her to him. "But most of all, what I've never had with anyone else that I do with you is being in love."

She sat there just drifting in infinite comfort. Then after a time she somehow made the effort to put her mind in gear again. She couldn't just drift into this. She had to think. She pulled herself slightly upright but not away from him. There was no doubt what he was getting at. This was the moment of truth. She had to tell him.

"Carlton, I have to tell you something." She held out her left hand. It was the most difficult thing she had ever done in her life. "This ring—I told you it was a Christmas present—it was. But it's also an engagement ring."

Carlton's face was suddenly stormy. "Who? Why didn't you tell me?"

"David Fraser. He's in Scotland now. I . . . ." She floundered helplessly. It seemed impossible to explain.

"Do you love him?" The words seemed more of a challenge than a question.

"I—I don't know. I thought I did, but I haven't seen him for such a long time."

"I could never have thought you capable of such deceit, Stephanie. Of such cruelty."

She could bear his anger, but the pain she saw in his face was too much. She turned away. "Please, Carlton, I didn't mean for it to be like this. Everything just got out of hand."

"So, history repeats itself."

"What?" She turned back toward him, her brow furrowed.

"My grandfather lost his heart to your grandmother. She chose a Scotsman instead too." He got clumsily to his feet and strode across the room.

Stephanie felt he was dragging her heart with him. "Wait, please."

But the door slammed behind him.

Three weeks later the Idaho legislature passed the tax credit for rehabilitating substandard housing. The next day the gavel rang through the chambers as they adjourned *sine die,* freeing Stephanie to go to Scotland.

Since that awful night when she told Carlton about David, she had seen the attorney general no closer than across the capitol rotunda. Whenever he happened to come into view, her heart lurched so loudly she felt as if he could hear her. But he never once looked her direction. Twice she tried leaving messages with his secretary, but he didn't return them.

There was nothing left in Idaho for Stephanie. Or was there? Why couldn't she simply go back to the plan she'd had for her life before everything got confused with men? She could continue in the legislature, build her political base. When the time was right she could run for US Congress. The sky was the limit, and she had her foot on the first rung.

Somehow the picture she painted didn't sound as thrilling as she used to imagine such a scenario would be. But at least she had a choice.

She was just back at Sue's with her arms full of books and papers from her freshly cleaned-out desk when the phone gave its familiar jangle.

"Mom!" Stephanie greeted her mother's voice. "How are you?

Elizabeth went on at some length about how marvelous both she and Eliot felt, how complete his recovery was, and how happy they were to hear that Boyd was settling in working on the family farm with Clarey and Tommy. "Thank you so much for helping him, dear. I feel so bad that he didn't feel free to turn to us—but I'm so glad you were there. I think I was too hard on both of you."

"Oh, Mom, don't blame yourself." Stephanie longed to reach out to her mother. She heard the note of unsureness in Elizabeth's voice, and she wanted to comfort her. "I'm sorry too, Mom. I'm sorry about being so—so—brittle toward you in the past. I realize now you were just trying to help."

"Yes, I was. But I see now that I overdid it. Ever since you were born in the middle of that awful blackout, I've wanted everything to be perfect for you. I loved you so much. I didn't want you to have to go through all the hard struggles I did."

"Yes, I read about all of that in Grammie's journal. I think I understand so much better now."

"I hope so. It wasn't that you weren't good enough, you know. It was never that. It was that you were so wonderful I was afraid I wouldn't do a good enough job raising you. I always believed one had to work so hard at everything. But it seemed the harder I worked on you, the more I drove you away. Then you went off on your own and did just great."

"Well, I didn't do too great on my own, Mother." She told her about her experience on Bald Mountain and her commitment to the Lord.

"Oh, my dear. I'm so glad. It's the key to everything." A loud sniff came down the wire. "I know I should quote Scripture or say something profound, but I can't think of a thing. I'm just so happy!"

After another sniff Elizabeth said, "Your father wants to talk to you. 'Bye now. I love you."

"I love you too, Mom."

Then Eliot's deep voice came on. "Steph, congratulations on the fine job you've done there."

"Thanks, Dad, but I don't feel I've done so great."

"That's not what I hear—I've been talking to Bill Harding and Frank Detweiller. They tell me I've got a hard act to follow when I come back."

The line went silent for a moment as Stephanie registered what her father had just said. She swallowed. "Oh, Dad, that's great." She hoped her enthusiasm didn't sound forced. "I'm so glad you're well enough to come back."

And she really was. But it did narrow her options.

31

On March 29 the last ground combat troops left Vietnam, and Stephanie finished packing her last bag. Tomorrow she would board the plane to Glasgow with very mixed emotions. But the person going with her held no such reservations.

Kathryn clapped her hands like a girl, her eyes shining. "Just think. By this time tomorrow we'll be in Scotland. It seems like it took Merrick and me about a month to get there. I don't remember exactly how long it was, but we took the train clear across the United States. Then we sailed on the *Carpathia*—that was the ship that rescued some of the people on the *Titanic* later—then a train again the length of England."

She closed her eyes, and Stephanie turned back to the packing.

A few moments later Kathryn spoke again. "It's so good of you to take me with you, dear. I'd dreamed of it for so long, but I'd given up on really going back. It will be so lovely to go to Fiona's wedding."

Stephanie murmured agreement and snapped another suitcase shut.

"And your wedding too, of course. Do you think you and David will marry soon?"

"I guess so. I don't really know, Grammie. We've been apart so long. I feel like we need to get acquainted all over again."

That night she didn't sleep well. Visions of David floated behind her closed eyelids. But at least half the faces she saw had Carlton's dark hair and saucy half-grin. Then the expression would change to one of anger and hurt.

She woke long before her alarm rang. She knew what she must do. She couldn't go without saying good-bye to Carlton.

His phone rang endlessly in the dark chill of the early morning. At last a very sleepy-sounding Ada answered. "What's that? You want to speak to Mr. Sperlin? . . No, he's gone. For about a month he said . . . No, I don't know where you can reach him."

So there was nothing she could do. She considered writing him a note, but couldn't think what to say.

All the way to the airport, sitting beside Kathryn and behind Eliot and Elizabeth, Stephanie tried to memorize every scene out her window. Would this be the last time she ever saw her beloved valley?

At the airport Eliot signaled a porter to help with their luggage. A man in a dark suit opened Stephanie's door and held out his hand to assist her. The moment she touched the warmth of his palm she knew.

"Carlton! What are you doing here? Did you come to see us off?"

"See you off? Not on your life. I'm not letting you just walk out of my life and never see you again. Remember at Sun Valley I told you you were never to walk out on me like that again? Well, I'm going to see that you don't."

"But I have to go."

"Right. I know you do. That's why I'm going with you. If I can't have you myself, I want to see the man who bested me."

It took all of Stephanie's will power not to throw herself into his arms right then. But it would be unfair to all of them if she didn't see David again before making up her mind. She flipped her hair over her shoulder and gave him an impudent smile. "Good. I was wondering who we'd get to carry all this luggage." She thrust her carry-on case into his hands.

The only awkward moment of the trip came nine hours later when David met them at the Glasgow airport. She introduced Carlton as an old family friend, but the two men eyed each other like sparring partners in a boxing ring.

Her own heart had lurched when she saw David. He was handsomer than she had remembered. Here in his native setting, he shone even more than he had when transplanted in Idaho. Now she remembered why she had promised to marry him.

And yet Carlton, standing beside him . . . Oh, what was she going to do? She couldn't stand to hurt either of them. But the longer she delayed the more pain there would be for everybody.

It was Kathryn's wide-eyed enthusiasm for everything around them that smoothed over the difficulties of the moment. Especially when a piper in front of the airport began playing "Amazing Grace."

Kathryn stopped and put her hand to her throat. "Now, that's the finest music in the world. I want a piper playing 'Amazing Grace' at my funeral." She said it with such enthusiasm that it wasn't a sad thought at all.

The road from the airport seemed unbelievably narrow. It wound sharply along rushing waters beneath steep, green hills. Tiny lambs tottered behind their mothers over fields dotted with yellow flowers. Time and again Stephanie turned to check on her grandmother. But always Kathryn's eyes were turned to the hills her Merrick had so loved.

Stephanie was thankful for David's casual chatter about the country they were driving through and for Kathryn's intermittent reminiscences, because Stephanie couldn't think of a thing to say.

They arrived at Selkirk in time for tea. A radiant Fiona greeted them at the heavy, carved door of Woodburn Manor, sprawling beneath its assorted towers and turrets.

"Fiona, you're more beautiful than ever!" Stephanie kissed her. It was true. Fiona's white skin glowed with a new radiance. Her long black hair, pulled back with a simple red ribbon, bounced glossier than ever. Tendrils escaped their band and curled around her face.

Their hostess turned with bright eyes. "Oh, and here's my Callum."

Even in the midst of the quandry she was in, Stephanie immediately liked the angular, sandy-haired Callum Douglas with his bright freckles and wide grin.

Fiona and Callum ushered them into the parlor to meet the rest of the family. Stephanie smiled and nodded at all the introductions but was thankful that Kathryn took the lead in responding.

"Little Robbie." Kathryn took the big hands of Fiona's grandfather in both her own and gazed long at him, shaking her head. "I don't suppose you remember me at all."

"Oh, but there's where ye're wrong, my lass. You were the first person I'd ever seen who could stand up to Grandpa Eagan. That wasn't a sight I'd likely forget."

Fiona's mother, Barbara, who was indeed as beautiful as her daughter had described her, urged everyone to sit down. Then she served them cups of rich, steamy tea and wheat scones dripping with butter and honey.

The food was delicious, and Stephanie was famished, but she found it harder and harder to swallow as the conversation swirled around her. For now, at last, she knew what she truly wanted. She knew the right end. But she couldn't figure out the means to get there without causing

287

even more hurt to a wonderful man who had already been deeply hurt.

No, there was no longer any doubt in her mind. One look at David, and she had known. He was handsomer than the picture of him she had held in her memory. His shining red-gold hair was more romantic than she had remembered it. His voice was more delightful than her ear had recalled, as he refilled Kathryn's teacup and quoted, "We'll tak a cup o' kindness yet for auld lang syne."

And Scotland was the green, sheltered escape she had imagined—even farther away than she had imagined from the hurly burly of the battles she had fought in Boise. She was in the enchanted never-neverland she had dreamed of with her prince charming.

But now she saw that she had miscast the man for the role. David had filled the dreams of a girl open for infatuation. He had all the outward requisites. He offered a fantasy of escape whenever life got to be more than she wanted to cope with. But that was all—infatuation and fantasy, romance and escape. They were wonderful stuff for a fairy tale, but not what she could build a whole life on.

She remembered what Carlton had said he wanted in the one he would spend his life with: shared goals and values, working together and praying together. She didn't even know David well enough to know if they had any of those things in common. In all the time—what was it, four years?—she'd known and dreamed of David Fraser, that was all it had really amounted to—dreams. A few head-spinning kisses, a handful of poetic letters, and her dreams of escaping from the pressures of the world she lived in.

Her relationship with Carlton had been tested in the heat of the work-a-day world, in the fire of a political battle. Carlton with his solid common sense and shining faith was true gold. There wasn't anything they couldn't face together—argue about if necessary—and certainly pray about together. Now she couldn't imagine how she possibly could have been so slow to see the light.

Her problem was, how could she possibly handle this without hurting David, who had already lost one love to another man?

Lord, help me untangle this mess. Show me what to do.

The doorbell jangled, and Barbara crossed the room to answer it. The woman was lovely in a soft brown skirt that matched her softly waved hair. Her peach sweater brought out the same tones in her skin. Stephanie watched Kathryn's eyes follow her. And Stephanie knew Kathryn was remembering Fiona's telling them that Barbara would have married Uncle Boyd if he hadn't been killed in the war. She hoped she hadn't been wrong to bring her grandmother to a place that held sad memories as well as happy ones.

"We have more guests," Barbara announced.

Everyone turned toward the door where she stood with two young women and a young man who looked so much like David he had to be his brother.

"Mary McKee." Barbara presented the girl with curly blonde hair, wearing a dark blue skirt and sweater.

Stephanie caught her breath at the name. Oh, no. This was the girl who had broken David's heart—his Highland Mary. Now Stephanie could never tell him she was in love with another man.

"And David's brother, Gordon, and his wife, Lucy," Barbara concluded.

Stephanie was sure she had misunderstood. She whispered to Fiona, sitting next to her, "Did she say *Lucy* was his wife? Not Mary?"

David, who had stood with the other men when the women entered the room, turned to Stephanie. "Oh, aye. That's the Mary I told you about. She's been nursing in Kenya. She just came back last week."

For several heartbeats Stephanie looked from David to Mary. Though they stood across the room from each other, there was no mistaking their feelings.

Stephanie, long known more for her courage than for her subtlety, jumped to her feet and threw her arms around David. "How wonderful! Now you can marry Mary, and I can marry Carlton!" She slipped the ring from her finger and handed it to David.

The rest of the tea party was a blur. Later she remembered David's kissing her before he handed her into Carlton's arms. And she remembered hearing Mary saying, "Oh, thank goodness," in a voice that was clouded with either tears or laughter. She couldn't tell which. But mostly she just remembered being deliriously happy and feeling that everyone around her was in a similarly idiotic state.

Two other days would stand out in her memory of the trip that turned out to be the fairy tale she had always dreamed of—only better, because it was based in the reality of her love for Carlton and the joy they shared with those around them: Fiona and Callum, David and Mary, and especially Kathryn.

One was the day when they armed themselves with cameras, sweaters, and plenty of just-in-case rain gear and set out in Callum's Range Rover for a sightseeing excursion. As they drove through the marketplace, Kathryn's voice took on a note of excitement. "Oh, here's where Merrick cast the flag. He was magnificent."

Stephanie leaned forward and clasped her shoulder. "I know, Grammie. I read it in your journal." She could see it in her mind from her grandmother's description.

They went on up the High Street and stopped before the bronze statue of a medieval warrior brandishing a tattered flag. Kathryn sounded even more excited. "Oh, I never thought I'd get to see him. That's Fletcher the Warrior. Merrick contributed five pounds to help build him."

Stephanie grabbed her camera. "Grammie, could you stand in front of the statue? I'd love to have a picture."

Carlton helped Kathryn to a secure footing in front of the granite base, while Callum told him about their local hero. Fletcher was the only Selkirk warrior to survive the

Battle of Flodden Field, and he had returned with the enemy flag.

"That's right. And Merrick's mother was descended from him," Kathryn continued, as the men helped her back into the Rover. "That makes you descended from him, Stephanie."

"Now I know why you're such a fighter." Carlton grinned at his future wife.

The other special day was the day of Fiona's wedding in the little gray stone kirk near the marketplace. The church was filled with ferns and daffodils, and the sun shone on the altar through the stained glass window.

The bride wore a traditional white wedding dress and veil but, in true Scottish tradition, also wore a length of plaid attached with a brooch to her left shoulder and looped across front and back to be knotted on her right shoulder. The plaid matched the tartan of her groom, resplendent in kilt and velvet jacket with lace jabot.

David and Mary, also wearing their family tartans, stood with the bridal couple for the traditional service.

Stephanie turned to look at Carlton. The jewel-toned light of the church was doing wonderful things to his beloved features. She thought of the unknown years ahead: success or failure, sickness or health, richer or poorer—and she knew that above everything else she wanted to be wherever he was to love him. She smiled at the triteness of the thought, but the commitment truly was "for better or for worse." Whatever it was to be, it had to be together.

Then the music began. Stephanie knew she had never heard "Savior, Like a Shepherd Lead Us" played more beautifully than it sounded on bagpipe and organ. She took her grandmother's hand and held it tightly. When the song ended, Stephanie turned and saw that Kathryn's eyes were misty. "She could have been no lovelier if she had been my Boyd's very own. Nor could I have been fonder of her—it's like having part of Boyd back."

And Stephanie knew the feeling was mutual, when the bride kissed Kathryn at the reception at Woodburn Manor. "You've made our wedding so extra special by coming. We want to name our first son Boyd."

Kathryn's eyes glowed. "And if it's a daughter?"

"Kathryn, of course—if you don't mind."

Kathryn smiled and nodded. "'One generation passeth unto another, and the sun also rises.' I'm sure there'll be many rising suns on the generations of this family."

Epilogue

They had been back from their honeymoon just two months. Just long enough for Stephanie, with the help of the sturdy Ada, to make a start on the redecorating and reorganizing that needed to be done on the big, white Georgian house on Warm Springs Avenue.

Stephanie greeted Carlton at the door with a kiss late one afternoon. "Just a quick, quick dinner tonight, my love. Then we need to drive over to Kuna."

"Is it your grandmother?"

Stephanie nodded and led the way to the kitchen where a pot of chicken soup simmered on the stove. "Mother called this morning. Grammie's just so very, very frail. Oh, Carlton—" she turned into his arms "—life and death—it's all so overwhelming."

Shadows were long across the alfalfa fields, and the gold of the setting sun shone on black and white cows in the pastures, as they drove across the lovely green farming valley to Kuna that evening. Roses climbed along the fence and bloomed by the door of the old farmhouse that had been home to three generations of Stephanie's family.

Mavis and Clarey, Alex and Leonard, Elizabeth and Eliot all sat in the living room sipping iced tea when Stephanie and Carlton entered. Stephanie would have liked to embrace them all at once. Her family.

"Boyd and Tommy are still in the barn," Elizabeth said after greeting her. "Go have a nice visit with Grams. Then we'll all have some chocolate cake with this iced tea."

As Stephanie led Carlton back to the wallpapered, carpeted bedroom, she thought of the single room with muslin divider it had been when Kathryn Esther Jayne and her papa pioneered here.

Kathryn was sitting up in bed, a pile of fluffy pillows at her back. A breeze was blowing a fresh, new-mown hay scent in the window, and music played on the record player.

"Grammie." Stephanie went to her and kissed her.

Carlton sat on the other side of the bed and reached across to hold his wife's hand. "We've something to tell you." He grinned at Stephanie, and she grinned back.

"You're going to be a great-grandma," Stephanie said.

"Well, it's about time." Kathryn smiled at both of them, her eyes twinkling. "You know, I've been thinking a lot about Jules lately. He would have been so happy about you two. Jules and I should have wonderful great-grand-children."

She looked at Carlton. "He was one of the best men on earth, your grandfather. Next to my Merrick he was the very best. And you're just as fine." She squeezed Carlton's hand. "I hope I'm here to greet Jules's great-grandson. But if I'm not, maybe you can read a little of my journal to him."

"Oh, Grammie." Stephanie's eyes burned, and her throat closed.

"If I can't tell him myself, you tell him—tell all your children. I want them to know that life isn't easy, but it's wonderful. And God is there. Even in the darkest times. He's always there. And His righteousness can be passed from generation to generation. You'll tell them all, won't you?"

As a pledge, Stephanie and Carlton kissed her parchment cheeks simultaneously.

The record in the corner played "Amazing Grace" on the bagpipes. Kathryn closed her eyes with a smile on her lips.

Author's Note

Because so much of Daughters of Courage has been drawn from my own family history, I hasten to tell you that I never wanted anything less than a career in politics. I was the little girl who took one look at a Snake River Stampede parade and said, "I will be queen someday." In 1959 I was.

I have, however, always been involved with my lawyer husband in working for good government in our state, which included investigating the 1971 rock festival at Farragut State Park. I also once accompanied him to a legislative committee hearing, carrying his briefcase because he was on crutches—from spraining his ankle on the slick, wet marble of the capitol steps.

I believe doing the research for this book has made me a better citizen. Now I really know how laws get passed. Thank you to my friends Gail Bray and Kitty Gurnsey, both legislators of experience and dedication, for their help.